Justice in the Making

Justice in the Making: Feminist Social Ethics

Beverly Wildung Harrison

Edited by
Elizabeth M. Bounds
Pamela K. Brubaker
Jane E. Hicks
Marilyn J. Legge
Rebecca Todd Peters
Traci C. West

Westminster John Knox Press
LOUISVILLE • LONDON

The lines from "Natural Resources" are copyright © 2002 by Adrienne Rich. Copyright © 1978 by W. W. Norton & Company, Inc., from *The Fact of a Doorframe: Selected Poems 1950–2001* by Adrienne Rich. Used by permission of the author and W. W. Norton & Company, Inc.

"The Dream of a Common Language: Toward a Normative Theory of Justice in Christian Ethics" by Beverly W. Harrison was first published in the *Annual of the Society of Christian Ethics* (1983): 1–25. Used by permission of the publisher. "Feminist Realism" by Beverly W. Harrison was first published in *Christianity and Crisis* 46 (July 14, 1986): 233–36. Reprinted by permission of the publisher. "Feminist Musings on Community" by Beverly W. Harrison was first published in *Holy Ground* 8, no. 1 (July 2001). Used by permission of the publisher. Beverly W. Harrison's foreword in *Welfare Policy: Feminist Critiques,* eds. Elizabeth M. Bounds, Pamela K. Brubaker, and Mary E. Hobgood (Cleveland: The Pilgrim Press, 1999), vii–xi, is copyright © 1999 by Elizabeth M. Bounds, Pamela K. Brubaker, and Mary E. Hobgood. Used by permission. "Human Sexuality and Mutuality" by Beverly W. Harrison is from *Christian Feminism: Visions of a New Humanity,* edited by Judith L. Weidman. Copyright © by Harper & Row Publishers, Inc. Reprinted by permission of HarperCollins Publishers, Inc. "Niebuhr: Locating the Limits" by Beverly W. Harrison was first published in *Christianity and Crisis* 46 (February 17, 1986): 35–39. Reprinted by permission of the publisher. Chapter 11, "On Harry Ward," Beverly W. Harrison's review of Eugene P. Link's *Labor-Religion Prophet: The Times and Life of Harry F. Ward,* was first published in the *Union Seminary Quarterly Review* 39, no. 4 (1984): 316–22. Used by permission of the Publisher. "Restoring the Tapestry of Life: The Vocation of Feminist Theology" by Beverly W. Harrison is from the *Drew Gateway* 54, no. 1 (1985): 39–48. Used by permission of the publisher. "Feminist Thea(o)logies at the Millennium: 'Messy' Continued Resistance or Surrender to Postmodern Academic Culture?" by Beverly W. Harrison is from *Liberating Eschatology: Essays in Honor of Letty Russell,* edited by Margaret A. Farley and Serene Jones (Louisville: Westminster John Knox Press, 1999), 156–171. Reprinted here by permission of Westminster John Knox Press. Beverly W. Harrison's "Dorothee Soelle as Pioneering Postmodernist" was first published in *The Theology of Dorothee Soelle,* edited by Sarah K. Pinnock (Harrisburg, PA: Trinity Press International, 2003). Used by permission. Beverly W. Harrison's dictionary entry for "Socialism-Capitalism" is from the *Dictionary of Feminist Theologies,* edited by Letty M. Russell and J. Shannon Clarkson (Louisville: Westminster John Knox Press, 1996), 264–266. Reprinted here by permission of Westminster John Knox Press. "Social Justice and Economic Orthodoxy: Structural Evils Neglected" by Beverly W. Harrison was first published in *Christianity and Crisis* 44 (January 21, 1985): 507–23. Reprinted by permission of the publisher. Beverly W. Harrison's "Toward a Feminist Liberation Hermeneutic for Demystifying Class Reality in Local Congregations" was first published in *Beyond Clericalism: The Congregation as a Focus for Theological Education,* edited by Joseph C. Hough Jr. and Barbara Wheeler (Atlanta: Scholar's Press, 1988) 137–51. Reprinted by permission of Barbara Wheeler. "The Fate of the Middle Class" by Beverly W. Harrison was originally published in *God and Capitalism: A Prophetic Critique of Market Economy,* edited by J. Mark Thomas and Vernon Visick. Madison, Wisconsin: A-R Editions. Used by permission.

Book design by Sharon Adams
Cover design by Night & Day Design

First edition
Published by Westminster John Knox Press
Louisville, Kentucky

This book is printed on acid-free paper that meets the American National Standards Institute Z39.48 standard. ∞

PRINTED IN THE UNITED STATES OF AMERICA

04 05 06 07 08 09 10 11 12 13 — 10 9 8 7 6 5 4 3 2 1

Library of Congress Cataloging-in-Publication Data

Harrison, Beverly Wildung, 1932–
    Justice in the making : feminist social ethics / Beverly Wildung Harrison ; Elizabeth M. Bounds . . . [et al.], editors.
        p. cm.
    Includes bibliographical references and index.
    ISBN 0-664-22774-0 (alk. paper)
    1. Feminist ethics.   2. Feminist theory.   I. Bounds, Elizabeth M., 1956–   II. Title.

BJ1395.H37   2004
170'.82—dc22   2004054994

*To all those who rise
to resist the oppression of women and
to all who work together teaching and
learning justice making.*

Contents

Preface

The six remarkable women whose names appear here as editors are responsible for the appearance of *Justice in the Making: Feminist Social Ethics*. Four years ago, shortly after my retirement, several of them approached me to propose reprinting a number of my essays, along with a few previously unpublished pieces, in a volume that would introduce feminist Christian social ethics. I was astonished to discover that they had already discussed the value of such a project and had gathered a group ready to sign on. They even volunteered to look through the several piles of unpublished materials, including lecture manuscripts and tapes, that I had located while cleaning out my crowded and messy office before leaving New York!

For several years, people had been urging me to make the writing of a general introduction to feminist ethics my first retirement project. I had found this suggestion unsettling. First of all, I had found inadequate the several books already published to serve that need and wondered how I could do any better. Further, the very notion that one person could adequately "introduce" the theory, practice, and multiple topics of this burgeoning field seemed to me pretentious in the extreme. Indeed, I felt my own work in Christian feminist ethics opposed the traditional idea that a solitary "expert" could unilaterally expound on the "how-to's" in ethics. However, the preliminary ideas raised by the women envisioning this volume began to move my imagination in a fresh direction. So we agreed to meet and explore the possibilities.

All six of these women had been advisees of mine during their doctoral studies. Happily, for our purposes, they represented a range of seniority in years of teaching—ranging from tenured professors to recently appointed assistant professors. While none were from my first generation of Ph.D. advisees, they represented a range of generations among the wonderful graduate students in ethics, theology, religion and society, and philosophy of religion that I had worked with during my years at Union Theological Seminary. Not only were all published scholars, but each is, by my lights, a masterful practitioner of the lovely art of doing ethics that engages each of us as academics and as intellectuals. All also exemplify the mix of academic rigor and activist advocacy for justice that makes me proud not only of them but of dozens of women and men with whom it has been my privilege to work.

Because some readers may be approaching my work for the first time, it may be well to observe at the outset that the approach to justice operating in these pages differs considerably from that found in many contemporary philosophical discussions. The conception of justice here is not the one found in standard liberal political theories—a balancing of interests or divergent notions of good, along with certain minimalist commitments to fairness. Although these "thin" theories of justice may well have their place in public discussion, I have long believed that several of the traditions rooted in the texts Christians and Jews call Scripture provide an alternative conception of justice. Beginning with truthful acknowledgment of injustice as the result of wrongful past practice, this notion requires an ongoing commitment to finding fresh ways of "undoing" past wrongs and initiating connections that enable life together. Such a conception is easy to dismiss as utopian, but given the scope and scale of existing injustice I also believe it is the only conception able to confront the massive evil characterizing those imperial and patriarchal social orders, our own included, that have shaped the modern world.

Perhaps the most important commonality of these six editors is that each holds a teaching position that enables her to focus and specialize intensely in Christian and/or religious ethics. Though three teach in religious studies departments and work chiefly with undergraduates and three teach in theological schools and teach both professional ministerial and doctoral students, all insisted from the outset that my work, even my earlier essays, continues to be of value for their ongoing teaching and writing. And they reminded me that since most of this material is no longer in print, it was harder and harder to draw upon for use in the classroom. Their insistence at first astonished me. But, as we pondered the possible materials and format for this volume, my reluctance to revisit work that felt reflective of the past, and my scepticism about whether there was an audience for such a book, gave way to enthusiasm, and by this point in the project, incredible gratitude. The gift of their collaboration was grace-filled beyond belief! Their extraordinary generosity included journeying to gather at the place where I now live, a beautiful tract of land that my companions and I call "Redbud Springs," for several days one summer. After our first meeting, these six women committed themselves to the time required to bring the book to fruition, which involved a second and a third gathering. Each editor financed her own travels to Redbud. Readers should know that not only is each of these women extraordinarily busy, but that all also are unbelievably effective classroom teachers, from whom students and colleagues expect much. Each is also gifted as a lecturer and academic consultant, much in demand in church and academic forums. They are all also currently engaged in ongoing major scholarly projects themselves, and several are well known for the innovative research they are undertaking for foundations active in academic change.

The sheer spirit of commitment each bequeathed this little project has left me in a state of awed thankfulness for which no words suffice. Their willingness to devote precious hours and days to our work has left me humbled beyond measure. More than anything else, of course, it was the prospect of their company and the pleasure of collaborative work with them that sealed my resolve to complete work on this book before any other to which I am committed. And it was the certain knowledge that each would find herself personally and professionally empowered by our mutual work which enabled me to accept with equanimity the extraordinary gift they bestowed by giving priority to executing this project.

I wish my literary skills were up to portraying a picture of what it was like to be part of this group. I have been blessed frequently as a feminist scholar, with the joys of extraordinary colleagueship and with the experience of pleasurable shared work. My ongoing participation (for twenty years!) in the Feminist Ethics Consultation of the Northeast and the experience of working in the Mud Flower Collective on *God's Fierce Whimsy*,[1] had long since confirmed my commitment to communal work. Yet nothing in my previous experience prepared me for the efficient and delightful collaboration I observed and participated in as *Justice in the Making* came together. Articles were selected and arranged with the greatest ease. The interviews were shaped and executed in ways that delighted this elderly senior. Careful notes of our discussions were quickly rendered into publishable texts, and twelve-hour workdays left everyone tired but exhilarated. And in between the long hours of work, we caught up with each others' professional and personal lives and projects, offered feedback on proposed ideas, and discussed endlessly the challenges of theological and undergraduate education, all the while assessing and condemning the backlash always threatening the possibilities of feminist transformations. How does one say, "Thank you, dear sisters" for such a gift? I also particularly want to thank Carter Heyward for being the theological muse in my pilgrimage toward a new relationship with my Calvinist theological traditions.

The personal and professional meaning of this experience for me has continued to unfold even as the project has come to conclusion. It is truly a life-enhancing experience to revisit one's professional career and theoretical development in the ways required by the shaping of such a book as this. Not only did reviewing earlier manuscripts lead to revisiting assumptions and assessing changes in my ways of understanding the world, but the interview questions formulated by the editors reprieved nearly fifty years of work, study, and life choices, and, among other things, reminded me of much I hoped to do that I have not as yet completed. I have come to realize that the struggle to counter the backlash against feminism must go on with renewed energy, especially in the face of growing lies and misrepresentations of the Christian Right. And themes and questions that I have long set aside must be taken off the shelf and reengaged. It is crucial that we find ways to mobilize a new generation of *practicing* feminists to resist the simultaneous trivialization and romanticization of women's lives. For years I have referred to the current political ethos in this nation as friendly fascism. I never say this now without the most sober awareness that speaking this way in "Bushwhacked"[2] America is dangerous, since those in power try to block any criticism of their presumed competence to reign. This means that the ongoing work of justice in the making is the only road for any who care concretely for the well-being not only of women and children but of little planet Earth and all its inhabitants, including our many four-legged companions. Feminist Kate Millett once wrote that "the work of enlarging human freedom is such nice work that we're lucky to get it."[3] May more and more of us join together in this work!

Beverly Wildung Harrison
Redbud Springs
Christmas 2003

Notes

1. Mud Flower Collective, *God's Fierce Whimsy: Christian Feminism and Theological Education* (New York: Pilgrim Press, 1985).
2. See also Molly Ivins and Lou Dubose, *Bushwhacked: Life in George W. Bush's America* (New York: Random House, 2003).
3. Kate Millett, *Sexual Politics* (New York: Simon & Schuster, 1990), xii. This is one of the favorite quotations of my very dear friend and collaborator, Dr. Marvin Ellison, who was the first of a long line of wonderful advisees.

Editors' Introduction

To be sure, the full world historical project that feminism envisages remains a distant dream—that is, that every female child in each and every community and culture will be born to share the full horizon of human possibility, that she will have the same range of life options as every male child. This is, and remains, "the longest revolution." But this revolution, for which we have every right to yearn, will come sooner if we celebrate the strength that shines forth in women's lives . . . [and] learn what we are to know of love from immersion in the struggle for justice.

—Beverly Wildung Harrison,
"The Power of Anger in the Work of Love"

In 1980, Beverly Wildung Harrison gave her inaugural address at Union Theological Seminary, New York, on the occasion of her promotion to full professor of Christian ethics. The event opened with a memorable procession. At Harrison's invitation, well over fifty lay, academic, and clergy women colleagues—"arrayed in garb of breathtaking color"—swelled the ranks of academic faculty from Union and related institutions.[1] Harrison's lecture that day, entitled "The Power of Anger in the Work of Love," challenged traditional Christian understandings of women's moral agency in ways that resonated with Christian men and women across the globe. Mimeographed copies of the lecture circulated widely in the United States among women's groups, influencing the development of a generation of lay activists and scholars. Within a year, Harrison's address had been translated into seven languages and has since become a classic in Christian ethics courses around the world.

Over the course of her career, Harrison's intellectual contribution has been considerable. She began work in 1956 as a campus minister at the University of California, Berkeley, where conversation with young faculty in the social sciences shaped her interest in the broad reaches of social theory. After six years at Berkeley, Harrison returned to Union, where she had previously earned a master's degree in religious education, to complete Ph.D. requisites and begin doctoral studies in Christian ethics. Harrison subsequently worked as an assistant dean of students at Union. In that role, she offered pastoral support to women students. In turn, they raised her awareness of the varied ways graduate theological studies marginalized women, and Harrison began to speak out about the role of women in theological education. In 1968, Harrison was named assistant professor of Christian ethics at Union, later becoming one of the first tenured women in the theological field in a major Protestant seminary that included doctoral studies. In the mid-1970s, the small number of feminist faculty activists and Ph.D. students doing ethics in the northeastern United States came together to form the Feminist Ethics Consultation. This group nurtured the emerging field of feminist ethics, providing space for intellectual development and personal support for the first generation of feminists working in religious ethics. In 1983, Harrison became the first woman president of the Society of Christian Ethics, a remarkable achievement given that women made up less than 5 percent of the membership at that time.

In terms of her published corpus, her book *Our Right to Choose: Toward a New Ethic of Abortion* remains the most substantive theological assessment of the morality of abortion in the last twenty years. In addition to *Our Right to Choose*, Harrison has written numerous articles on abortion that have been widely anthologized in philosophy, religion, and medical ethics textbooks. Her collection *Making the Connections*, first published in 1985, offers integrative analyses on selected topics that helped pioneer the field of feminist social ethics. But Harrison's unrelenting passion as a teacher and activist led her to give precedence to concerns other than her publication agenda. In many ways her contributions have been most profoundly expressed through personal relationships, leadership, and teaching engaged in with hundreds of people throughout her thirty-five-year career as a professional ethicist. While she often devoted herself as a stalwart supporter of the professional development of feminist colleagues, her influence in the larger academy is also evident in the number of former doctoral students, both female and male, teaching and working in universities and seminaries. Likewise, her influence in the church is apparent in the large number of lay justice activists and concerned clergy she has mentored and befriended over the years.

PROCESS OF COLLABORATION

After her retirement in 1999, a group of Harrison's former students began discussions with her regarding what kind of support she might need to publish some of her speeches and papers that were not readily available. This task was motivated both by our familiarity with her particular contributions to feminist social theory,[2] which we wanted to make accessible to a larger community, as well as our desire to be able to teach her approach to social ethics in university and seminary classrooms.

From our first meeting together, we intentionally modeled our working arrangement as a collaborative process in order that this project would not just result in a volume of critical feminist ethics, but that our process itself would embody the doing of feminist ethics. Throughout the three-year production process, we engaged one another in dialogue about the discipline and work of Christian feminist ethics and how Harrison's work illuminates the ongoing tasks of liberatory feminist ethics. Together we selected articles and speeches we thought most relevant to these tasks. We organized the pieces into sections and divided up editorial responsibilities.

Working within a feminist collective has significantly shaped this collection of some of Harrison's previously published and unpublished works. Each section includes excerpts from conversations that we have had with Harrison about the pieces included here and the ways in which her thought has developed over the years since the original delivery or publication. While we teach in different settings (college, university, and seminary), locate ourselves in different communities of accountability, and have multiple research agendas, we all share a multidimensional approach to feminist social ethics that privileges critically appropriated experiences in dialogue with traditional sources of theological traditions and scripture, read through critical social theory. This approach, which we learned from Harrison, undergirds our work together in this volume and has enabled us to support one another in our disparate theo-ethical efforts.

It is of great importance to us that this material be useful for the ongoing task of teaching and learning. We believe that the ideas reflected here will help readers make connections between systems of belief and forms of political control that will probably not be made by the commentators who regularly appear on television news programs or by most preachers during weekly sermons. This book invites us to ask critical questions about how to transform some of the injustices in our society that will also most likely not be raised in standard social science textbooks or strategy sessions of neighborhood or union meetings. In addition, we feel strongly about the need to teach this material because of our passionate commitment to the work of ethical analysis and moral reflection. Ethics always involves critical questioning, and one of the best ways to elicit such critical thinking is through teaching and learning.

OVERVIEW

In this collection, Harrison navigates the academic disciplines and social movements associated with liberative-feminist Christian ethics. These readings offer a sojourn with this skillful and insistent guide across the messy terrain of social theories and practices that have influenced our lives and shaped our vision in this late capitalist[3] period of the twenty-first century. For Harrison, it is the social value of claims within Christian and other religious and moral traditions that provides us with a much-needed moral compass. In clarifying, pushing, and prodding the way forward, she helps us recognize and claim liberative ground for ourselves and our communities.

This collection brings together a diverse set of essays marking the progression of her contribution to this field from the early 1980s to the present. It shows Harrison refining earlier insights, revisiting Protestant and feminist legacies, and providing rejoinders to current debates and issues. Excerpted conversations with the editors update and amplify Harrison's views throughout the volume. Readers can follow the course she has charted in developing key notions of such concepts as justice, spirituality, political economy, community, embodiment, and sexuality. For her such concepts can only be understood as rooted in human experience, especially the experiences of women and other marginalized persons, and as mediated through critical social theories. Those who are new to religious and feminist ethics will find these materials to be a lively and accessible introduction to the field.

Critical "snapshots" of late capitalism and its attendant neoliberal public policy and academic initiatives mark an important stream within Harrison's work. If any single idea undergirds her approach in almost every essay in this collection, it is her commitment to a historical materialist reading of concrete social realities. Of particular importance is the way she works to counter the invisibility of politics and economics by clarifying the moral implications of political economy. Corporate market mechanisms now control political power, directing institutions of government that once were sustained by our common political life and making abstract individualism "a hideous existential reality."[4] While attention to the social and cultural dynamics of globalization and its impact on people in local communities, ecologies, and cultures is on the rise, too many current religious ethicists take for granted the legitimacy of present economic arrangements that shape political power. In contrast to this dominant approach, Harrison's work here questions the assumption about the primacy of capitalist markets and corporate power as moral proxies and, in so doing, represents a critical edge of liberative feminist methodologies. For her, economics must always be political economy, the study of interlocking economic and political systems.

In doing this work for justice, Harrison has consistently located herself within Reformed Christian traditions. This location is ambiguous since she has long been aware of the failures of patriarchal Protestant theological liberalism. These failures include deference to existing power, excessive need for respectability, and preoccupation with abstract doctrine rather than concrete human suffering. Her own feminist conversion enables retrieval of the voices and praxis of women as role models and intellectual companions. Through this work, Harrison envisions a radical Protestant ethic charged with the task of "reappropriating all our social relations, including our relations to God, so that shared action toward genuine human and cosmic fulfillment occurs."[5]

Over the course of this volume, one can observe the complexity of Harrison's thought in response to changing social realities and the variation of her "voice" as she articulates Christian ethics for different audiences in the academy, church, and broader society. In her work with laity in the church and her students in the academy, Harrison has shown a driving commitment to encourage and make a place for women and others at the margins. She challenges the subjugating ways in which women's intellectual contributions, their gifts of ministerial leadership, and their reproductive capacity and sexual identity have been defined. Harrison's relentless critique and bold notions of justice, solidarity, and academic integrity interrupt oppressive patterns in our thinking and acting and empower struggles for a new world.

The preface by Harrison, which precedes this introduction, reviews current themes in her present work and how the collaborative nature of this project characterizes her own methodological commitments. This introduction provides an overview of the book, which is divided into three parts, each including an introduction, a group of related articles, and interviews that illumine and update Harrison's approach. The essays are not necessarily in chronological order as the dates in the contextual notes for each one demonstrate.

Part 1, "The Tasks of Liberatory Feminist Ethics," identifies and considers formative aspects of Harrison's ethical method. Her critical perspectives on justice, community, sexuality, and welfare policy are put forward in these essays, indicating several critical base points for the overarching project of feminist ethics.

Part 2, "Working with Protestant Traditions," covers two topics. Chapters 10–12 show Harrison's active engagement with the heritage of modern Christian ethics, particularly twentieth-century figures who have influenced her work. Here she challenges, extends, and on occasion rejects the work of such well-known ethicists as the Niebuhr brothers, as well as those who are less well remembered, such as Harry Ward, John Bennett, and James Luther Adams. Chapters 13–15 show the contrasting development of feminist theo-ethics and Harrison's self-understanding in relationship to significant foremothers and sisters. Reading through the pieces in this section, the reader can see how Harrison's aim has always been to broaden the work of constructing and expanding theological knowledge, especially through concrete participation by diverse voices.

Part 3, "Christian Ethical Praxis and Political Economy," considers the importance of class and political economy in the work of critical feminist social ethics. Harrison theorizes class as foundational to the work of economic justice and political ethics and questions capitalist social relations and culture.

In the afterword, the editors signal the ongoing significance of Harrison's writings and point to future directions for feminist work as they invite others into the ongoing and changing work of liberatory feminist social ethics. The volume concludes with a bibliography of Harrison's published work.

USING THE BOOK

We hope that this volume will be used for active teaching and learning. We believe critical reflection about how we should treat one another, while not sufficient by itself, can enhance our social relations and help to create a more compassionate and just world. Reading and discussing the essays in this volume is one way to engage in such critical reflection.

When we envision the kind of teaching and learning from this book that will be most beneficial, it is our assumption that teaching is fundamentally a process of mutual interaction. It requires substantive engagement among teachers and students, in dialogue with the material, where each participant's experience and existing viewpoints are valued, and spiritual, emotional, and intellectual growth is encouraged. We hope that this volume will be used in a variety of contexts— from undergraduate and graduate classrooms to community-based settings such as book groups, church-based adult education, and women's support groups. We think it is crucial that communities participate in defining key notions such as justice, interpreting historical traditions of belief, and both understanding and shaping our social-political-economic relations. We hope these essays are a springboard to such an engaged process.

There are many ways to engage with the material included here. We want to suggest a few questions and activities to spark your own creativity and to invite you to make it relevant to the context of your own work and communities:

Throughout the volume, Harrison describes the difference that feminist thinking and activism makes for formulating theology, ethics, and social theory (including theological, moral, and social-scientific theoretical approaches) as well as for shaping women's self-perceptions and sense of agency. Identify this "difference" feminism makes for Harrison. Do you agree with her? Disagree with her? Why?

Find personal stories and examples in the interviews and compare them with the scholarly articles. Where do you see connections and differences? How do you think Harrison came to some of the arguments she makes in the scholarly essays given her personal experience described in the interviews?

In these essays, do you see Harrison drawing on (1) Christian faith, (2) spirituality that is not distinctively Christian, (3) secular sources, or all three? Show specific instances to support your categorization and give reasons for them.

How would you connect religion or faith with one of the major issues raised in the book, such as methods of "doing ethics," interpretations of historical traditions of belief, or analyses of our political economy and struggles for social justice?

Personally engage a specific idea in a subsection or article of this book. For example, after exploring Harrison's theological influences in part 1, think about the influences on your own theology. Do the exercise on family history in the essay "Toward a Christian Feminist Liberation Hermeneutic for Demystifying Class Reality in Local Congregations" in part 3.

Read the afterword and reflect on what the editors propose about the work of feminist liberatory ethics. What would you add? Where do you disagree? What ideas are most relevant to you and the concerns in the community in which you live?

Notes

1. Beverly Wildung Harrison, *Making the Connections: Essays in Feminist Social Ethics*, ed. Carol S. Robb (Boston: Beacon Press, 1985), 3.

2. It is important to clarify that in Harrison's view theology is *itself* a social theory and that, in this volume, the term *feminist social theory* refers to theological/religious, moral/ethical, and other social scientific/critical theory.

3. The term *late capitalism* is used by many social theorists to designate the most recent structural shifts in the now singular, global political economy of capitalism. In particular, it refers to centralized economic control mechanisms of the post-World War II period—the International Monetary Fund, the World Bank, world trade agreements, and the political institutions that determine market and trade activities so as to shape international flows of wealth.

4. Beverly Wildung Harrison, "The Dream of a Common Language: Toward a Normative Theory of Justice in Christian Ethics," p. 24 in this volume.

5. Harrison, *Making the Connections*, 245.

Acknowledgments

Even though there were seven of us revising essays and editing this volume, we could not have completed this project without the support and contributions of many other people.

For their contributions of ongoing encouragement and supportive work that allowed us to focus on our work when we gathered in North Carolina, we would like to thank Carter Heyward, Sue Sasser, and Lisa Nafzinger. We also give a special thank you to Marvin Ellison for coming up with the title for this collection.

For their assistance in some of the more technical labor of gathering, transcribing, copying, and editing this material, we would like to thank Beth De Ford, Jane Ellen Nickell, Patricia Rivenbark, Carrie Roberts, Ruth Rudell, and Sandra Tucker. We would especially like to thank Jennifer Janzen-Ball for compiling the bibliography of Beverly's work and Julie Pfau for final manuscript and index preparation. Thanks also to Stephanie Egnotovich and Dan Braden of Westminster John Knox Press.

For institutional support in varied forms, we would like to thank California Lutheran University, Elon University, Emanuel College of Victoria University/University of Toronto, Emory University, Drew University, and St. John Fisher College.

Part One

THE TASKS OF LIBERATORY FEMINIST ETHICS

Introduction

Jane E. Hicks and Traci C. West

*It is no secret that I am one who works from a perspective of liberation the-
ology and, therefore, aspires to a social ethic (all ethics being social) aimed
to challenge not merely unjust acts, but structures and institutional patterns
of power and their attendant structures of privilege.*

—Beverly Wildung Harrison,
"The Dream of a Common Language"

Part 1 highlights Harrison's distinctive feminist liberation methodological frameworks and starting points. She uses the term *feminist liberatory ethics* to denote
work that seeks revision of Christian tradition away from past oppressions, that
stands in solidarity with marginalized voices, and that uses women's experiences
as criteria for reconstructive directions in Christian ethics. The essays here show
Harrison reflecting upon feminist ethics as an emergent discourse. She addresses
a variety of different audiences, including church-based Christians, professional
theological ethicists, and women activists and academicians. These writings illumine Harrison's own developing method as well as her pioneering role in the
overlapping fields of Christian and feminist ethics. Taken as a whole, they serve
to introduce basic concepts, language, and conversations, and to illustrate her
approach to policy analyses, particularly in the area of sex and gender ethics.
Several other themes found here related to economic ethics and feminist
transformations of ethics and theology are developed further in essays found
elsewhere in this volume. The editors have organized materials in this part in a

general movement from theoretical consideration of approaches and principles to methodological insights developed in conjunction with specific issues.

The piece titled "The Dream of a Common Language: Toward a Normative Theory of Justice in Christian Ethics" was her presidential address to the Society of Christian Ethics, where she emphasized the importance of visionary images and metaphors in our ethical deliberations. As is characteristic of her ethics, she depicts a feminist liberationist principle of justice as the "animating passion" of Christian moral life. For Harrison, the root of our desire to act for justice grows out of our longing for right relations. Harrison's second essay, "Doing Christian Ethics," is a brief, accessible introduction to basic concepts of ethics, including what might be called levels of moral discourse.

"Feminist Realism" continues the justice theme, showing how right-related community is implicated in the abortion debate. Harrison's ethic of procreative choice, developed in essays and especially in her earlier work *Our Right to Choose: Toward a New Ethic of Abortion*, calls for creating a world in which genuine personal and reproductive choice exists, where conditions for bearing and raising children are more just and more deeply embedded in respect for and support of women's wider well-being. She also contends that genuine conditions for reproductive choice do not yet really exist for most women and that they are essential for all women, whether they themselves favor reproductive choice or not.

The final three essays, "Feminist Musings on Community," "Foreword to *Welfare Policy [feminist critiques]*," and "Human Sexuality and Mutuality," illustrate Harrison's methodological insistence upon historically locating any ethical discussion. This insistence comes through her criticism of spurious claims about how well existing families and family values actually nurture community, wrongheaded assumptions that privatization will succeed where government welfare policy has "failed," and silences in traditional Christian theology and history about human sexuality, "especially its seamier side." In each article, Harrison invites recognition of the historically situated and contingent nature of our knowledge, noting the material and ideological interests that are served by certain ways of thinking about social reality.

Two interviews with Beverly Harrison form "bookends" for the articles and speeches in part 1. The first interview provides an overall introduction to the ideas that are found here, with reflection on some of the experiential and intellectual influences on her work. Her recollections about audience and her own intellectual development place some of these materials in context. This interview also allows a glimpse of her views on issues such as race and racism, which are not otherwise emphasized in this volume but are crucial to her conception of liberative ethics. The closing interview offers a substantive account of Harrison's current views on sexual ethics. Her reflections give an expansive framework for how our culture shapes the meaning of sexuality and the concerns a feminist sexual ethic must include. For Harrison, our liberatory tasks are both as concrete and as visionary as the global sex trade, current environmental crises, and notions of queerness demand.

Harrison wants us to remember that ethics is an ongoing, fully human activity, one that is never finished because human historical existence constantly frames and reframes questions of the meaning and value of human action. Respect for past spiritual and moral traditions is essential, but as human activity continuously reconfigures the historical present, those traditions must be critically revisited and reassessed in light of new dilemmas.

Chapter 1

Making Connections: Becoming a Feminist Ethicist

Interview by Traci C. West

West: *This opening section of the book highlights key elements that are a consistent part of your approach to social ethics as a feminist Christian. How would you briefly summarize the most important overarching assumptions for your various methods of doing feminist liberative social ethics?*

Harrison: I want to emphasize my desire to situate our lives as well as our moral reflection in structural (deeply institutionalized and historically embedded) patterns of oppression that shape us not only as individuals but also as communities, cultural groups, and nations. Feminist liberative ethics must address the gender and sexual injustice rooted in a deeply embedded misogyny that includes both contempt for women's competence as thinkers and agents of change and also hatred of strong women who will not surrender to malestream hegemonies[1] of all kinds. It also must expose the distortions compulsory heterosexuality inscribes on all women. A liberating ethics must include careful attention to class dynamics (blockages in access to wealth and political power) and to white racism (the continuous practice of Euro-American cultural supremacy).

West: *This section includes some essays that I would describe as implicitly feminist and others that more explicitly and passionately reflect feminist commitments as essential* *for formulating Christian ethics. Could you reflect for a moment on the development of your feminist approach to social ethics? I am also interested in the evolution of your understanding of race, and of whiteness as an aspect of your feminism. But first, how did you become clearer about the need for developing an explicitly feminist formulation of Christian social ethics?*

Harrison: Your question in relation to these particular essays is helpful to me, because when you all chose the essays that should go into this section, I realized you had included a version of my very first public lecture, "Doing Christian Ethics," in which, speaking as a Christian ethicist, I also "came out" as a feminist ethicist. Since the late 1960s, I had been reading and discussing feminist writing and had identified myself as a feminist in feminist circles. But this particular lecture was given to a large group of church-based women, most of whom were either unaware of or already hostile to feminism. (Back then, much as today, feminism was treated with contempt, albeit with less meanness and libelous misrepresentation than is directed at us today.)

The portion included here has been revised and combined with another talk that was part of a later annual lecture series sponsored by the Union Theological Seminary Women's Committee. As I recall, there may have been over four hundred women present for the first lecture and almost as many at the second. In those days, these audiences would also have been as white as a Protestant churchwomen's group gathered by a white seminary could be. We were almost all of European ethnicity and oblivious to white racism as most educated white women were back then. (Believe me, I include myself in this generalization!)

Most of the women in my audience were not only churchwomen but also supporters of Union, and thus came from fairly liberal congregations. They were a wonderful crowd, and very eager to learn about ethics. Even so, it was a challenge to introduce the idea that women's lives are a serious source of moral experience, and that our experiences enabled and empowered us to do moral reflection and be moral agents. At the time of the first lecture, it took a certain courage to speak as a feminist. That's why, as you can see, I cast the issue of doing Christian ethics in terms of women's experience as childrearers. While I doubted most of these women would understand they possessed genuine intellectual gifts, I was sure that many would respond to the idea of valuing their parenting skills. I think that well before I published anything as a feminist, I had decided that working with children and teaching children was where human moral formation began, and since women did this work, we knew more about doing ethics than many men— even professional ethicists! (Fortunately, many feminist men have now figured this out.) I also learned from lectures such as these that there is little or no difference between talking with churchwomen and talking with academic women. What are you doing in the classroom? You're trying to get people to image themselves as performatively competent to think well and act well—to do ethics.

But even as I began to be aware that women's experience and our performative abilities needed to be taken into account, I simultaneously began to see that many of my earlier questions of malestream theology, philosophy, and ethics were rooted in my experience as a woman. My discomfort with a male academic monopoly even in college had led me to read any books by women that I came across! More and more, I came to admit to myself that malestream Christian ethics was seriously off target.

For perhaps the first time in my life I felt enabled to believe that I had really urgent work to do, work that was deeply needed by other women, who were becoming excited and mobilized by my approach. As a result, my work as a feminist became not only personally and intellectually liberating for me as an individual, but it also was suddenly connecting me deeply to other women's lives. Until this began to occur, I had never experienced confirmation that what I thought really mattered. Not surprisingly, I began to take myself seriously, and a subtle sense that I was crazy for undertaking the effort to be a theological ethicist suddenly dissipated.

I understood that my identification with feminism had begun in a deep intellectual loneliness. During my first years as a faculty member at Union, I had felt the pain of real invisibility. As the only woman present, I began to notice that I often made a point only to have a male colleague make exactly the same point later, as if I had not spoken. I have heard many women academics and other pioneering women speak of having this experience. Whenever they do, I wince with pain, remembering how much that hurt.

When I first developed this hermeneutic of suspicion that women's wisdom had been omitted, I still did not realize that my understanding of women's lives and experience was obscured by my location in white, middle-strata, "old line" Protestantism. For example, when I was talking to these groups of women, it never crossed my mind to consider whether what I was saying related to poor welfare mothers or any other women whose material-cultural world was profoundly different from mine. My suspicion of the power of my social location to blind me to my "whiteness" and my identification with dominant values had not yet developed, not to mention my total lack of awareness about compulsory heterosexuality. My critical consciousness about these important matters developed later, and was shaped and fueled less by books than by my concrete encounters with women intellectuals whose different ways of looking at the world taught me that there could be no generalized or collective idea of "woman."

West: *What about your own background and personal history? Can you give some examples of how your consciousness of your own social location developed?*

Harrison: A few examples should illustrate how I began to discover the meaning and grasp the complexity of class dynamics and ethnicity.

I grew up in a small, prosperous farming town (Luverne, Minnesota) that was racially homogeneous. My family was a successful business family, and we were among the town's elite, even though my father had already lost two businesses in the Depression before I was born. In my sophomore year of college, a sociology professor asked us to take a reading from the work of Karl Marx and think about how his ideas about class related to where we grew up. That assignment absolutely transformed my way of understanding my family politically and economically. Reading Marx, I discovered that there is no real wealth and power in villages or small towns. Real wealth belongs to urban elites, and the scope of their wealth and power is often invisible. The middle strata or business strata always comprises the town's elite and identifies upward to the actual wealth-owning group. I learned the liberative power of naming class in my own history the first time I read a few chapters of Marx. There was no class pride in this, however, and my family bore the marks of self-deprecation that such "little capitalists" always carry.

My family on my mother's side had experienced anti-German sentiment before World War I, and as a result, overidentified with the U.S. cause in the war. That side of my family also was composed of anti-Jewish Protestants. My grand-fathers believed that because Jews did not accept Christ, they were inferior. My family began to deal with this deeply embedded anti-Semitism and anti-Judaism only when my older siblings went to college; my sister was the first to protest the family's subtle culture of contempt toward Jews shaped by our conservative German Lutheran roots.

The subject of racism had always been particularly painful for me to think about because even when I was very young my mother made clear that the institution of chattel slavery in this nation had been evil. She had also told me that we were strongly Republican because Abraham Lincoln had freed the slaves and Harold Stassen, her favorite statesman, had led the way in integrating the National Guard in Minnesota. My first experiential lens for confronting racism was through my mother's eyes and her tortured conscience. But I lived in a culture and region that had no tortured conscience about the racism closest at hand. I grew up less than thirty miles from the Pipestone Reservation and in the area of the Lakota people. The immigrants who came to South Dakota and Minnesota, my forebears among them, never acknowledged that these peoples had been deprived of their land by the U.S. government.

When the Mud Flower Collective was studying our lives in relation to each other in *God's Fierce Whimsy*, it was painful but healing for me to revisit the dynamics of race and ethnicity in my own background.[2] Initially I felt trapped by these terrible contradictions. I was ashamed and confused. I think many white women start where I started. Our silence about racism is maintained because of an agonizing guilt about it. However, in my mature years, I have realized that guilt is an antirevolutionary emotion, which we must work through so that we can get on with effective liberative work.

West: *In relation to issues of race, would you describe how your thinking has emerged on theorizing whiteness and understanding whiteness? In "Feminist Musings on Community," you write, "Every person who is serious about community today must begin with the blinders we wear to otherness, the whiteness that blinds us to our own cultural imperialism." And in your "Foreword to* Welfare Policy, *[feminist critiques]"* *you talk about "the deeply racist antidemocratic values" that are part of the public debates about welfare policy. I know that this is something that you've been thinking about, and I am wondering if there is more that you'd like to say about it.*

Harrison: You've asked a huge question, because I think the most exciting intellectual work of the last decade has been the development of whiteness studies, which has enabled the theorizing about white racism to become clearer and more concrete. We are better able to name the daily impact of an unconscious whiteness. I have also learned a great deal about the construction of racialized barriers through reading critical race theory written by black legal scholars such as Kimberle Crenshaw, Patricia Williams, and Kendall Thomas.[3] Of course, I also appreciate all of the contributions to the theorizing of white racism by womanist religious scholars and by black activists/scholars such as Bernice Johnson Reagon, Barbara Smith, Audre Lorde, Angela Davis, and June Jordan.

When we first started celebrating Women's History Week at Union, back in the seventies, we invited Barbara Smith to do the first keynote, and then invited Audre Lorde the next year. Reading their work, meeting them, and talking with them, even briefly, completely transformed my way of thinking about the relationships between white and black women in the United States. At both lectures, the first question asked by white students was "How can white and black women become friends?" I was amazed when both of these powerful black feminists gave an identical answer to the question: "Tell me what your politics are, and I will tell you if we can be friends."

West: *Barbara Smith and Audre Lorde were pioneer black feminists who helped to shape and define "second wave" U.S. feminism, and too few people remember that fact.*

Harrison: These experiences and many years of reading black women social theorists, even before I began to read the great black novelists and poets such as Alice Walker and Toni Morrison, taught me that only a practice of political solidarity would enable me to understand white racism in a new way. My stumbling efforts to build solidarity with some of these women and with other black activists such as Florence Kennedy taught me that the only way to deepen my theoretical grasp of white racism was to try to act in ways that enabled black women's voices to be heard.

Even so, the effort to retheorize racism has been a slow process. It took a while for me to rid myself of liberal notions that racism is chiefly a matter of personal bias and to learn that it has nothing to do with biological difference or fear of "color difference." I have been greatly helped here by the social deconstructionist approach, one that teaches white women like myself to understand and demystify the subtle unearned privileges that our whiteness confers. And in the last decade or so, the insistence of postcolonial theorists from the global South that white racism is chiefly a form of cultural arrogance—deep cultural supremacy, if you will—has opened my eyes to the ongoing oblivious assumption by us white people that our way of being is the only true way.

We need to remember when we theorize race that mere ethnic prejudice is not synonymous with racial bigotry. Racism is ethnic prejudice *plus* long-term patterns of historical violence done by one culture to another. Acting viciously toward another group always leads oppressors to develop theories that justify this cultural supremacy. These racialized supremacist notions function in turn to justify treating our victims with contempt. The unspeakable historical violence that has been embedded in our Euro-American social and cultural patterns means that white supremacy operates as a cultural chauvinism so deep that we often do not even see how it works. Just as we have invented heterosexuality as "normal" in order to force people to conform to compulsory heterosexual preferences and patterns, so we have invented justifications about black inferiority to justify our violence and to hold white power in place. We have invented the idea that racism is a problem of *color* variation in order to keep people of darker hue where we want them. Our deciding what black folks want and need is never seen as violence toward them.

We live in a global village in which the political and economic power of the United States has spread cultural imperialism (i.e., white racism) in largely unnoticed ways, and we have used our cultural supremacy to embed division and conflict within other communities and nations. As always, through all of this, women of color are the underside of all the undersides.[4] I tremble for our planet as I see Eurocentric cultures reproducing racisms everywhere. And we can never forget that racism as ethnic atrocity and arrogant cultural and economic hegemony also simultaneously fuel new forms of gender and sex oppression. This is why we must keep the focus on white racism central when we interrogate the historical consequences of Euro-American capitalist patriarchy. I also must say very clearly here that few of the essays in this book represent where I am now in the project of retheorizing white racism. I still intend to publish additional analytic reflections on why white racism is so difficult to see and even harder to resist.

West: *Another matter, not unrelated to racism, might need clarification here. I refer to the question of the range of sources needed for feminist ethical work. One of the ongoing debates among Christian ethicists is about the relationship between Christian theology and moral philosophy. Would you describe how you relate these two sources?*

Harrison: That's a complicated question. It's important for folks studying ethics to remember that there were two big debates in the seventies and eighties among my generation of scholars. One debate was a general one about whether the Christian ethics scholar should use theology *and* philosophy, while the other was over whether social ethicists should rely on social science or philosophy (chiefly moral philosophy).

The first debate grew out of a disagreement between Karl Barth and Emil Brunner in Germany during the Nazi period. Barth argued that Christians should stay away from generalized, abstract philosophical work, while Brunner took the other side of the debate. From reading them, I agreed with Brunner, who used philosophical sources as well as theological and biblical ones in formulating his ethic. It's important to remember though that both Barth and Brunner were working at an earlier time and neither knew a broad enough range of types of philosophy and natural and social science to deal with this question optimally.

The second debate about philosophy and social science was one I always thought was what Jim Gustafson called "a misplaced debate." Insufficient attention was paid to the various ideologies that were shaping *both* social science and philosophy. In my view, Christian ethicists should use any sources that illumine a social problem. We need a strong hermeneutic of suspicion about morals and moral traditions, and should always be asking, "Whose voice are we hearing here?" Christian theology, moral philosophy, and social science and/or theory should all be scrutinized for assumptions that lead us to misread the nature of human agency or the actions and policies being proposed. And all of this work must be situated within a critical understanding of our historical moment. Any source that deepens our grasp of what we are doing and contributes historical perspective and insight should be used.

I need also to say that I don't think a lot of people in the Christian ethics guild understand very well the complexity of sources I use when they label my work. Some people call me a Greek—that is, one who is not biblical and who is shaped too much by moral philosophy. Others assume that I am just a rabid feminist leftie who got all of her ideas from Karl Marx. My educational background was deeply shaped by my undergraduate majors in philosophy and modern history. (I minored in religion and am glad I did because my college religion adviser, Robert McAfee Brown, urged me to get as broad a base as possible.) I realized very early on that choosing between using Christian tradition, which for Protestants meant an emphasis on the Bible, or using insights from moral and social philosophy was a phony decision. I read everything historically, which means that for me there is nothing fixed or final or essential about philosophy as a discipline. And there is nothing fixed or essential about theology or about how Christians read and use the Bible. Philosophies and theologies are concrete historical traditions, and we have to orient our work to both.

The influence of John Bennett, my doctoral mentor, was great. He believed strongly in what were called in his day revelation and natural reason, and he believed that both came to us in historically changing ways. I always thought he did ethics better than those who used only theological sources because such a narrow method easily leads to biblicism and to weak or misleading scriptural interpretation. No religious academic theorist should imagine that what we are doing cannot be transcended. Our grasp of moral wisdom changes, and what we say must remain open to falsification in light of new learnings. What science is about is a process of falsifying existing truth claims. Ruling out new insight and new wisdom and being closed to intellectual counterarguments is stupidity, not divine revelation or inspiration!

I always found the more traditional moral philosophers, such as Immanuel Kant and his followers, interesting and helpful in thinking about ethics even when I also thought they were wrong, or when they abstracted and overgeneralized truth or lost track of historical particularity. To be honest, I have especially enjoyed post-Wittgenstein analytic moral philosophy because those writings helped me discover how often so-called intellectual debates are, in fact, merely conceptual confusions. And this material helped me clarify what matters are relevant and irrelevant to ethical thinking and analysis.

In any case, I am convinced that it is intellectually suicidal to try to produce one's Christian ethical approach out of a single dialectical source or even a single theological tradition. In teaching methods in ethics courses, I tried to get students to focus on the ways in which theology, philosophy (social and moral philosophy), and theories of scientific inquiry could usefully interact. But there must be some convergence in the perspectives we bring together in our inquiries. This is a point where feminism as theory became increasingly important to me, as it helped me see that my discontents with the abstractness and nonsituatedness of what I learned to call malestream traditions were rooted not in my biological gender but in my appreciation for women's cultures. In the early part of *Our Right to Choose,* I voiced this objection very clearly. I became dissatisfied with how white males read well-known philosophers. When, as a young man, Cornel West began teaching at Union, we used to talk a bit about this. We both appreciated the Marxist and American pragmatist traditions, because both assume that one's intellectual horizon is fundamentally shaped by the social commitments one makes to the future, the experience of social transformation and the community one seeks to serve. Theory arises in practice and is corrected in turn by that practice.

West: *In "The Dream of a Common Language," your presidential address at the Society for Christian Ethics, you stress the need to challenge abstract and overly universalized principles when conceptualizing justice for Christian social ethics. Is there anything you would like to add about the importance of including questions of justice at the center of liberative feminist ethics?*

Harrison: For me, the present task of feminism as theory is reimaging justice in a way that makes it the only possible context for thinking about collective and personal human agency. That's our formidable intellectual task. To engage the justice question is to engage the question of right relationship between groups and between persons, of being decent human beings and decent communities in our relations with each other. It is way past time for us to become decent inhabitants of our violated planet. We only begin to understand justice if we engage in the struggle for it, the struggle for better relations. I was persuaded long ago by Marx's claim that we can never compose a full and adequate theory of justice in a deeply unjust world. However, Marx was wrong to discourage us from trying to "think justice" as we seek it. It was his antireligious bias that led him to fear that visionaries would ever also be effectual actors.

I stand in the intellectual traditions of critical theory—that is, the social, philosophical approach first developed in Germany and later in France that believes that we get to better ways of knowing by interrogating and demystifying any and all truth claims. Anything that is currently held to be "truth" in politics and religion must be questioned in order to see whose voice, whose self-interest, is being expressed in this claim. Since we do not have consensus about what the good society should look like—that is, what the perfect commonwealth of God would be—we have to *work* toward a deeper social consensus through struggle and through examination of claims and counterclaims. However, we cannot wait for the resolution of this debate, since we must face the immediate challenge of life together as human beings. We will never arrive at a definitive or fixed theory of justice, or, for that matter, love or compassion. As moral persons and professional ethicists, we should not be preoccupied with designing perfect sets of norms (action guides, virtues, or values). Instead, we need to clarify what norms should be prioritized, and then *act*. I do believe there is a growing global consensus "from the underside" about the priority of basic human rights. Alas, the importance of human and other species' rights isn't a matter of deep widespread concern here in the United States. We had better awaken to the fact that we are becoming the globe's moral pariahs.

Of course, we also need the theological dimension in finding empowerment for the future. We need imagination, vision, and hope to forge ever-fresh strategies for making justice. We need never to forget that there can be no deep love and no deep compassion where there is no passion for justice, the form God/the sacred takes among us.[5]

Notes

1. The use of "malestream" referring to male dominant mainstream traditions can be found in a variety of feminist work. See, especially, Mary O'Brien *The Politics of Reproduction* (Boston: Routledge and Kegan Paul, 1983).
2. Mud Flower Collective (Katie G. Cannon, Beverly W. Harrison, Carter Heyward, Ada Maria Isasi-Diaz, Bess B. Johnson, Mary D. Pellauer, Nancy D. Richardson), *God's Fierce Whimsy: Christian Feminism and Theological Education* (New York: Pilgrim Press, 1985). The Mud Flower Collective was an interracial group of feminist theological educators.
3. See Kimberle Crenshaw, Neil Gotanda, Gary Peller, and Kendall Thomas, eds., *Critical Race Theory: The Key Writings That Formed the Movement* (New York: New Press, 1995).
4. This way of characterizing the historical location of women of color comes from James H. Cone, black liberation theologian and Harrison's long-time colleague at Union.
5. Here Harrison alludes to a work by her favorite theologian. See Carter Heyward, *Our Passion for Justice: Images of Power, Sexuality, and Liberation* (Cleveland: Pilgrim Press, 1984).

Chapter 2

The Dream of a Common Language: Toward a Normative Theory of Justice in Christian Ethics

This is the 1982 address given by Harrison at the annual banquet of the Society of Christian Ethics when she was the first woman president of the society. Here she lays out some of the distinctive dimensions that liberative feminist theo-ethics contributes to our understanding of justice. The essay was originally published in the Annual of the Society of Christian Ethics *(1983): 1–25.*

My assignment has been made doubly difficult by the eminent performances of my two immediate predecessors in this position, Douglas Sturm and Daniel Maguire. In 1981, Sturm chose as the topic of his presidential address "The Prism of Justice: *E Pluribus Unum,*" and in 1982, Maguire discussed "The Feminization of God and Ethics."[1] Those of you who know me well will appreciate how soundly they encroached on some of my central preoccupations!

I am keenly aware that my presence on this platform is not unrelated to the growing sensibility in this society to the matter of gender justice. I am here, honored as a number of women deserve to be, for the accelerating, creative contribution of women as a group to our common work. I speak tonight with an acute sense of accountability to these other women. Yet, despite my commitment to the urgency of gender justice, I will not rehearse themes that Dan Maguire so elo-

14

quently advanced last year. Had his effort not been so adequate, my topic this evening, marking the occasion when the first woman addresses this society as its president, would surely have had to be different. I would have focused more directly on gender justice and its meaning for us all.

Douglas Sturm's able and thoughtful address of two years ago also made me reticent to follow my intuition concerning what I should be about here. It was he who mused at the outset, "Why the Presidential Address and the Annual Banquet were cast together to begin with I do not pretend to know unless it was intended as a jaundiced commentary on the one or the other, given the maxim that one must, in this world of woe, take the sour along with the sweet. . . . Reveling in the pleasures, we must not forget the pains of the *Civitas Terrena*."[2] Like Sturm, I am painfully aware that justice is hardly a topic for after-dinner revelry.

As I pondered this occasion, I decided to risk presumption in addressing the matter of justice so soon after Douglas Sturm had, not because I was left unsatisfied by his perceptive analysis of current concepts of political justice. On the contrary, his gentle and irenic probing of the principles of justice, their strengths and limits, need no emendation. I agree with him that any principle of justice is bound to have strengths and limitations. I also believe with him that at the level of theory we should all be as pluralistic in our conception of justice as possible. However, and I know he would agree, pluralism could have the last word only if all human activity were suspended, because action, and even inaction, inherently involve some prioritizing of principles. Because I am an activist who is also a scholar, I tend to think normatively about prioritizing the principles of justice.

I have chosen to retread familiar ground, then, because the matter of justice is with me a central preoccupation. It is inevitable that on this occasion the incumbent of this office muses on his, or for once, "her" concerns for the "state of the art" in which we are mutually engaged. When I do so, my mind turns inexorably to the question of justice, and more especially to the place of justice in our work, both at the level of the theories we employ and the way in which the concern animates or fails to animate our work.

I also want to acknowledge awareness that the strong disposition I felt to speak of justice here was not unrelated to the fact that I am a woman and the first female president of this society. However, precisely how this urgent inner response had worked to shape my intention did not become clear to me until after I had finished a first draft of my text. At that point, my beloved colleague Mary Pellauer shared with me a splendid essay by the social theorist Carole Pateman entitled "'The Disorder of Women': Women, Love, and the Sense of Justice."[3] Contemplating Pateman's analysis of the social theory of liberalism, and more particularly liberalism's axiomatic assumptions about women's nature, triggered my deeper awareness of what had been going on with me. What Pateman identifies, from Rousseau to Freud, is a firm tradition "that women lack, and cannot develop, a sense of justice."[4] While the substance of her exposition was hardly new to me, it precipitated recognition of what had been working in me, below the level of consciousness. In the years of struggle to own my own competence and power as a working Christian ethicist, I have come to know myself well enough to realize that I fling myself in the face of a sex-role stereotype with an alacrity born almost of instinct. Ergo, the topic of the evening!

MY PERSPECTIVE ON A THEORY OF JUSTICE

It is no secret that I am one who works from a perspective of liberation theology and, therefore, aspires to a social ethic (all ethics being social) aimed to challenge not merely unjust acts but structures and institutional patterns of power and their attendant structures of privilege. You are well aware of the thesis of liberation theology that structures of power and privilege thwart and dehumanize not merely individuals but groups of persons who as a result must live out their lives without the degree of self-direction appropriate to the human person and without the necessary participation in the human community that would make it possible for "community" to be understood as genuinely encompassing them. From such a position, or rather, from such a commitment, justice appears not merely as a juridical notion, nor as a "regulative ideal," nor even as the "first virtue of social institutions," although this important contention of John Rawls[5] is surely an improvement over earlier liberal conceptions of justice. For me, justice is more than all of these. It is our central theological image, a metaphor of right relationship, which shapes the *telos* of a good community and serves as the animating passion of the moral life. I have no hope of justifying such a conception of justice in so brief a time as is available to me tonight. The operative word in the subtitle of this address is *toward.* What I do intend to do is press the thesis that a radical conception of justice as rightly related community may be claimed legitimately as *the* core theological metaphor of a Christian moral vision of life, in much the same way that many have claimed love, in the form of *caritas* or *agape,* as Christianity's central theological-moral metaphor.

However, I certainly do *not* mean to suggest that any notion of justice as core theological metaphor for Christian ethics provides a full and adequate normative theory of justice. One cannot derive a full conception of obligation or principles of justice sufficient to adjudicate the social conflicts that occasion our concrete moral dilemmas from theological images and metaphors. No Christian ethicist, in my assessment, has persuaded the moral philosophers that *agape* yields a distinctive or sufficient theory of moral justification, and none will find that a radical theological notion of justice fares any better in this regard. I do not aspire to derive my moral theory exclusively from my theology, nor do I think that Christian ethicists ought to so aspire. Morality is the work of our *common* life, and the particularities of my convictions and my participation as a Christian, grounded in the way I have experienced revelation in my community, must answer not only to my community's sense of narrative and vocation but also to the sensibilities, principles, and values that inform the conscientious efforts of other morally serious beings. Not to acknowledge this is to me sheer Christian chauvinism of the sort which is indefensible in a pluralistic world. The "blessed disorder" created by the collapse of the *corpus christianum* has enabled us, quite properly, to live free of nostalgia for the day when theology alone could dictate the terms of an ethic for society.

As I understand the matter, however, central theological images and metaphors do function in our ethics to provide what I still hazard to call a teleological impulse, one which profoundly shapes our understanding of our purposes and directions as moral agents and moral communities. Teleology serves that dimension of our moral theory which Dorothy Emmet has aptly presented in her excellent work *The Moral Prism*.[6] There she describes two quite different types of teleology. "Teleology A" is an approach to moral justification that involves consequences or the identification of concrete ends. By contrast, theological images and metaphors provide what Emmet calls "teleology B"—a purposive sense of vocation or lifestyle. I would also insist that theological images and metaphors of justice encompass what Emmet characterizes as the axiological or aesthetic dimension of moral theory. They shape our sense of what sort of community would be beautiful to behold. Our images of justice provide intimations, imaginative envisagements, of what constitutes the good of the whole society. So while theological notions of justice specify neither the range of concrete goods and values for which we ought to strive in the immediate future, nor principles of sufficient specificity to adjudicate conflicts of interest, they do ground our sense of purpose and order our direction as moral agents and communities. They give some clues for prioritizing our principles and identifying our concrete goals.

As a result, I believe that it makes a considerable, even overriding, difference to the enterprise of Christian ethics whether or not we construe a vision of justice to be substantive and central to our *theological* vision. It is, I believe, a failure to discern the shift on the part of liberation theologies toward locating a radical conception of justice at the center of not only a theological *ethic*, but of *our vision of God*, which accounts for much of the considerable misinterpretation of these theologies in North American academic settings.

LIBERATION THEOLOGY AND ITS CRITICS

I cannot take the time to defend liberation theologies from the myriad of misreadings to which I believe they have been subject. But just to assure you that I *am* familiar with them, I will rehearse the well-known charges of liberation theology's detractors. Many have proclaimed liberation theologies faddish at best, and at worst neither authentically theological nor adequately ethical. The ethics of liberation theology, insofar as they yield any, are said to be crassly utilitarian, violating canons of universalization in ethics. Our theologies are deemed subversive of God's transcendence, substituting a humanism in which the hegemony of oppressed and marginated communities as a historical force displace divine will as *the* source of human good. And of course, in the eyes of many, liberation theologies are hopelessly entangled in the ideological battles of the day in a way that other, presumably less passionately partisan approaches avoid.

Others, including liberation theologians themselves, have defended liberation theology from these accusations far better than I can do here.[7] Even so, a brief comment on each is necessary to clarify why a more serious appreciation of the viability of liberation theology in ethics is in order. About the charge of ideological entanglement, perhaps the less said, the better. Let it suffice that I believe our world is filled with ideological conflict because there is deep and basic disagreement regarding the historical direction in which we ought to move. I presume that no one denies the pervasiveness of ideology. However, I do believe that many neglect its source in basic and life-rending disagreements about the future. My assumption, then, is that when there is genuine social conflict, ideology is both intense and inevitable, such that *no one* can stand above it. To claim or imply otherwise is to deny the basic conditions of temporal process and human historicity, on the one hand, and the reality of our finitude, on the other. It is also to fly in the face of everything we have come to understand about the sociology of knowledge over the last century. I happen to believe that explicit ideological commitments and loyalties are far less subversive of the fragile canons of human fairness and far less corrosive of authentic community than approaches which purport that objectivity is a state of being, or even the proud possession of a socially detached, academic class. Objectivity in the pursuit of knowledge and in morality is, I submit, functionally subservient to the wider social requirements of fairness and public accountability. Few of us honor many of these requirements most of the time. There are numerous ways to monitor ourselves in terms of fairness and accountability, and assuming a stance of objectivity—that is, attempting to detach ourselves as completely as possible from our specific interests—is one such method. However, theories which make objectivity as disinterestedness the whole of "fairness" and construe *it* as adequate public accountability tend rather seriously to obscure the interest served by any social location and to every purported appeal to fact, value, or norm. In any case, to acknowledge the pervasive character of ideology in our world is also to recognize that such conflicts will ineluctably leave their mark on every theological and ethical position, without exception, rendering the charge of ideological entanglement empty of critical substance. In my opinion, it would be a boon to the quality of our debate if we ever reached this point of awareness and moved on to specific substantive disagreements.

The charges aimed at liberation theologies regarding the inadequacy of their ethics are more complex, and cannot be responded to here sufficiently. I am inclined to think, however, that much of the unease among academicians on this issue derives as much from our own cultural provincialism—our lack of in-depth understanding of what other cultures and peoples are enduring—as from genuine inadequacies in the ethics of those engaged in liberation theology. We are, after all, deeply provincial, we Americans, with little empathy for persons and groups whose situations and life circumstances are far different from our own. And as academics, we are inclined to bond ourselves to the current common language of two formerly remote provinces of the Roman Empire, or at least to the Husserlian and Ricoeurian dialects, and then complacently to imagine that we have probed the deepest wisdom of the world!

It is also an obvious fact that liberation theologians as a group do not come from communities where the sort of differentiation between theology and ethics intrinsic to our academic specialization prevails. The sustained attention to moral theory and styles of moral justification, together with the degree of elaboration of specific problems and decisions, which many of us take for granted as indices of "competent ethics," are, to be sure, not always forthcoming in the writings of liberation theologians. I do not, however, believe that it is the less specialized character of their writings which chiefly accounts for the ethical differences between liberation theologians and many U.S. academicians. Rather, these differences obtain due to liberation theologians' different analyses of existing society and their different communities of accountability, which are so unlike those many U.S. academicians choose to serve. It also goes without saying that liberation theologians are not striving, like many of us, to formulate a social ethic for society as a whole or one attempting to impact well-established institutions and the consciousness of their leaders. To me, a seminal moral difference in the ethical situation of liberation theologians, and others who construe the Christian ethic differently, is that they, unlike some of us, do not begin with the axiomatic assumption that the present order of society deserves, at least to a considerable degree, a take-for-granted mantle of moral legitimacy.

Certainly, modern Christian theologians and ethicists in the West also have been concerned that a Christian ethic offer critical challenge to the existing order of things. However, when the critical element is presumed to inhere either in already elaborated theological tradition or in rationality functioning in abstraction from engagement in situations on injustice here and now, critical sensibility can, and frequently does, lead to a paralysis of action. It promotes a kind of "pox on all your houses" attitude in which theoretical purity, whether theological or moral-philosophical, is more valued than doing that which makes for justice. Many contemporary theologies of the neo-orthodox tradition and contemporary moral philosophies that take established moral convention as their starting point project, I submit, a strong, if sometimes subtle, bias against social change, assuming the axiomatic viability of major patterns of our social world.

It is with the accusation of theological deficiency in liberation theology that I begin to focus my central thesis. The charge directed at liberation theologians concerning our presumed theological functionalism and humanism, including our failure to give divine transcendence an assured place at the center of Christian theological vision, can only be clarified if we recognize the centrality of justice as a normative *theological* conception. Let me say, though, that with respect to the many Latin American liberation theologians who, along with feminists, have borne the brunt of this accusation, I am persuaded that the charge is, simply put, wrong. To be sure, Jose Porfino Miranda has contended that theism, as a general problem, is in principle irresolvable in a world so filled with injustice as our own.[8]

However, as Gustavo Gutierrez and Juan Luis Segundo, among many others, have made plain, the Latin Americans are serious about affirming divine transcendence, but will not do this by sustaining the sharp either/or dualism of Christian theological formulations which bypass the agency of human communities in history. They insist, rightly, that the abandonment of the two-tiered metaphysics of an earlier worldview requires thoroughgoing reenvisionment of how God's transcendence interrelates with the potency of human activity.[9]

What I believe is at issue between these liberation theologians and a good many of their critics is precisely the continuing reservations of the latter in the face of bridging the presumed unbridgeable gulf between God's action and human agency. The spirit of the early Barth still breathes heavily in much modern mainstream Christian theological ethics, despite the resolution of Barth's dualism in his late embrace of the radicality of human freedom.[10] By comparison with most established Christian theologies, many Latin American liberation theologians have posited a radically different way of stipulating *how* divine transcendence and revelation is mediated to human beings. For them, as for many of us, divine transcendence is mediated not through tradition as given but through *praxis*, concretely understood both as engaged solidarity with the poor and disinherited and as critical reflection on the Christian tradition in light of that engagement.

As a feminist theologian, I am astonished that the dominant understandings of transcendence are still considered unproblematic in so many quarters. Many feminist theologians have indeed gone much further than other liberation theologians in challenging traditional notions of divine transcendence. And I believe that we have some way to go before we can face the point insisted upon by our renegade sisters, especially those post-Christian and non-Christian interpreters of feminist spirituality who insist that traditional theological claims to divine transcendence have operated *actively* and *directly* to subvert a sense of our own power and responsibility for the world and the way things come to be. Some, such as the Wicca theologian Starhawk, have embraced a radical doctrine of divine immanence and a pluralism of spiritual powers, which Starhawk contends is *necessary* to place respect for the real, existent cosmos and its creatures at the center of our moral concern.[11] Those who would summarily dismiss such theological arguments as warmed-over and much discredited pantheism, an evil from which Christian orthodoxy long since delivered us, at the very least should respond to this analysis concerning how appeals to divine transcendence shape—or rather misshape—our sense of responsibility and accountability for our world.

Many Christian feminist theologians have also insisted that theological claims to transcendence must answer to the way they mold our sense of moral agency vis-à-vis justice. Not only have they analyzed the effect of masculinist-idolatrous deformation of our conceptions of moral agency and of God, but they also have joined Jewish thinkers in identifying the intrinsically anti-Semitic character of christological development.[12] And they have joined black theologians, female and male, in elucidating the way the superiority of light over darkness in our dominant theological paradigms of transcendence sustains and legitimates racism.[13]

JUSTICE AS THE FOUNDATIONAL THEOLOGICAL IMAGE IN LIBERATION THEOLOGIES

To be fair to Christian liberation theologies, it simply must be understood that all of them posit as *the* appropriate, concrete correlate of the active love of God, the human longing and capacity for active struggle toward justice born of the aspiration for *rightly related community*. Just as Marx apparently felt that any theory of justice under capitalism would mask alienated social relations, such that no notion of justice could envision the well-being of species-being, given a thoroughly unjust, class-stratified society,[14] so many liberation theologians have maintained that dominant theological theories of transcendence reflect alienated, objectified social relations. The corporate human experience of divine presence is, they presume, largely subverted by structural oppression and the exploitation of some groups of human beings by others at a systemic level. Our atheistic ethos attests that we do not live in a just world, nor one in which the longing for right relationship is widespread. In keeping with Gutierrez's thesis,[15] we are not atheistic by virtue of our appreciation of the world as truly worldly, but by virtue of our rejection of the prophetic task of justice.

We do not, from a liberation perspective, possess blueprints for a just world. It is only by virtue of our engaging in the struggle for justice—a struggle we must suppose will endure for as long as time and history continue—that we gain intimations of what rightly ordered community and God's transcendence may mean. Such intimations are *never* abstract, and we cannot, some liberation theologians insist, transmute the foundational metaphors and images such intimations provide into *ideal ends*, traditionally understood, without transmuting our ethics back into abstract idealism. Gutierrez's widely misunderstood insistence on the centrality of utopia in theological reflection is related to this point. It is his contention that utopia is *annunciation*, not denotation, and he warns that without properly utopian thinking, that is, properly annunciatory utterance, faith cannot endure.[16] People must have hope that something more than the present order of things is possible if they are to act together in the face of dehumanizing power.

So too, Jules Girardi, whose central image is of a world "where there are no excluded ones," intends to elicit not a programmatic agenda but a metaphor of transformation.[17] Dorothee Soelle's invocation of "the phantasie of possibility" as the ground of our praxis as Christians also needs to be read in this light.[18] The phrase which I borrowed from feminist poet Adrienne Rich for the title of this evening's address, *The Dream of a Common Language*, is another such seminal image.[19] I should hasten to add that Rich might well not approve my co-optation of her title, for she is among the proponents of the new feminist spirituality who believe that Christianity is intrinsically implicated in the legitimation of male control of women. However, like the liberation theologians, she warns mightily against premature abstractionism in our language of justice, given the realities of the world in which we live. I often quote from another of Rich's poems, precisely to remind myself of how often, as a moralist, I violate her strictures against the inflation of language:

> There are words I cannot choose again:
> "humanism" "androgyny"
>
> Such words have no shame in them, no diffidence
> before the raging stoic grandmothers:
>
> their glint is too shallow, like a dye
> that does not permeate
>
> the fibers of actual life
> as we live it, now . . .[20]

Like many liberation theologians, Rich also understands the concrete and immediate task of the moral life, not as the proclamation of a *general solution* to the brokenness of human life, but rather as the unmasking of what she calls "the lies, secrets, and silences" that sustain and legitimate existing unjust orders of power.[21] For her, as for liberation theologians, there can be no premature proclamation or universal formulae for the general resolution of the problem of our broken and unjust community. Parenthetically, I would add that it is this refusal to formulate a general theory for the resolution of this brokenness which has created the impression that liberation ethics violates the canons of universalizability in ethics, at least as many Christian ethicists currently construe them.[22] In response, liberationists insist that any such scheme of general resolution would violate the conditions of historical existence. Yet these concrete liberation images and metaphors of justice, by comparison to conservative and liberal theories, do imply a quite different, and morally compelling, notion of what society may be, and alternative understandings of politics and social power.

WHAT THESE NOTIONS OF JUSTICE IMPLY
FOR OUR CONCEPTION OF SOCIETY

As I have said, the notion of justice at issue here does not presuppose the validity of the given structures of society and community, such that justice enters, as in organic or conservative theories, to adjudicate the conflicts between individual well-being and common good. Here, individual well-being and common good live and breathe or die together. Nor is society, as in liberal theories, conceived of as a contractual ordering of common life between already existent autonomous individuals, such that liberty and equality struggle in a perpetual trade-off. An organic theory of society yields a conception of justice which has as its central concern the need for each to receive her or his due. Because, to speak in modern sociological parlance, the macrostructure of society, organically conceived, is largely impenetrable, the task of justice is thought best focused on seeking to assure that each receives her due.[23] Liberal contractual theories see large sectors of society as merely voluntary. Only the family and related orders are conceived as essentially social because they are "of nature," prior to society. My communitarian bias leads me to believe that such liberal notions of society hardly yield a conception of justice at all until they are reformulated, as John Rawls and innumerable others in our time have proposed, to reconceive liberty as a principle of "equal liberty,"[24] thereby providing a theoretical basis for moving beyond monadic individualism's purportedly inevitable zero sum war between liberty and equality. I am enough of a liberal to believe that a good society will maximize liberty, but it will also never confuse it with privilege. Liberty is a *nonrelational* notion, which is why it has so little usefulness in moral discourse or in theories of justice. Nozick and other libertarians have done nothing at all to disabuse me of this conviction.[25]

Concerning the conception of society, then, there is some continuity between organic theories and liberation perspectives, in that each accepts the inexorable and irreducible sociality of all reality, and understands the social patterns of society as the matrix from which the individuation of human life and community proceed. But organic metaphors fail to illumine the radically historical nature of society. A clear conceptual break with organic metaphors, which imply that the structures of our social world are ineluctably shaped and controlled by their origins, is also required. The prior question in a radical notion of justice is not the question of what is our due, but whether the status or station into which we are born is itself just.

By contrast to conservative theories, the historical conditions under which liberalism arose made it largely unnecessary to accept primal sociality as a given. Liberalism's contractarian conception of society gained plausibility historically precisely because it enabled a radical break with prescribed and inherited roles and means of access to power. The rising class that elaborated the liberal theory of society generated economic power to pose against the established political order. But though liberalism invoked and enabled what Michael Lewis called "the individual as central sensibility,"[26] its conception of the individual was abstracted from our actual, intrinsic social relations. Furthermore, its normative social conception of community was limited. Civil society, understood as the arena in which egoistic interests of individuals are adjudicated, hardly encompasses interdependent relationships. Furthermore, the liberal conception of civil society placed most of the generative sources of social power, especially economic production and exchange, outside the sphere of politics, or legitimate communal accountability.[27]

Liberalism has surely fallen upon hard times, assailed by libertarians who resent the reformist amelioration of its early narrow definition of the proper scope of civil society, and also by radicals, because we believe it has largely come to represent, in the words of Dee Brown, author of *Bury My Heart at Wounded Knee*, an "almost reverential attitude toward the ideal of personal freedom for those who already [have] it."[28] The central virtue of liberalism, the sensibilities it commends to us for respecting persons as such and as members of the moral community will, I believe, not survive unless its fearfully abstract sense of both person and community is recognized. The manner in which liberalism construed the relationship between the individual and civil society abstracts social relations from most social power, and construes politics as the competition of interest groups and denies that production and the market are sources of political power. Classes, castes, and alternative nondominant cultures are obliterated in the theory of this rationalized ethos, and within liberalism, all are construed merely as *interest groups*. Furthermore, it is assumed that all existing social power can be controlled and redistributed by the continuous balancing of interests and constitutional provisions for procedural fairness. But the generative source of much contemporary social power, the production and control of wealth, is untouched by the mechanism aimed to sustain civil society. And now, the unchecked social power of those who control our economic life has made liberalism's abstract individual, free of communal ties, a hideous existential reality, and has all but absorbed the fragile institutions created to sustain civil society.

WHAT THESE NOTIONS OF JUSTICE IMPLY ABOUT POLITICS AND SOCIAL POWER

We may not, I submit, find our way back, unless we reorient not only our sense of how the relationship of person and society shapes community but also our conception of *what social power is* and what the task of politics must be. Like its theory of the individual, liberalism's core theory of social power is inappropriately abstract. Power is an inexorable given in society. Perceived chiefly as dangerous to individual interests, power is to be balanced and checked. The task of politics here is to contain the quest for power that relentless egoism breeds. This task is largely a negative one, though liberalism's fascination with power contradicts this conception of its faintly dirty face.[29] Because it is in politics that we expect everyone to let it all hang out, pursuing interests with abandon, justice is valued precisely as the checking of unbridled power and the successful balancing of interests. To be sure, the task of justice is endless, for power abstractly roams the world, ineluctably moving from right to left and back again. Humanity may move ahead a little (and liberalism values that little even less than it should), but do *not* get your hopes up, because the struggle for power alone is basic to politics and human nature.

But social power, we liberationists insist, has a human face. It is something we human beings collectively and individually *generate*. Social power also has a very definite history—and *that* is the problem. If alienating power controls our world, and it surely does, the answer is to release the thwarted power of those whose lives are otherwise denied the human participation that right relationships generate. Because our relationships to each other are given, the social question is not the contractual one—When and for what activities shall we come together?—but rather, What are the conditions and patterns of the social relationships in which we now exist that thwart right relationship? The question then becomes, How may we alter these to enable *common effort* for *common well-being*? Power, from this viewpoint, is neither inherently tainted nor simplistically benign. The generation, distribution, and direction of social power are shaped by the patterns of social relations that characterize any society. Alienated and alienating power, so widespread in our world, is power which stands over us, determining our fate apart from or in opposition to our own power of self-direction and our power to participate in the shaping of our common lives and future. If we do not construe our "social problem" this way, our well-intentioned policies inevitably exacerbate precisely those class and group antagonisms engendered by human action in the past. And to resign ourselves to the inevitability of these ancient antagonisms is precisely to eschew responsibility for shaping our common life.

The goal of liberation politics, I submit, *is to forge new and very concrete bonds of community*. In the barrios of Latin America, base communities of people, including Christians, seek literally to forge out a form of interdependent common life which the most brutal repression cannot stamp out. So too in South Africa, the Philippines, and Korea. Why is it, I ask myself, that so many people like us—white and relatively affluent—do not hear in the calls for solidarity (not just advocacy or concern, but *solidarity*) with the poor a call to community? Why is it that in a world where those of European extraction are a tiny minority, we do not hear in the demand of black liberation theologians for our commitment to black reality as normative human reality, a hopeful invitation to us to forge new bonds of community?[30] Is it not the case that the politics of liberation make little sense to us, and frighten us so badly, precisely because the longing—our will and desire—for genuine community is so nearly dead among us?

WHAT WOMEN SEEKING LIBERATION HAVE TO TEACH ON THESE QUESTIONS

In closing, I will be presumptuous enough to suggest that the deepest analysis of disordered power and the parables for new community are coming in our time from women, both white marginated women and women of color.[31] It is, I submit, not at all surprising that female persons in our time have perceived the *subtler* modes of disordered power. Justice, we have learned, must begin in the bedroom. And the search for community must begin concretely there and in the way we relate in the workplace, and in all those interpersonal spheres so long and so romantically assumed to be "natural," and therefore arenas where norms of love function directly, uninhibited by "social egoism." Women are insisting that we need a revolution of "small changes,[32] which will imbue culture with the personal transformative power to sustain political change humanely. So we have been insisting that love, power, *and* justice be brought together because they belong together! "The personal is the political and the political personal" is a serious slogan forged of such understanding. It is hardly novel to suggest that love is the doing of justice. I am aware of how many of you have also said this.[33] I do believe, however, that women struggling for liberation have something critical to teach, especially about the role of the body and of passion in forging the connections between love, power, and justice.

Carol Pateman, in the essay referred to earlier, explains that the liberal view of women's deficiency in justice is rooted in the assumption that we females are set so intrinsically in the order of the family—an order presumed central to the state of nature rather than to civil society—that we cannot escape the entrapments of biology and therefore the consequences of sensuality and sentiment. Justice, liberals presumed, demands *dispassion*, and women cannot be counted on to manage that! So love is women's work, and justice, men's. All liberation theologies celebrate the materiality, the carnality, the physicality of life. But we women, who have long had sensuality imputed to us, in our time have decided to embrace this sensuality, said to be ours by nature, with a vengeance. When we say we are "our bodies ourselves,"[34] we mean, among other things, that we have come to understand that the human body is the integrated locus of our perception *of all reality*. Through it, by touch, sight, and sound, we experience our relations to the world. Through our deep responsiveness, our passion, we experience longing for connectedness to the whole. But our passion is more than this. *It is also the source of our energy*, which is to say, *our power to act*. Love in the pursuit of justice is effectual acting upon the longing to make right relation. And doing so does make for justice.

No liberation theologian in our time has put more concretely what this merging of passion and love with justice as right relationship implies for our theology than has Carter Heyward. Out of her own experience, and wrestling with the devastating portrayal of the reality of the Holocaust forged by Elie Wiesel, she posits that, quite literally, "the realm of God" *is* the power of relation. But it is also here in the power of relation which is the realm of God that the deepest struggle between good and evil transpires. Here our longing for relation, and our fear of the sort of power that merges from right relationship, forge a divine-human drama on whose outcome our common well-being depends. Heyward puts it this way:

> The constancy of fear—of whatever we cannot control (dominate); (the fear) of *dunamis*, relational power itself—insures the constancy of injustice. Injustice is not, finally, the result of too many good people doing nothing, but rather of too many frightened people doing something so thoroughly, systematically, and often thoughtlessly, that even these same people—good people trying to live in right relation to one another—cannot un-do the systemic evil simply by living good lives day to day. . . .
> Justice is the fruit of human passion, deep love that is willing to bear up fear and tension and uncertainty in relation to persons, issues, and possibilities known and unknown.[35]

In conclusion, I hazard what for traditional and liberal Christianity is an unthinkable thought: that the images of justice engendered by liberation struggles imply that to do the prophetic task of justice, we must make love, passionately, in the world.

By now, some of you must surely be musing, "Aha, you see, she is but a typical woman after all. Having urged us to ponder justice and argued that it must be our central animating theological image, she ends merely by prescribing love."

Well, yes! If at this point, this is your frame of mind, I feel obliged to try to remind you that you should have been forewarned. For after all, what more could be expected, from one of those who, by nature, are bound to passion?

Notes

1. See Douglas Sturm, "The Prism of Justice: *E Pluribus Unum*," *Annual of the Society of Christian Ethics* (1981): 1–28; and Daniel Maguire, "The Feminization of God and Ethics," *Annual of the Society of Christian Ethics* (1982): 1–24.
2. Sturm, "Prism of Justice," 1.
3. Carole Pateman, "'The Disorder of Women': Women, Love, and the Sense of Justice," *Ethics* 91, no. 1 (1980): 20–34.
4. Ibid., 20.
5. John Rawls, *A Theory of Justice* (Cambridge, Mass.: Belknap Press of Harvard University Press, 1971), 3.
6. See Dorothy Emmet, *The Moral Prism* (New York: St. Martin's Press, 1979), esp. 5–17, 42–61.
7. In addition to liberation theology texts cited elsewhere, see Matthew L. Lamb, "A Distorted Interpretation of Latin American Liberation Theology," *Horizons* 8, no. 2 (Fall 1981): 352–64; Christian E. Gudorf, *Catholic Social Teaching on Liberation Themes* (Washington, D.C.: University Press of America, 1981); and Robert McAfee Brown, *Theology in a New Key: Responding to Liberation Themes* (Philadelphia: Westminster Press, 1978).
8. Jose Porfino Miranda, *Marx and the Bible: A Critique of the Philosophy of Oppression*, trans. John Eagleson (Maryknoll, N.Y.: Orbis Books, 1974), 254ff.
9. See Gustavo Gutierrez, *A Theology of Liberation* (Maryknoll, N.Y.: Orbis Books, 1973); and Juan Luis Segundo, *The Liberation of Theology*, trans. by John Drury (Maryknoll, N.Y.: Orbis Books, 1976). I do not accept Segundo's astonishing identification of Christian revelation with maleness on pp. 37–38 n. 55.
10. See, e.g., Karl Barth, *The Humanity of God* (Richmond, Va.: John Knox Press, 1960).
11. See Starhawk, *The Spiral Dance: A Rebirth of the Ancient Religion of the Great Goddess* (San Francisco: Harper & Row, 1979), esp. 9ff. See also Starhawk, "Ethics and Justice in Goddess Religion," in *The Politics of Women's Spirituality*, ed. Charlene Spretnak (New York: Anchor Books, 1982), 415–22.
12. See, e.g., Rosemary Radford Ruether, *Faith and Fratricide* (New York: Seabury Press, 1974); Carter Heyward, *The Redemption of God: A Theology of Mutual Relation* (Washington, D.C.: University Press of America, 1982); and Dorothee Soelle, *Christ the Representative: An Essay in Theory after the "Death of God"* (Philadelphia: Fortress Press, 1967).
13. See, e.g., Cornwall Collective, *Our Daughters Shall Prophesy* (New York: Pilgrim Press, 1980), esp. 38–48; Starhawk, *Dreaming the Dark: Magic, Sex, and Politics* (Boston: Beacon Press, 1982); Cherrie Moraga and Gloria Anzaldua, *This Bridge Called My Back: Writings by Radical Women of Color* (Watertown, Mass.: Persephone Press, 1981); and Gloria Hull et al., eds., *All the Blacks Were Male and All the Women White* (Old Westbury, N.Y.: Feminist Press, 1981).
14. I agree with Allen W. Wood, "The Marxian Critique of Justice" and "Marx on Right and Justice: A Reply to Husami," in *Marx, Justice, and History: A Philosophy and Public Affairs Reader*, ed. Marshall Cohen, Thomas Nagel, and Thomas Scanlon (Princeton, N.J.: Princeton University Press, 1980).
15. Gutierrez, *Theology of Liberation*, 189–202.
16. Ibid., esp. 232ff.

17. See Jules Girardi, "Class Struggle and the Excluded Ones," trans. (and circulated) by New York Circus, from *Amoe Christiano Y Lucha De Classes* (Sigueme, Spain, 1975).

18. See Dorothee Soelle, *Beyond Mere Obedience* (Philadelphia: Fortress Press, 1982).

19. Adrienne Rich, *The Dream of a Common Language, Poems 1974–1977* (New York: W.W. Norton & Co., 1978).

20. Adrienne Rich, "Natural Resources," in Rich, *Dream of a Common Language*, 13.

21. Adrienne Rich, *On Lies, Secrets, and Silences: Selected Prose, 1966–1978* (New York: W. W. Norton & Co., 1979).

22. I subscribe to the thesis that universalization has a key role in moral reasoning, both as a rational criterion for testing action guides themselves (what sort of society would it be if everyone did the proscribed or prescribed action, etc.?) and also as a test of acts (I should do what I would want anyone to do in the same or highly analogous circumstances). I believe, however, that some Christian ethics assume inflated and unjustified theories of universalization; for example, that there is a hierarchy of obvious and unexceptional moral principles, or that a Christian ethic must be committed to an abstract, ideal formula of the good, whose meaning is unspecific and unrelated to context. Persons who construe a Christian ethic in this way seem almost invariably to accuse those with a different moral theory of being "unprincipled." The assault on liberation ethical approaches that follows, predictably, invokes such claims as that liberation theologians are reductionistically utilitarian, embracing violence (as though violence were a moral norm in these perspectives) or eschewing love. Such criticisms seem to derive from ahistorical and asocial abstractness in the use of moral theory and from the tremendous ambiguity of such abstracted theory as to what is meant by the "over-ridingness" of moral principles.

23. My point here is not to rule out the problem of the person's standing vis-à-vis the community but to observe that the traditional natural law starting point—*sum cuique*—does not enable the question of the moral viability of a given social structure to be focused centrally in moral debate. It is a matter of starting point in the theory of justice which is at issue.

24. How far Rawls's "justice as fairness" goes in incorporating "equal liberty" as a foundational consideration in the theory of justice is, quite properly, a matter of dispute. But Rawls may be read as at least recognizing the basic problem of classic liberal theory (*Theory of Justice*, 33, 195–251, and passim).

25. See Robert Nozick, *Anarchy, State, and Utopia* (New York: Basic Books, 1974).

26. See Michael Lewis, *The Culture of Inequality* (Boston: University of Massachusetts Press, 1978), part 1.

27. This generalization requires further qualification in terms of the ideological development of liberal neoclassical economic theory. The classical theorists, including Adam Smith, David Ricardo, and Karl Marx, focused on both production and exchange, whereas the trend in neoclassical theory is to ignore questions of the social character of production and construe *the* basic "economic activity" *as* exchange.

28. Dee Brown, *Bury My Heart at Wounded Knee* (New York: Holt, Rinehart & Winston, 1970), v.

29. Some may object that this characterization of politics applies only to realism, not to liberal theories of politics. I construe the political realist tradition, including Niebuhr's Christian realism on the side of its political theory, as an amalgam of classical and liberal elements. Because political power is posited as given, the questions of its origin *and* its generation are not examined. Yet its conception of and confidence in political process as the source of the balancing power in society seems to me consummately liberal.

30. See, e.g., James H. Cone, *A Black Theory of Liberation* (Philadelphia: Lippincott, 1970); James H. Cone, *God of the Oppressed* (New York: Seabury Press, 1975); and Allan A. Boesak, *Farewell to Innocence: A Socio-ethical Study on Black Theology and Power* (Maryknoll, N.Y.: Orbis Books, 1977). My point is that black liberation theologians have fared no better than Latin American liberation theologians at the hands of white, dominant traditional theological interpreters. In a world where people of color are overwhelmingly the statistical norm, the call to acknowledge that blackness is normatively human is still heard as an outrageous and threatening claim. If this were not so, some sage among us would surely have thought to accuse Cone of the "naturalistic fallacy"!

31. See, e.g., Alice Walker, *The Color Purple* (New York: Harcourt Brace Jovanovich, 1982); Elisabeth Janeway, *The Power of the Weak* (New York: William Morrow & Co., 1981); and Pam McAllerter, ed., *Reweaving the Web of Life* (New York: New Society Publishers, 1982).

32. This phrase is from Marge Piercy, *Small Changes* (New York: Fawcett, 1978). This is the critical point often missed in assessing feminism—that social change must integrate cultural *and* political transformations. That many purported radical theories of politics dichotomize culture and politics, either by denigrating politics or by marginalizing cultural dynamics in social change, is obvious.

33. So many colleagues have done suggestive work here that on reflection I hesitate to identify any works for fear of injustice to others. However, I will cite a few which have been helpful to my thinking on these matters: Daniel Maguire, *A New American Justice: Ending the White Male Monopolies* (Garden City, N.Y.: Doubleday, 1980); James B. Nelson, *Embodiment: An Approach to Sexuality and Christian Theology* (Minneapolis: Augsburg, 1978); Gene Outka, *Agape: An Ethical Analysis* (New Haven, Conn.: Yale University Press, 1972); and Gibson Winter, *Elements for a Social Ethic* (New York: Macmillan, 1966).

34. Boston Women's Health Book Collective, *Our Bodies, Ourselves* (New York: Simon & Schuster, 1973). This work has been a powerful influence in transforming women's self-understanding during the past decade.

35. Isabel Carter Heyward, *The Redemption of God: A Theology of Mutual Relation* (Washington, D.C.: University Press of America, 1982), 135–36.

Chapter 3

Doing Christian Ethics

This text includes revised excerpts from a speech that was originally entitled "Rules, Roles, and Relations: Finding Your Way in Christian Ethics." Harrison delivered this speech during the early 1980s as part of an ongoing series at Union Theological Seminary sponsored by the Women's Committee, a group of Protestant laywomen. It offers a helpful introduction to basic assumptions of Christian ethics.

I knew when I agreed to present this lecture, offering an orientation to thinking ethically as a Christian, that before I finished I would hate myself for accepting, that I had let myself in for one of the toughest assignments I could think of. That may surprise you, for, after all, I teach Christian ethics, and you may be wondering what could be so difficult about doing a brief introduction to my own field.

Years ago, when I was a young campus minister at the University of California, Berkeley, before the free speech movement and the turbulent 1960s, Berkeley undergraduates were very angry about the quality of teaching they received at the university. Besides listening to these student concerns, I also made it my business to find out how faculty felt about the relation of teaching to their disciplines. One professor, in particular, interested me, and his view of teaching impressed me very much. He was a world-renowned chemist, a senior professor at the university. He surprised everyone by announcing that he would teach the introductory course for freshmen in his department, since he agreed with student complaints about the quality of teaching they were receiving. The reason he agreed (or so he said) was that he believed that there were not enough senior professors teaching introductory courses in his field. "A good introduction," he said, "is possible only if you have mastered the full intricacies of your discipline." He explained that you have to be a specialist for a long while to be good at general introductions in your field. Simplification of complexities is not simple at all!

If this is true of natural science, how much more so of ethics! The language of ethics, precisely because it is analytic, not empirical, is terribly ambiguous. Ethical reflection is critical questioning of our evaluations of the world. Scientific language, what we call knowledge of the world, is chiefly empirical or descriptive. Ethical discourse involves judgments about what is right or good in a moral sense. (I'll say more about the term *moral* in a minute.) Scientific logic aims to describe or, better, to enhance our understanding of what is true by efforts to *falsify* existing knowledge. Ethical inquiry, by contrast, seeks to do two things—to improve our ability to reflect on and also to choose better or worse ways of shaping our personal or social actions. "Doing ethics" is not like "doing chemistry" because there is usually a consensus in science at any given point about what chemists are defining. In ethics, as we shall see, there are several different ideas about what criteria make something moral.

We must ask, Who is the expert in ethics? Is it someone who can help us define ethical terms and understand what philosophers and theologians who lived before us believed about ideas in books on Christian ethics, someone who can persuade us to be concerned about these matters? Or is it the person who is almost invariably thoughtful and kind, someone who does admirable things, someone about whom—if you were asked what you admired about her—you would exclaim, "She is such a good person"? The professional ethicist is, in the first instance, proceeding much as the chemist might proceed. The expert is *describing* what others have held to be ethical. On the other hand, the person you describe spontaneously as "good" is *practicing* what the professional ethicist calls "values," "virtues," or "principles."

Since professors of ethics do not agree on what it means to "do ethics" in the way that professors of chemistry do about what it means to "do chemistry," there are large areas of disagreement in how to evaluate matters morally. For example, some theologians and philosophers give priority to finding the correct principles of action. In fact, these ethicists define morality as governed by "rightness" rather than by goodness. Such ethicists are usually called *deontologists*, a Latinate term that means duty or obligation-centered ethical thinking. Deontologists believe that what makes actions or decisions moral are the principles we follow in our actions. Another way to characterize such ethics is to think of this sort of moral thinking as imperative centered: Do this! Do not do that! There is much of this kind of ethical thinking in Christian ethics. Not all deontologists take the same view of the status of moral principles, however. Some philosophers and theologians believe that there are a few preeminent and largely unchangeable moral principles, while others of us believe that there are many moral principles and that they are often in conflict. We will return to this disagreement.

Other ethicists define morality by identifying which values or virtues are most important, and these ethicists are usually referred to as *teleological* theorists—those who characterize the moral by defining what is good, or by assessing the results or consequences of our acts or social policies. To think of what is central to ethics this way is to shift the focus of ethical reflection from locating principles and rules to considering qualities to be realized in our actions and imaging the *consequences* of what we do.

These two theories have many variations among professional ethicists that are beyond the introductory matters that require our attention here. An important point here, however, is that these disagreements are theoretical—they are about definitions of what constitutes the best way to think about ethics. But there are ambiguities in doing ethics that are not merely theoretical. There are important practical disagreements that we need to keep in mind as well.

For example, you can be said to be doing ethics when you drop what you are doing in your kitchen and rush to the side of a neighbor whose child has been taken suddenly ill. Or you may be said to be doing ethics when, faced with an agonizing question of how to communicate to a child why you are distressed by a course of action she has adopted, you call up a friend and ask to talk to that friend about how to deal with the child. When you and your friend have clarified your options about what to tell the child, you then have to communicate what you decided to say. Notice that I said that when you were thinking about what you would say to the child you were "doing ethics," and that you were also "doing ethics" when you were instructing the child. There are layers and layers of "doings" that come into play when we think and act, all of them a part of "doing ethics." Is it any wonder that teaching ethics is a challenge?

There is fairly widespread agreement among professors of ethics that the subject of ethical discourse—its referent—is best limited to the sorts of human action over which we have some control. Ethics isn't about my knee jerking when my physician hits it with a reflex hammer! It is about those aspects of my actions that I can consciously change or alter. In the English-speaking world, philosophers usually call the aspect of our actions that we control our "conduct." What makes our conduct and our thinking about our conduct so complicated is that everybody everywhere controls some of their actions to at least a certain extent. However, what is also clear is that not everyone cares to put energy and effort into doing ethics as we are speaking of it here, that is, thinking *and* acting well (always remember, though, that thinking *is* human *activity*). Some people just do not want to do ethics; they are intellectually thoughtless (uninterested in reflection) or morally insensitive (uninterested in being virtuous). Others, by contrast, may be actively opposed to our particular moral approach so that they want to do ethics quite differently, often observing different values.

These days we hear a lot of people say that in our society there is a loss of ethical standards or a lack of concern for morality. I can't take the time this morning to consider fully the accuracy of this widespread claim, but I do want to make one important observation about it. We who are interested in Christian ethics need to notice how often we and others, when questioned about our actions, answer in ways that imply that our actions are done for reasons that have nothing to do with moral rightness or goodness. What we appeal to are expectations that are dictated by very mundane and limited considerations. The same people who worry most about the so-called loss of moral standards or ethical concern often fail altogether to notice that our society, in fact, operates so as to exempt large classes of our actions from any broader moral standards, insisting instead on the use of limited short-term considerations. I submit that currently the most common determinant of what we are to do is what our jobs or our station in society dictate.

Someone who teaches school is told that the only thing that matters is to get her pupils to do well on standardized tests, period! Forget about any wider considerations. The person working for a corporation is told that he must function in a certain way because the bottom line requires it! We are assured, over and over, that the proper goal of economic activity is profit, period. All our action at work is to be aimed to that end. The student is told that the aim of education is to get the degree, period. The doctor is told that the goal of her practice is to do something about the patient's current complaints, period—or to spare the dying patient pain, period. All of our actions or strategies are too often narrowly focused on predefined goals, excluding important moral questions about the rightness of roles, rules (action guides), and relations, and also about how and for whom something may be good. More and more parts of our lives have become subject to amoral standards, that is, they are judged by whether something works or is profitable. They are no longer within the sphere of ethics, where we would consider whether our activities contribute to our own and others' well-being. Thus, if we complain about the loss of ethical standards, we had better examine exactly what it is that we will not submit to critical scrutiny, what it is that we, in our social practices, exclude from questioning.

I want to leave another thought with you today as well. It is that the problems of doing ethics, of deliberating about what we are to do and examining what really is right and good to do, is a task for everyone. Furthermore, each of us must do that reflection; we each must deliberate for ourselves. For complex philosophical reasons that I can't lay out here, the person who merely follows orders or acts out someone else's imperatives is not considered a conscientious or morally mature person. Such externalized morality is not, at least to most moral philosophers, really living out "the moral point of view." This also means that certain kinds of Christian ethics that teach us to merely follow God's orders do not get high marks from these philosophers. I, for one, think the philosophers are right on this point: The purpose of studying Christian ethics is most assuredly not just to learn what our orders are. Rather, we are discerning what we are to do by wrestling both with what others have taught about Christian practice in the past and with what has changed and what is required of us in the present. Ethical renewal, getting a clearer sense of standards of personal and communal ethics, comes as much from noticing what has changed and what needs to be done differently as it does from reverencing the past. Unfortunately, there is a lot of confusion about this among those who teach Christian ethics.

If you stop to think about it, you will see that the very idea that what we need is external moral authority is mistaken. It is not for the preachers or professors to tell us what proper Christian standards ought to be. This is not to say that we ought not to listen to, and ponder, and argue with those who are concerned for our moral formation and for their own. Only that (here again there is wide agreement among professors of ethics) if you opt out of the process of reflecting and clarifying your own conduct, you are, in a fundamental way, also opting out of the hard work of being a moral person.

Let me be clear here. I am not saying that the main point of reference for doing ethics is ever an isolated person asking, "What am *I* to do?" In my ethical approach, our identities always begin with "We," since we are relational beings, rooted in inescapably social lives. However, a lot of moral philosophers have believed that ethics is chiefly about the individual moral agent. Here I think we Christians have particularly to dissent and argue that Christian ethics is about moral community, that we always start with a "We" question, and only secondarily consider an "I" question. Of course, the "I" question is still important, because the hardest moral dilemmas are those that arise precisely because someone judges that she must break with the existing loyalties and existing "we-relations." The most important moral revolutions take shape at just the points where we discover the inadequacy of the moral claims someone has taught us to believe. It is the discovery that what we have so far accepted as good is not good enough, and that we must do something differently, that makes us aware of the power and creativity of moral discernment. Such discernment requires us to challenge the accepted practices and the conventional wisdom of our families, our communities of faith (i.e., religion), our cultural or class affiliations, and, perhaps especially in this century, our nation.

There is also a new moral problem in our time that deserves mention and attention here. This new moral problem is that everything most of us have learned about ethics to this point in our history reflects a certain understanding of the human person, one that has developed out of European and North American philosophical/religious traditions and contexts. When we discuss morality we often stress that good ethics require us to seek and to express a universal point of view. Today, however, we are having to rethink whether and to what extent our assumptions about the right and the good are more culture-bound than we have realized, and to ask whether and to what extent they reflect the biases or even the prejudices of our culture. Today no one can doubt that morality is shaped by cultural assumptions; one cannot just assume the supremacy of one's own cultural values without submitting one's views to cross-cultural scrutiny.

It is important here to understand that *cultural* relativism—the descriptive fact that different cultures have different values and moral systems—is not exactly the same thing as *moral* relativism as it is commonly understood. Moral relativism involves the assumption that we must offer justifications for the roles, rules, and relations we privilege in our ethics and not just speak *ex cathedra* without accepting others' challenges and objections. We must recognize that ethical claims *are contestable in principle*. However, the term *moral relativism* is itself an ambiguous term. It may cover very different notions—from the idea that different cultures have different norms (roles, rules, and relations), all of which may have some moral standing, to an extreme relativism in which a person believes that all moral norms are totally subjective and arbitrary, the private preferences of the person who utters them ("there is nothing right or wrong, but my thinking makes it so"). How cultural relativism affects moral relativism is a big question, one I cannot get into further here. Obviously, a Christian ethicist is not an extreme subjectivist in the second sense, but I suspect that we must all learn to be moral relativists in the first sense. This means that we must also learn to value cross-cultural discussions of our ethical proposals that will require all of us, secular and religious people alike, to suspend any dogmatism about our own moral supremacy and to submit our normative claims about moral goods or about roles, rules, and relations for questioning and contestation by others. I suspect the road ahead for religious ethics will be filled with new and interesting moral debates.

To this point I have been talking mainly about what philosophers call "the moral point of view" and have said little about the distinctive features of a Christian moral position. It is my view that we Christians, or other religious folk, do not have anything distinctive to contribute about the logic of moral discourses or the variety of relevant norms. Instead, our distinctive contribution lies chiefly in what I call the aspirational dimension, which goes beyond the level of debates about deontology or teleology as consequentialism. This dimension is what philosopher Dorothy Emmett calls teleology B—the horizon that we aim for in our agency.[1] Traditionally, Christians have named this "the kingdom of God."[2] What does it mean to live toward or in the presence of this kingdom? Theologically, Christian discourse calls us to act out of and into several horizons of inclusiveness, redefining the "we" in several directions. One direction supports the aspect of we-ness that is often expressed theologically as humans bearing the *imago dei*. All human beings are children of God, and none can be treated as outside the circle of divine blessedness. We cannot draw a moral distinction between those we consider moral peers and those who stand outside the moral community. This dimension or horizon of inclusiveness is rooted in Christianity's Jewish roots, and this sort of inclusiveness also appears to be widely shared by the best readings of most other religio-moral traditions.

There is another transformation of the "we" relation that is also claimed as distinctive of the Christian story. Rereading the Jesus story for the radicality of his teaching leads us to insist that the Christian ethic also requires redefining our moral priorities so as to shape our actions in the direction of solidarity with the most dramatically excluded, what Jesus identifies as "the poor."[3] Our relationships must be redefined so that we stand with, and where necessary, advocate for, those situated outside of voice and recognition, those who live and act beyond the socially constructed barriers which favor the powerful.

This means that we must remember that those who are divided from us by such barriers will not automatically trust us, and I submit that they should not. They will not hear our request for them to be loving toward us, nor our claim that we are, in fact, loving toward them, unless the quality of the "we" relationship between us changes. When we fulfill our obligations to them, acting upon our principles, we must do so as people who stand *with* these excluded others. We must meet them as sisters and brothers, not speaking from above, as their superiors, but meeting them in mutuality. The claims Jesus makes upon our moral agency require that movement toward solidarity, the elimination of "otherness," be present. Only through the changing of our "we" relations can our claims about love as the key to the Christian ethic and as central to principles and obligations of action become persuasive.

The religious vision of Jesus, then, requires transvaluation, not merely of rules and obligations but, most importantly, of our social relations. When his hearers heard Jesus discuss what it means to participate in the kingdom, they asked him, "*Who* then is my neighbor?" Christian ethics and Christian community are born of commitment to this sort of neighbor solidarity. Invoking the principle of "love" is not the revolutionary note in Jesus' moral teaching. It is, rather, the critical criterion he offers—that our love be aimed at those who have suffered exploitation and injustice—that sharpens and specifies the direction of our efforts. The transformative force of the Christian ethic, what the ancient prophets called hospitality to the stranger, defines the most urgent strangers as those who are currently the most excluded ones.

In light of this, we may well ask, Doesn't the Christian ethic present us with such demanding norms that, by its standards, no one could ever be moral? In point of fact, it is probably wise to recognize that Jesus' approach to morality should never be treated as merely an abstract and formal ethic of unchanging norms. What he calls us to is a lifestyle of questioning, challenging, and correcting moral traditions, and what he teaches is that we need to learn to live as moral gadflies who help to create new approaches to community, new ways of being with and for each other.[4] It is by listening to those whose voices are not being heard that we begin to see what moral complacency and conventional wisdom cannot yet see. Doing Christian ethics is good work because it is always full of new insight and surprises.

Notes

1. This formulation is taken from Dorothy Emmet, *Roles, Rules, and Relations* (Boston: Beacon Press, 1975). Harrison found many of Emmet's formulations helpful and used her *Moral Prism* (New York: St. Martin's Press, 1979) in her introductory course in Christian ethics from its publication until her retirement.

2. Shortly after this lecture was given, Harrison adopted the practice of speaking of the "Commonwealth of God," in keeping with usage characteristic of the Reformed tradition of Protestantism. She has also used the phraseology suggested by Ada Maria Isasi-Diaz—"the kin-dom of God." See Ada Maria Isasi-Diaz *En La Lucha (In the Struggle): A Hispanic Women's Liberation Theology* (Minneapolis: Fortress Press, 1993), xi; *Mujerista Theology: A Theology for the Twenty-first Century* (Maryknoll, N.Y.: Orbis Books, 1996), 125.

3. Harrison realizes that this presentation does not include reference to more recent ecological perspectives. Querying anthropocentrism was, for her, made possible through the influences of her colleague Larry Rasmussen, and of Carter Heyward. See Larry Rasmussen, *Earth Community, Earth Ethics* (Maryknoll, N.Y.: Orbis Books, 1996); and Carter Heyward, *Flying Changes* (Cleveland: Pilgrim Press, forthcoming).

4. See Carter Heyward, *Saving Jesus from Those Who Are Right* (Minneapolis: Fortress Press, 1999). Even before the publication of this book, Heyward and Harrison were in substantive agreement on this reading of the Jesus tradition. This section of the lecture has been emended to sharpen Harrison's original text.

Chapter 4

Feminist Realism

In this article, drawing upon her analysis of abortion in Our Right to Choose, *Harrison helps identify a feminist moral agenda for analyzing evaluative assertions about the termination of early fetal life and about attitudes toward children, and for distinguishing between them. It provides a model for linking theory and practice in feminist moral analysis. This article was originally published in* Christianity and Crisis *46, no. 10 (1986): 233–36, and was reprinted in* Ethics in the Present Tense: Readings from Christianity and Crisis 1966–1991, *edited by Vivian Lindermeyer and Leon Howell (New York: Friendship Press, 1991). Harrison was a long-standing contributing editor to and supporter of this progressive Christian magazine, which was cofounded by Reinhold Niebuhr, John Bennett, and others in 1941 and ceased publication in 1993.*

Feminism generates a profound commitment to social justice. This commitment originates in an awareness of the fundamentally relational, interdependent, and finite character of life. At the same time, feminist reflection on the particularity and diversity of women's lives and on the integrity of their historical struggles cautions us against thinking too rigidly about what social justice and morality mean. Because religious feminism sets the context for my thinking about abortion decisions, I want to elaborate on some of its particular insights.

A feminist religious vision urges us to understand social justice within the radically pluralist nature of creation. As feminist theory affirms and celebrates, reality is not given and static, but is an ongoing, changing process. The world and the cosmos are inexhaustibly rich in potential for moral fulfillment in spite of the active and powerful presence of evil. Moral life that is authentically feminist must honor this insight.

Ethical reflection does not consist in the static repetition of inherited patterns of obligation. Such patterns help us locate the claims the past bequeaths to us. But thinking ethically requires us to take these claims and continuously test and reformulate them. It requires us to reorder values and to forge hope and virtue out of conflicting values. A feminist religious ethic enables us to grasp that all our "I" decisions—including a decision about a specific pregnancy—are made "in a world in which there is a call to do good, a call to be generous, a call to self-fulfillment," a world, also, in which "it is certain that creation both recovers from wrong decisions and continues to be alive to the processes of creation" (Jean Lambert).

A caveat: We should not talk about abortion dilemmas in a way that removes them from the living *continuity* of women's lives. The approach we need is an ethic of procreative choice, not merely an ethic of abortion. In one sense, abortion is a negative therapeutic or corrective act, not an act of positive moral agency at all. From the standpoint of a woman's experience, we have to ask a more basic moral question: What am I to do about the procreative power that is mine by virtue of being born female? In thinking about this question, in acting on this question, one consideration remains paramount: the active moral agency to create a world where conditions actually exist that enable women to exercise real choices about the role of procreation in their lives. A genuinely reflective, value-respecting morality cannot fully develop where conditions of choice are absent.

Our moral arguments either for choice or about particular abortion decisions must never be severed from our historical analysis of the absence of choice. (This interrelationship is not understood by some writers, notably Sidney Callahan and Madonna Kolbenschlag, who criticize pro-choice feminists for excessive individualism and voluntarism.)

Feminists recognize that human fertility and reproduction have always been shaped by human activity, decision, and control. We must be suspicious of any purported feminist theory which does not recognize that basic social institutions, including the church, are implicated in institutional systems of control aimed at dictating the use of women's reproductive power.

The recent availability of legal, elective abortion provides, at best, an increased degree of self-directive power. It enables women to maneuver more meaningfully amid incredible pressures and limited options. For many, the availability of abortion does little more than increase the margin for survival. It certainly does not assure full and optimal conditions for spontaneous choice or even for full deliberation about choice.

We make a dreadful error, in thinking about abortion decision making, if we do not acknowledge that the conditions needed to choose to bear and rear children are worsening. The accelerating pauperization of women and their dependent children is a massive and global phenomenon. While the conditions for procreative choice among the minority of the really affluent improve dramatically, the possibilities for providing food, shelter, health care, and adequate education for children deteriorate for most. Increasingly, children are dependent—*exclusively* dependent—upon the maternal lifeline. It is those who neglect this historical setting who are individualistic in their ethics.

THE MORAL SITUATION

Here then is the full complexity of the moral situation in which we must set a discussion of criteria regarding abortion: We need the guidance moral reflection can give, but we must insist that women be *fully realistic* about what it means to have children. The historical situation suggests that the decision to bear and raise children is likely to be made either out of an immense amount of psychological denial—for females are still rewarded with spiritual approbation for unconscious conformity to a naturalistic myth of women's fulfillment—or out of a well-considered commitment that requires an element of moral courage.

How much moral courage do feminists have a right to expect of ourselves and our sisters? No more than the prudential wisdom our theological-moral tradition has commended to men. No doubt without full conscious intent, traditionalist Christian moral theology has managed to make the pregnant woman the most conspicuous exception to the general rule that theological fidelity enables us to live conscientiously even when we must act in situations where none of the options are optimal morally. (All females are excepted, but *especially* the pregnant woman.)

We can envision some of the elements of optimal decision making, but we must do so while remaining aware that individual cases are not simply occasions to express consistent value commitments or principles of action. They are rather particularly vexing settings for value-balancing decisions where an individual woman most frequently has little power to shape the moral quality of life. Individual women do *not* bear all of the moral accountability for the complex social-moral equation that confronts them when a pregnancy is unplanned. (Why then are the most censorious denouncers of the morality of women who do choose abortion often those who accept no part of the moral burden for altering the many constraints on women's lives?)

NURTURANCE IS ACTIVE

Certainly one of the values most normative for the feminist moral vision—and the one "feminists for life" distort and make the exclusive norm—is our obligation for "caring" and "nurturance" of others. I see no reason to retreat from this value in feminist approaches to abortion decisions. It is a distinctive feature of women's culture and women's historical experience to nourish a fundamental respect for the irreducible moral value of nurturance. This, however, is an active, not a passive value; it can be expressed in myriads of ways, through all of the social roles in which we participate.

What we must be clear about is that active caring and nurturance are not the same as some "natural" female (or worse, "feminine") need for motherhood which, if denied, renders us morally inept. Here again, an insufficiently historical feminist theory tempts us to confuse the irreducible value of active caring with some purported "special vocation" of motherhood. It tempts us to place women who don't choose this vocation outside the moral pale of true femininity, to make them enemies of feminism.

But the social institution of motherhood is as historical as any other, even though bourgeois ideology portrays maternal desire as the peculiar, ahistorical "essence" of womanhood. When feminists join this ideology of motherhood with nurturance, caring, and all active efforts to maintain a familial quality in our common life, we fall into the trap of being bourgeois propagandists. Unfortunately, Christian feminists are particularly tempted by this pitfall.

We all know at heart that good mothering requires clear and consistent differentiation between a child and a parent. Its goal is always mutual empowerment and the transformation of infant dependence into mutuality. That is not the same thing as entrapment in "maternal thinking." A compulsive maternalism has its own forms of pathology and provides a poor basis for social decision making of any sort. It tends to romanticize dependency, and, as philosopher Sarah Ruddick has shown, it makes it difficult to maintain distance from personal feeling when that is appropriate to moral discrimination.

Compulsive maternalism (like paternalism, of course) also erodes a woman's (or a man's) capacity for growth and self-direction; it invites us to seek our fulfillment indirectly, through manipulation of another's need. The often unconscious use of another's dependency to provide ego enhancement for oneself is surely the besetting sin of parenting. We can say that child-rearing requires extraordinary artfulness in the moral expression of caring precisely because the child's dependency makes him or her vulnerable to aberrant caring. In other words, especially under modern conditions, motherhood is a morally demanding relation; it therefore ought not to be entered into lightly. That is certainly no reason for insisting that women who find themselves pregnant are moral degenerates if they discern they are not at this point well equipped for the assignment.

Romanticizing motherhood threatens also to tilt the understanding of caring and nurturance in feminist ethics away from an insistence that shared or mutual relationship is the morally highest mode of caring. It is perfectly legitimate to insist that in having children women should not be motivated by a strict and legalist sense of obligation. I am suspicious of all "motives to maternity" that do not participate in a gracious recognition that children are not mere helpless, dependent, or innocent beings but rather, in all their adamant separateness, abundant sources of joy, appreciation, and wonder. Should any women choose childbearing who do not see this?

A SHIFTING MORAL EQUATION

I also tend to think that the inability of many women to differentiate between a moral evaluation about terminating early fetal life and a moral evaluation of one's attitude toward children stems from an inability to distinguish claims regarding dependency. Appeals to "fetal innocence" and "helplessness," for example, resonate deeply for those raised in the Christian tradition. Unfortunately, traditional Christian symbolism yields a special valence to such claims because in it only what is *not* sexual is seen as truly innocent. Clearly, in orthodox Christian tradition, a pregnant woman is perceived as tainted; only fetuses can be "truly innocent." No matter how much we value early fetal life, we cannot say that only fetal helplessness counts as a relevant moral claim. That would give absolute privilege to the fetal-maternal relationship. To opt for childbearing always means we take a path toward realizing some critical moral value. But it also invariably involves excluding some other moral values. Pressure not to consider the conflicting claims of the many values involved only aggravates the socially underdeveloped ability of women to recognize that everything in life requires continuous value balancing and moral choice.

I recognize the need for a shifting moral equation within the ongoing process of gestation. Until neurological development has occurred, the claims of a woman's well-being and of her existing obligations have a clear, overriding validity. Adequate understanding of gestation leads me *not* to impute intrinsic value to a fetus—certainly through the first four months of pregnancy.

Nor does my conviction that a woman should extend active human value to her fetus in later decision making lead me to think in terms of some overriding "right to life" prior to birth. It does mean that weightier considerations are needed to justify late abortion. And it means that I would want second-trimester abortions to become a rare exception.

A feminist moral agenda includes active efforts to encourage women to detect pregnancy early and—if the pregnancy is unplanned—to make decisions about it with speed and clarity. In fact, more and more women are learning to do this. The mean term of abortions has dropped in the United States in all areas where abortion services are adequate. The experience in Sweden also makes it clear that further reductions can happen, but only in a society that respects women's right to choose. Failure to extend this respect through social policy aimed to encourage early decisions only increases many individual women's ambivalence and evasion.

Certainly morally dubious reasons for having an early abortion exist, as do morally vacuous reasons for carrying a pregnancy to term. Obviously, the rightness or wrongness of these decisions inheres in the violation of responsibility to one's own integrity and to relationships with male partners, family, and others. But even when a woman considering an unwanted pregnancy does not share my views about fetal life, and considers the fetus to be already a human life, I would still urge that she not treat the moral prohibition against taking human life to be an unexceptional rule.

It is morally wiser for a woman deliberating about abortion early in pregnancy to recognize that she has an *active* obligation to think of the embryo or fetus *not* as an existing human life, but as a powerfully potential soon-to-be human life that will require deep moral commitment and claim her obligations dramatically. The most conscientious decisions at this point in pregnancy can be made only if a woman or girl can free her imagination to ponder what it may mean to have a child. There is much to be gained morally from helping pregnant women to learn to think this way.

I reject any position that portrays as "frivolous" or as "matters of mere convenience" reasons for terminating pregnancy that relate to the basic material and spiritual conditions of a woman's own life as well as her obligations to others. A woman must consider how a specific pregnancy affects her plans for her life. How can our deliberations over unplanned pregnancy have any genuine moral quality if our plans for our life count for nothing, if reasons based on our goals are considered trivial?

HOW MUCH MORAL COURAGE?

My principled recognition for the increasing moral ambiguity of late abortion does not lead me to conclude that good reasons for early abortion have no weight at a later point. The act itself becomes increasingly dubious morally as fetal life actively individuates and approaches stages analogous to the biological complexity of existing human life, but pregnancies can become unwanted at some point in the process. The life circumstances of a pregnant woman can change dramatically, and for the worse. Marriages come apart suddenly, jobs are lost, basic support systems collapse. There will always be some late abortions, and in my view many will be fully justifiable morally.

Furthermore, the largest number of late abortions are due to lack of access to affordable abortion services or to the current incapacity of the young to detect pregnancy. It is increasingly distressing to see so few people—including liberal pro-choice proponents—making connections between the rate of resort to late abortions and the largely successful "pro-life" crusade to limit abortion services (and in some cases, contraception) and cut off public funding for abortion. These connections make me even more willing to acknowledge that my reservations about late abortion must be held with great tentativeness. I want no part of anathematizing poor women or the confused, pregnant young.

One category of late abortions that is on the increase has to be considered a *sui generis* type of dilemma: The dramatic escalation of prenatal medical technology, in particular, the availability of genetic screening, has created a distinctive dilemma for many women and their partners. All but invariably, the dilemma arises for a woman who wants to be pregnant and have a child. She is confronted with information—some of it certain, much of it imprecise projection—about the health of her fetus.

Everyone who has faced this situation has attested to the extraordinary trauma involved. The pregnancy has proceeded with growing anticipation, shaped by general experience. But now the woman experiences yet a further testing of the values and moral commitments that led her and her partner to want a child: All will not be as they hoped.

For me, some cases pose no ambiguity morally. I rejoice that women who are carriers of some severe degenerative genetic diseases learn their fetus is afflicted in time to be spared the ordeal of watching a child die. Conversely, I am appalled that some few women and their mates are willing to use the new technology to select gender. For reasons I cannot develop here, I believe abortion-for-gender choice is an unqualified moral wrong.

But what of the greater number of cases where what is involved is some projection, often inexact, about mental retardation or physical disability? Discussion of these issues among women—deeply painful discussion—is only now beginning. It requires feminists to press value clarifications even further. I, for one, must confess that so far the issues raised have produced more agony than clarity.

On the one hand, it is obvious that the sin of "ableism" is at work in the widespread assumption that mental retardation and physical disability provide privileged reasons for having abortions. Clearly morally serious feminists must *not* share in such assumptions. They are fueled by sexism and by the "body perfectionism" hype that ravages the lives of the differently abled and also twists and warps the lives of many girls and women.

Yet when I ask myself what I would do in this situation, the limits of my values come screaming forth: "Not too much mental retardation! I couldn't cope!" Posing the question this way, however, has put me in touch not only with the bias and limits of my own values but also with the extent to which such a decision forces me to confront both fear and the genuine question of limits. With even greater urgency, I find myself asking again, How much moral courage do feminists have a right to expect from our sisters?

If realism in moral reflection is required at any stage in pregnancy, then surely we have some obligation to insist that it is even more appropriate here. Truth to tell, after struggling to envisage a personal response to such a dilemma, my chief reaction was relief. As a woman beyond childbearing years, I will never actually face the situation.

Increasingly, though, women are facing it. And I trust that women will forge the moral wisdom to deal with this dilemma also. My trust is no cop-out, but a confidence consistent with my feminist commitment.

Chapter 5

Feminist Musings on Community

This article concisely exegetes "community" as a key term for feminist liberative ethics. It appeared in Holy Ground *8, no. 1 (July 2001): 2.* Holy Ground *is the publication of Holy Ground, a women's center in Asheville, North Carolina, dedicated to offering programs for women focusing on feminist spirituality, peace, and justice. Beverly Harrison is an ongoing supporter and occasional participant in their activities.*

Among theologians, and among spiritually concerned women, there is much talk these days about community. But as I read the signs of the times, concerns about community are also reflected in every conversation that occurs about morals and public policy. The issues also hide in or lurk under every controversy around us. For example, all the talk by the religious right about "family values" is talk about community. What lies behind this constant invocation of "family" if not a longing for stability and closeness? Never mind that the other comment we hear over and over is "I come from a dysfunctional family" or "Is there any such thing as a nondysfunctional family?" Enthusiasts for conservative religion rarely note these contradictions rampant in popular discourse, nor do they speak with candor of the massive suffering and abuse so many people suffer and learn in families. If they faced those realities, they would have to think differently about a great many issues.

Instead, they appeal covertly to our need for community, and their endless talk of family values is aimed at the emptiness so many people feel. The longing for community so widespread among us can be triggered by this praising of the only experience of community many know. But it should be obvious that our attraction to the closeness of family really bespeaks both the love we feel toward our families but also the emptiness and alienation of our relationship to the other dimensions of life. It is notable that many people long for closeness and for the sort of acceptance we dream of and wish for from childhood onward.

But are the needs of early childhood an adequate measure of community? The romanticized family gives some clues to community, but when it is the only model we have for what community is about, our imaginations are impoverished. We grasp for the best model we know for what it means to be cared for, to matter to others, wishing that everyone could be as close as brothers and sisters. The religious Right also encourages us to fear anyone who does not share this longing. Those who doubt the importance of family are construed as anticommunitarian. Many theological accounts of the importance of community are suffused with this culture of family romanticism, and are closely allied with the patriarchal and antifeminist reactionary religion.

While there is no question that community is critical to any adequate spirituality, theological integrity also requires facing squarely the serious limitations of imaging community primarily within the constraints of family, most especially the nuclear family of late modernist capitalist political economy. There are several limitations to the family metaphor that reinforce social injustice. To some extent the metaphor encourages us to equate community with biogenetic connection and ethnicity, and worse, by extension with shared culture and the comforts of cultural familiarity. Is it any wonder that black feminists and womanists and other colorful women have pointed out how insensitive white women are to diversity and difference? Biological familialism leads us to presume that community is present when similarity and shared culture is present. Community seems to have nothing to do with encountering the unfamiliar, the new, that which stretches and challenges us. And with the images of family foremost when we reflect on community, we tend to imagine that community is primarily a matter of warm feeling and subjective liking of others.

Because we women rightly value the arts of family making, arts that do contribute to community building, we may at times forget that the true measure of community building is love infused with justice. Feminism began with the insistence that justice is as important in the bedroom as in the wider society. THE PERSONAL IS POLITICAL transformed many women's expectations of what they deserved and challenged the limits of privatized notions of community. But too much feminism, facing the society's violent reaction to its retheorizing of society, has slipped back into thinking only about interpersonal relations. By contrast, deep feminist spirituality is about how we interrelate our personal and social relations; the measure of our ethics is, like that of the ancient Hebrews, about hospitality to strangers, whether those strangers are "the others" within or beyond our family. So every person who is serious about community today must begin with the blinders we wear to "otherness," the "whiteness" that blinds us to our own cultural imperialism, our religious ignorance of what others reverence, our fear of the poor and our pervasive classist arrogances exhibited in contempt for those more vulnerable economically.

And we must measure all religion and all spirituality by whether or not they lead us to struggle against the boundaries that turn all four-legged and two-legged compatriots into "others" we can justify treating as those who hold nothing IN COMMON WITH US. If we do not long for a world where there are no excluded ones, our theological vision of community simply is not deep or wide enough.

Chapter 6

Foreword to *Welfare Policy*
[feminist critiques]

This essay first appeared in Elizabeth M. Bounds, Pamela K. Brubaker, and Mary E. Hobgood, eds., Welfare Policy [feminist critiques] *(Cleveland: Pilgrim Press, 1999), vii–xi.*

The publication of *Welfare Policy: [feminist critiques]* is for me an occasion for rejoicing. Grounded in the present public controversy over so-called welfare reform, the ten chapters published here, along with afterwords from noted womanist and *mujerista* theologians, model a genre of feminist ethics, informed normatively by radical reading of Christian or related religious traditions. However, the distinctiveness of this book lies in a theological perspective that is also profoundly and unapologetically political, rooted in advocacy for a policy that aims at women's well-being, a position situated outside the mainstream of current public policy debate.

Readers who do not follow the subtle shifts of academic theology and ethics in the academy may be surprised to hear me say that this wonderful collection of chapters is the first of its genre, but that it also could (if trends continue) be the last of the genre as well. Why is this so? Ours is a time when new and sometimes subtle forms of neoliberal theology and ethics are impacting every area of theological and religious studies, including feminist work in women's studies. While producing often-artful cultural criticism, much newer feminist theology is nevertheless dismissive of positive claims to religious or moral knowledge and is subtly antipolitical. Today's cultural critic (postmodernist jargon for any and all intellectuals who reread established intellectual traditions) frequently aims to deconstruct political, moral, and religious interpretations as such. Some recent feminist theology, and even some feminist religious ethics, rereads in ways remote from the actual dynamics of our historical situatedness in a political economy which, as never before, is restructuring the lives and life conditions of every man, woman, and child on little planet Earth.

Such a retreat into apolitical feminist work follows a neoliberal enthusiasm for the erasure of politics and relegates cultural criticism to academic enclaves where the presumed rites of cultural radicalism go on. Much such academic work supposes that novel speech-acts uttered in classrooms or published in books are a sufficient politics of change. In this new neofeminist world, participation in public policy debate itself is often taken as a symptom that one has not understood the profundities of postmodernist critique. Imbibing the socially constructed right-wing attack on political correctness, enthusiasts for postmodernism often leave us without comprehension about this present world, where now everything is left to market forces. The current ideology of welfare reform itself is suffused with neoliberal moral and theological assumptions, including the deep and libelous assumption that private business can solve problems that the state heretofore has only mismanaged. Happily, the essays in this volume help unmask such welfare reform by locating these reforms in relation to global economic shifts that go unnoted in most of the public debate on the welfare question.

In their introduction, the editors provide a valuable account of the methodological assumptions that set these authors apart from ahistorical and antimaterialist genres of cultural criticism, which I find so disturbing. As they note, the genre of feminist ethical work presented here is liberationist, not liberal. It seeks to address the concrete patterns of human suffering, not only to illumine gender injustice but to show how the interstructuring of racism as cultural supremacy and class/economic privilege and labor exploitation interact with gender/sex oppression to shape ongoing public discourse.

Exposing the duplicity in welfare reform is not easy. It is central to the goal of this feminist ethical work to challenge the imposition of neoliberal ideology, so triumphant in the Reagan-Bush era and proceeding apace under President Clinton. The rhetoric of welfare reform aims to persuade us that serious efforts are being made at restructuring government spending. Welfare reform is a rhetorical concession that Clinton tossed his right-wing critics to prove his fiscal caution and his commitment to less government.

The contention here—that the state should address more vigorously issues of justice and undertake new initiatives at distributive justice—has an almost quaint ring in this political climate. The media fill the airwaves with analyses that suggest that state-initiated efforts at solving social problems simply do not work.

Welfare creates bureaucracy, it is said, and can do little else. Such arguments are merely propaganda, however, and they are wrong historically. The facts are that federal government initiatives can work and have done so consistently, reshaping society in a more democratic direction. Here and in every liberal Western democracy where public policy has aimed at change, state programs have made important differences. Most justice-centered programs do what they were designed to do.[1]

The problem is that the United States, unlike many European welfare democracies, never intended to do much for dependent children or poor women! It is a truism that the original Aid to Families with Dependent Children (AFDC) in our now downsized welfare program was created intentionally to be bureaucratic. Our nation, with its fierce tooth-and-claw-like work ethic, creates all social programs with rigid standards for eligibility so as to require administration by experts to discern entitlement.

Because we believe that it is necessary to ferret out ruthlessly malingerers and the undeserving, public welfare American-style is an endless, tangled process of demonstrating and documenting need. Is it not "the American way" to make the process of applying for public assistance so demeaning and so stigmatizing in itself that only the most desperate will ask for help? In the past, many welfare democracies (including Canada and most European nations) had programs in which moderate child-welfare subsidies were paid to each and every child born into the society. Such universal programs do not require costly administration and were the preferred pattern in most countries. Persons with disabilities and those receiving unemployment compensation or retirement benefits can benefit from programs that are designed to reduce administrative cost. By contrast, U.S. programs are created to search out and destroy unworthy claimants.

No one denies that there was an urgent need for reform in our former AFDC system. As the authors of these chapters make clear, however, the one thing that has never been tried is an approach that makes the survival and well-being of poor single mothers and their children a central value in the policy process itself. When the smoke clears from the present restructuring of AFDC, we may safely predict that this downsizing, said to be required by fiscal responsibility and the need for less government, will merely have further shifted the costs of bearing and raising children to poor and poorly educated women and to voluntary organizations such as churches and private agencies. The tiny savings in the federal budget garnered from ending federal programs will turn out to have been only an occasion to shift costs to state and local governments. Nor will these costs be accurately counted. Increased homelessness and poorer health and education will have a social cost that politicians will deny. Welfare reform is merely redistributing the cost of our social-moral contempt onto those already victimized by a death-dealing neoliberal theology in which God rewards only those who help themselves.

So long as deeply racist, antidemocratic values prevail in this public debate, and so long as the debate is shaped by scepticism that political solutions can work to enhance the common good, the welfare debate itself will further poison our already hate-filled society. In such an atmosphere, concern for real commitment to the common good will appear as naively idealistic, a holdover of an outmoded liberalism which threatens the enterprise, ingenuity, and creativity of deserving elites. In such an environment, issue-oriented, publicly concerned theological and ethical discussion, which this volume represents, can be easily brushed aside.

Readers should be clear at the outset that the crisis we face is not a crisis in our welfare system. The crisis is a loss of moral decency and fairness in the broader society. The authors of these chapters see this point clearly. Targeting poor women and their children and making them the issue is a way of evading the truth: that the problem is a political-economic system that privileges the wealthy and obscures its own profoundly antidemocratic value system by victim blaming.

What follows here should be read against a backdrop that insists that what government does shapes all our lives, for better or worse. All of us must learn to reread welfare reform as a matter that is addressed in every act of Congress, in every bill enacted into law. All tax policy and all appropriations are also public welfare decisions. Every public expenditure is the use of government for someone's welfare, and every wealth-producing activity left untaxed (read: profit making) is wealth accumulated without attaching social costs.

If the feminist ethical goal is a full rereading of our national welfare policy, then it is time for us to ask, Why is the Pentagon budget so privileged and central to our national welfare? Why are the defense industries, the banks, and those who own wealth-producing wealth allowed to live so free of any social accountability for the use of that wealth? What are we missing when we are forced to name the elimination of AFDC "welfare reform"? What is going on when welfare reform becomes the occasion for the muddled middle (not a class), who do indeed pay most of the taxes, to blame those who carry even more of the social costs for the wealthy than do the middle? The rhetorical ploys of the current debate quite erroneously lead those of us in the middle to suppose that the federal government is actively looking out for us rather than rapidly accelerating the overprotection of our corporate welfare system.

Any Christian or religious acquiescence to the rhetoric of welfare reform is deeply wrong; it is racist, sexist, and class-distorted nonsense. Our real agenda should be to recall federal, state, and local governments back to their responsibility for shaping policies that provide minimum conditions for human dignity. Those least well placed to earn the ever growing amount of cash required to buy human dignity in this society are not the enemy. We can devise better and more creative ways to support poor women and their children than the old model enabled. But we had better not do so until we grasp the truth clearly that poor women and their children are not the problem.

The problem is an antidemocratic economy that rewards those who already have wealth while, more and more, closing off conditions of economic access not only to mothers who stay at home with young children but to most working people as well. The middle sector of this society is being hurt by the same downsizing policies that punish poor single women. The same dynamics that are brutally reordering poor women's lives and punishing their children are those shaping ours as well. No amount of prosperity for the few can obscure the connections between the neoliberalized zeal for blocking state initiatives for welfare and the growing welfare system for the rich that this state currently enacts daily.

We have never needed serious, overtly political, feminist liberation theology and ethics more than we need such work today. So join me in resolving that this new liberation feminist reader on public policy will be only the first in a long line of such volumes.

Notes

1. I should have written "do a little of what they were designed to do, but not enough." BWH, 2004.

Chapter 7

Human Sexuality
and Mutuality

This essay was first delivered at a symposium on October 21–22, 1982, at Princeton Theological Seminary to mark the fifteenth anniversary of the adoption of the confession of 1967 of the United Presbyterian Church. It was first published in the Journal of Presbyterian History *61 (Spring 1983): 142–61. This revised version was published in* Christian Feminism: Visions of a New Humanity, *edited by Judith L. Weidman (San Francisco: Harper & Row, 1984), 141–57.*

We Christians know very little about our own history with respect to human sexuality, especially its seamier side. We must acknowledge this history before we move to embrace fine platitudes about the possibilities of human gender relationships. Otherwise we will be compromising a liberation theological hermeneutic by making contemporary Christian morality look better than it is or has been. In this connection, *Power and Sexuality*, a much neglected book by patristics scholar Samuel Laeuchli, is helpful. It is a study of one church council—the Council of Elvira, in Granada (now Spain), held in the year 309. This study discloses how and why the Christian tradition got into such trouble about human sexuality: "The Christian church, as the antiheretical literature shows in chapter after chapter, always tried to discredit its rivals as sexually inferior, an apologetic slander technique that has worked to this day."[1] In a time when that technique works only with those already frightened and vulnerable from other sources, it is time to ask: Where have we gone wrong?

CHRISTIANITY'S LEGACY OF HUMAN SEXUALITY AND GENDER RELATIONS

The problem, I submit, is the pervasive sex-negativity and fear of the power of sexuality in the Christian tradition.

In his fine book, *Embodiment: An Approach to Sexuality and Christian Theology*, James Nelson ponders the sources of sex-negativity in our tradition.[2] Nelson contends that two dualisms have embedded themselves deeply in Christian thought and perception. One is the spiritualistic dualism, which conceives of persons as body and spirit (or as body and mind), not as a unity but as an uneasy amalgam. Nelson rightly observes that such dualism had no place in the Hebraic spirituality that we Christians purport to honor in our appropriation of the ancient Hebrew Scriptures. But such dualism was a virulent force, characteristic of the terribly religious culture of late Hellenism into which Christianity was born. Nor was its influence on Christian perception of the world slow to emerge, as any reading of second-century theologians such as Justin Martyr, Tatian, Origen, and Tertullian makes clear. Furthermore, the growing attraction of asceticism in early Christian theology attests an escalating revulsion to the body as the source of temptation and evil. So "inferior" are bodily functions to many of the church fathers that sex is justified only for procreation. Procreative functionalism eventually became the meaning of sex in the Christian tradition, and for many influential theologians, such as Jerome, it was a very dubious necessity, literally justified only because through sex, more virgins and rigorous ascetic Christians might be born.[3]

The full force of Christian sex-negativism cannot be understood, however, without recognizing the interconnection between the spiritualistic dualism, with its antisexual and anti-body bias, and that other dualism—gender dualism—in which male is superior to female. The concrete, historical-social relations between men and women in Christian history has constituted an oppressive praxis which has shaped our theology. It is a truism of feminist analysis that in Western tradition, women have symbolized sexuality, animal nature, and body. Whether in the appalling biology of classical Hellenic philosophers such as Aristotle, or in the teachings of the church fathers, women, unless committed to asceticism and unqualifiedly "pious," are evil. "Woman's God-given role" is either to be dutiful and faithful mothers, or virginal ascetics. In fact, in the ascetic tradition, a woman became a man by renouncing her "natural" inclinations through rigorous ascetic practice. By a self-effacing piety, a woman, literally, became spiritual, overcoming her inherent blot as sexual temptress and her pure physicality by spirituality.

It goes without saying that male gender superiority, in its theological form as masculinist idolatry, is older than Christianity. The institutions of male control of women's reality have evolved over fifteen thousand years of history. We know now, thanks to feminist scholarship in anthropology and history, that there has been a great diversity in the sorts of institutions and social controls elaborated to keep women "in our place" and to construe male reality as normatively human. Because of this scholarship, however, we also know how deeply the central institutions of dominant religions are implicated in the legitimation of male superiority. Sociologist of religion Nancy Jay has demonstrated that numerous human religious systems, including Christianity, have developed blood sacrifice rituals that aim to replace human once-bornness of women by twice-bornness through a male deity.[4] Of course, ancient Hebrews did not invent patriarchy—in its concrete and original sociological form, the ownership of women and children by "the father"—nor were the dominant Christian fathers exceptionally creative among the intellectual elites of their day in embracing the ideal of sexual transactions with women as characteristic animality, which wars with genuine spirituality, and of women as the source not only of sexual temptation but of evil itself. But what the now massive and growing work of feminist scholarship forces us to confront is the lingering disvaluation of women which lives on in the praxis— that is, both the theological reflection and the practice—of Christians. And remember, only the good women—women more consistently self-sacrificing and ascetic than men—were celebrated in the church.

The usual theological response among Christian theologians to these facts is either to trivialize the matter, labeling so-called women's issues as of lesser import to the "real" issues of justice, as if the well-being of 51 percent of the human race had nothing to do with justice, or to reject them outright, as grounded in overwrought feminist mutterings. There are even suggestions that feminism threatens to reintroduce Canaanite Baal cults or other pagan practices into the seamless web of Christian traditions. Since feminists have all but concluded anyway that many heresies were to become so precisely because, in one way or another, they challenged these dualisms in which the orthodox were so embedded, the flip dismissal of feminist critiques only reinforces our suspicions or—in the case of Christian feminists—fears that Christianity may really be intrinsically a system of male deification.

We Protestants, not least we Reformed Christians, continue to believe that we have largely overcome these dualisms. Far too readily we wrap ourselves in self-congratulation that the Reformation broke the hold of these baleful dynamics of sexual asceticism through Protestant Christian history. After all, the ending of clerical celibacy proves this, does it not? To be sure, the Reformers, none more passionately than Calvin, embraced marriage almost as a duty. (Reviewing the civil ordinances of early Calvinist Geneva for my research on my book on abortion reminded me of how passionately Calvin and his cohorts believed that marriage was a duty. I would add that it had to be, for if men must marry women, whom they view as deficient in humanity, the external rule of "duty" necessarily must be invoked.)

The truth is that nothing in the Reformation can be read as a genuine reversal of this negative antisexual, antifemale, antisensuality heritage. Luther and

Calvin celebrated the nobility of "the good woman," but that was nothing new in Christian history. In fact, it was a mere reassertion of social convention. They revisaged the role of sexuality in marriage as involving more than procreation, but that was because marriage was so pivotal to their view of divine-human relations. We miss the problematic of current discussion if we do not also acknowledge that the Reformers embedded the marital relationship, and especially the child-centered family, as the central, sacralizing institution of "the household of faith."

Nor did the Reformation strengthen women's social role in society. The Reformers—as our Catholic feminist sisters remind us regularly—closed down women's religious houses, destroying the one clear institutional base of women's culture in the late Middle Ages. The Reformers and their followers did nothing to change women's role in the church. Furthermore, as historian H. R. Trevor-Roper reminds us, their followers joined the rising tide of witch hunting, the great European witch craze, which was *premodern* Christian Europe's most organized and systematic bout with *internal* genocide.[5] (The same period saw the external genocidal pattern of "domestication" of Africans by Europeans through the slave system.)

Until forced to change, then, the mainstream churches of the Reformation were, like the Catholic tradition before it, institutions which assumed that full spirituality and theological power resided with males. I have elsewhere observed the anomaly of the Christian church, which encouraged male-male bonding so powerfully, also having to support marriage—that is, intimate relations with social inferiors—as its central institution. I truly believe that homophobia in our churches is directly related to the powerful sublimated eroticism of a Christian tradition so fixated on masculine symbols, which also demands normative heterosexuality as its sexual norm.

In any case, the praxis of Protestant Christianity on these matters did not change in the centuries following because of any internal theological innovation. Such constructive change as there has been has come painfully and reluctantly, through confrontation with the historical justice movements of women in Western culture which call for conditions for women's fuller humanity. The emergence of gay movements has accelerated that pressure.

Even the most progressive of our theologians responded reluctantly, while the church deflected feminist calls for justice by adopting the nineteenth-century bourgeois romantic view that women are nobler and *morally* superior to men, the true mediators of nurturance and moral uplift, and are to be revered (read: pedestalized and patronized). Elsewhere I have documented the fact that in the early nineteenth century, it was still possible for Reformation theologians to speak of women chiefly under the image of Eve and the fall. By the end of the century, women in the church had been elevated to the other side of the traditional dualism—the devoted, mothering, virginally asexual "good woman," the only woman to whom Christianity had been able to relate.

In Reformed theology, even in its most progressive expressions, sexuality still remains shrouded in the mystifications of either "God-given" or "natural" existence. Whether in the theology of Emil Brunner, who lapses into natural law thinking under the rubric of "orders," or Barth's biblicist and silly exegesis of female "voluntary" subordination to male,[6] women, sexuality, and marriage are treated within an essentially ahistorical, acultural horizon. In spite of the celebration of the historicity of existence in Reformed theology, when these issues are before us, all are still treated either as paradigms for direct divine decree or "natural" determination.

Such a state of affairs, however, simply will not do. In our own time these mystifications about ahistorical sexuality are being unmasked, and if the church does not change, our theology will, more and more, be rightly judged to be intrinsically intertwined with the mystifications of masculine deification. Any communion which still rests so uneasy with human sexuality and with gender justice that it feels reluctant about contraception—which has, after all, made a major contribution to delivering women from what has been through history a source of unspeakable capriciousness and suffering for most women—still has a long road to travel before public confession will be transformed by evidence of liberating praxis.

RESOURCES FOR A NEW PARADIGM

The Rising Consciousness of Women

It is the presumption of liberation hermeneutics that contradictions within the praxis of the community of faith will be recognized most clearly, and challenged, by those whose lives are negatively affected by and marginated because of these contradictions. Not surprisingly then, the implications of our assumptions about gender relations and human sexuality are being challenged today chiefly by women. Those like myself—mostly white, educated, of the "middle strata" of this society—have experienced the taken-for-granted views of sexuality and gender relations embedded in Christianity as a direct invitation to our own subjugation as persons. Unlike racial and ethnic women and poor women, who are the majority of all women, we escape the double and triple jeopardy of racist and class oppression. We experience gender subjugation, even if sometimes subtly, as a pattern of marginalization and trivialization unintwined with other oppressions. We are the ones who, given the "pedestalism" of bourgeois life, have been socialized to believe that our sexuality exists only through our relations to and dependency upon men. We are those who have been invited, at the cost of loss of personal power, to deny that we are "our bodies, ourselves."[7] It is not surprising, then, that the book by this title, written by a women's health collective, has been high on the list of works targeted by the New Religious Right for removal from school libraries. This volume, predicated upon the assumptions of the newer feminist perspectives on sexuality and read by countless thousands of women, is but one of a vast library of works that contemporary women have written on matters related to the issue of sexuality and gender relations. Through these works, women are invited to revision our own being as self-directed, sensuous body-selves, as those who can and must direct our self-expression as sexual beings who

are responsible *agents*. As body-selves, sensuous centers of self-direction and relationship, our lives and sexuality are ourselves, intrinsic aspects of our being, and
we bear responsibility for the choices we make in terms both of sensuality and
relationship.

The empowering self-respect which has followed upon women's discoveries
around issues of sexuality has, I submit, been the generating source of the new
courage and activism of many women in these difficult times. For a woman to
recognize herself as an embodied psychosexual, spiritual unity means for her to
see that she is an embodied self, not merely that she *has* a body. This means,
among other things, that all our relations to others—to God, to neighbor, to cosmos—are mediated through our bodies, which are the locus of our perceptions
and knowledge of the world. Our senses—all our senses, including touch—mediate the manifold world to us. We are not split, "compounds" of mind and emotion, or body and spirit. Our emotions mediate our basic interactions with the
world. Our minds are an integrated aspect of our body systems, shaped by the
matrix of our sensuous being in the world.

Sexuality in This Paradigm

The discovery that our sexuality is intrinsic to who we are, that we are sexual
beings whose bodies ground *all* our relations to the world, that we are not merely
sexual through genital contact with males, has helped feminists make sense of the
dynamics of sexual subjugation throughout recorded history. It has also led us to
perceive that with bodily repression comes loss of a sense of our connectedness
to the rest of nature, to the cosmos, and to each other. From this perspective it
becomes clear that "individualism"—a sense of the self as genuinely autonomous
and independent, experienced as unrelated existence—is the result of misunder-
standing who we are as persons. While the equation of "person" with "individual" is not uncommon, such an equation is based upon misconception. A person,
as Reformed theologian John MacMurray rightly argued,[8] is a richly related, centered being, one whose ties to others are deep and complex. To be fully a person
is to be deeply related to others.

In this newer paradigm, then, our sexuality is not a "segment" of our reality.
Our sexuality is our total, embodied, sensuous connection to all things, as female
or as male. Because our embodied sensuousness is the ground of our being in the
world, it is also foundational to our sense of well-being, and to our "power of
relation" in and to the world. Furthermore, as we move beyond body/mind and
body/spirit dualism, we discover that our own well-being and our relationships
to others are not dualistic or antagonistic alternatives. Personal well-being and
deeply grounded relationship to others are *intimately interstructured possibilities*.
This means, literally, that who I am in my "power of relation"[9] determines and
is determined by my relationships, and that my well-being and that of the others to whom I am related depends foundationally on existing conditions of
mutual respect between us or upon the lack thereof. Women have been learning

this lesson of mutual empowerment, for we have been literally "hearing each other into speech."[10] We have been taking ourselves and each other seriously, as those who have the power to "name" reality, especially in those areas where men infrequently have heard us or taken us seriously.

All of us, then, literally call forth each other in relationship, and our power of being and capacity to act emerges through our sensuous interaction in relation. If our modes of relationship are not grounded in bodily integrity, and if our ways of being with each other preclude mutuality—which is the power, simultaneously, to affect and be affected by another—we cannot and will not have either personal well-being or community, which is to say, relations of mutuality, shared empowerment, and common respect.

Mutuality has been downgraded in our theological tradition and portrayed as a lesser good than *agape*—unrequited radical, divine love. But in a feminist paradigm, mutuality, or genuine reciprocity, is utterly foundational. There is nothing "higher." Without it, we are thwarted, broken beings who seek to avoid vulnerability—that is, the capacity to be deeply affected by another. Furthermore—and this is critical for our ethics—the absence of such genuine bodily integrity and mutual vulnerability leads to a distortion in our power of agency, that is, our capacity to act and be acted upon. Far from being a peripheral secondary or poor approximation of love, bodily integrity, self-respect, and mutuality are of love's essence. When they are present in relationship, that relationship evokes simultaneously self-enhancement and community or deep intimacy. Whenever one party is invulnerable, and therefore unwilling or unable to be affected by another, there is and can be no love present. And wherever bodily integrity is not respected, genuine other-regardingness is absent. How we relate as body-selves is paradigmatic of how we experience and express power.

Parenthetically, I should add that neither our Christian ethics nor our later, secular moral traditions in the West do justice to the concern of bodily integrity as foundational to our moral relations to each other. Consider, for example, our notions of human rights. Our liberal political traditions value, as foundational human rights, those conditions of relationship which already presuppose the basic, concrete conditions of physical well-being. We do not see food, shelter, and freedom from bodily control by another as moral requirements of a good society. This is no accident or mere oversight, for our founding documents were written and interpreted by men who owned slaves, who were not disturbed by a praxis which included ownership of other human beings, and who used black women's bodies as breeders of "property." These same men also did not see any contradiction in denying the rights of citizenship, and therefore the signs of full humanity, to the women with whom they shared their beds, who bore the children carrying their names. Because of these and other patterns of praxis that negate the full humanity of people, our liberal political and moral traditions do not ground human rights as basic conditions of well-being concretely enough, in a fashion that recognizes the basic embodiedness of humanity, and that acknowledges our basic relatedness as embodied, species-beings.

The "Problem" of Sexuality in the Feminist Paradigm

Given this understanding of ourselves as sexual beings—sensuous and related—the problem is not that there is too much sex per se. The fact is that we have very little sex that enhances our self-respect and sense of well-being and simultaneously deepens our relations to each other. The truth is that we cannot have one without the other—deeper self-respect and deeper intimacy. We have little of either in this society. For all our society's preoccupation with genital sexuality, there is little evidence that the result is a greater sense of playfulness, genuine tenderness, enhanced human communications.

In a feminist paradigm, our sexuality is problematic because it is entangled not only in the old dualisms but also in distorted patterns of power-in-relations. Women, especially, are "objectified," understood not as full human sexual beings but as sex objects who exist to fulfill male needs and are evaluated as idealized projections of that need. As sex object, a woman is to live as mediator of sensuality and affective support to men. But now men are also entering into objectification, living by "the looking glass effect"—that is, seeing themselves *through the eyes of* a purported lover. Objectified sexuality invites us to experience ourselves *chiefly* as objects of another, to experience sexuality as a power relationship in which we enmesh an other in seductive dependency or place ourselves in that position. To experience the power of relationship, there must be reciprocity, shared power, power exhibiting cocreative, mutually enhancing action. In the dominant paradigm of sexuality and gender relations, power emerges as control of another, whether as seduction, manipulation, or coercion. To be sexually valued means, too often, to have the other in our power or to "give over" our power of relation to another. Dynamics of ownership, control, or "possession" permeate our sexual relations. We speak of "scoring" or "making it" or "getting what we want" from the sexual partner.

I do not mean to say, however, that the problem of sexuality is merely the consequence of "bad," objectified *attitudes* about sex. Sexual objectification is not merely a matter of individual sensibility. The truth is that, in this society, our expectations about sexuality are overburdened because patterns of objectification and alienation are so widespread in our broader social relationships. Mutually enhancing, intimate, vulnerable relationships are rare in *any* dimension of our social relations. Our advanced capitalist economic system conditions us to experience all aspects of ourselves, including our sensuous labor, as "commodities" to be bought and sold. For the most part, people in this society have given up the expectation that work will enhance their self-respect, or that the power of relation will be expressed in the work they do. Instead, we see our work as a means to an end, as a means to economic security and to consumption. We should not forget that two intellectuals who so deeply changed our world, Marx and Freud, both agreed upon what it means to be a full human being. To be whole, they argued, we need to be able to love well and to work well. In the expression of our eros and our power to create through sensuous labor, we express our personal power, meeting the power of relation others extend. When we encounter these others as willing our good and we respond by willing their well-being, the "realm of God"—the power of relation—is released, and mutual well-being enhanced.

The growing sense of powerlessness of large numbers of people in the middle strata of this society is no chimera. Increasingly, we do not have the power of self-direction or mutuality in our lives. Again, we do not have one without the other. In such a situation, where alienation and objectification or the commodification of life is widespread, our anxieties grow, and the sense of something gone awry increases. However, the liberal ideology of this society, what Michael Lewis calls "the individual as central sensibility,"[11] prevents us from seeing and naming the problem. In such a context, we project our anxieties outward and "blame the victims"—those even more exploited and vulnerable than ourselves.[12] Witness the rising racism of our society, now "respectable" once again. And as economic exploitation increases, our society is rife with growing class antagonisms that we do not have even the conceptual frame to recognize. Resentments are expressed at every turn, but we do not see the connections between people's growing asocial actions and the dynamics of our political-economic order.

In the midst of all of this, the new Right seeks, consciously, to blame our social dis-ease upon the women's movement and gay men and lesbians. Uppity women and gays are, we are told, undermining traditional order. The use of sexuality issues in new Right propaganda is an organized response armed to exploit the widespread anxiety people are experiencing.[13] These strategies help to deflect discontent and to keep those who actually are in control safe and secure from scrutiny and accountability to the rest of us whose lives are shaped by their decisions.

In the face of all of this—the reality of growing powerlessness, the anxieties of things amiss in the society—people retreat from the "public" world of political and economic relations, turning to the "private" sphere—that is, to primary intimacy relations to ground their sense of personal well-being missing elsewhere. Our expectations for our intimacy relations are enormous, and, too often, these turn out to be too tender a need to sustain our self-respect adequately. We seek meaning, desperately, in interpersonal relations and expect our intimacy relations to deliver us from the loss of personal empowerment and self-respect suffered in other areas of our lives. We bring incredible expectations to our love relations with another, and for the most part, we are often bitterly disappointed. Our problem with sex amid all of this is not that we have so much of it, but that it is joyless, so earnest, so lacking playfulness and refreshment. Such overloaded sex does not participate in growing intimacy; it often exacerbates objectification.

We Christians have had a hand in increasing the pressures on sexual relationships, especially in marriage. By insisting that we are to be fully sexual only in marriage, by teaching people to expect so much of their primary intimacy commitments and to see their life partners as *the* mediating source of sexuality and intimacy, we have romanticized marriage and denied people a sense of their own sexual integrity. We have even taught sexual repression, for if one is to deny sexuality and sensuousness except in a marital context, one learns to shut off sensuousness and sexual *prob born w/ sex only in marriage*

feelings. And when sexuality is denied and repressed, our sensuousness does not go away. Sexual feeling denied reemerges, sometimes as compulsive sexual behavior, or as misdirected or compulsive need, and sex appears as a "foreign power," outside of ourselves, as a dangerous force which must be controlled.

This romanticization of marriage and family within the church must stop. Honesty requires us to begin to recognize that the American family is a battleground, where rape, battering, incest, and child abuse abound. Marital relations that actually involve tender sensuality and deep mutual respect are very rare among us. We are a needy people, a people who are not sensuous or at ease with sensuality but who use each other in a futile effort to enhance self-respect at the cost of another's sense of self. Men whose lives are thwarted in the workplace go home to express their sense of powerlessness and frustration through violence and coercion toward their wives and children. Needy adults exploit psychically vulnerable children to experience the sensuality they do not and cannot express in adult relations. In this situation, divorces frequently are not "forgivable failures." Just as often they are exemplifications of real maturity, a step in the process of reordering relations in the direction of self-respect and mutuality.

And even that symptom of sexual disorder with which I have some sympathy—the exploitation of sex in pornography—is more symptom than cause of this disease. It is important to recognize that pornography is not wrong because it is erotic. It is wrong because it is predicated upon an exploitative power of relation, one by which women are portrayed as objects of conquests, or as temptresses who long to be "taken" and controlled. Furthermore, pornography is very big business, and we will not be rid of it so long as there is profit to be made by it. In a sense, pornography is the ultimate displacement of sensual, mutual relationship by objectified fantasy. Many are more turned on by watching than by concrete sensuous transactions expressing love.

Toward a New Paradigm of Sexuality

The implications of all this for the church, its theology, and its ethics of sexuality are immense, but I can highlight only a few of them here. We must face up to the extent to which Christianity has been implicated in antisensual, antiwomen praxis, and how much our Christian teaching on sexuality has contributed to sexual repression and sexual objectification, and to legitimating marriage as a form of institutional control of women's sexuality.

The controversies over the role of women, and more especially gay people, are, I believe, intimately connected with defense of the old paradigm. The effort to entrench Christianity as the defender of the institution of normative heterosexuality is part and parcel of the effort to require conformity to the old paradigm of human sexuality. And in all of this, Christians project onto gay people unfaced anxieties about sexuality. As nonconformists to the social norm, gay men and lesbians are perceived as "really sexual," as those who express sensuality and embodied sexuality without constraint. Such projections must cease, and we must find our way to valuing, celebrating and making normative all deep, respectful, sensuous, empowering relationships, which, wherever they exist, ground our well-being and the bonds of mutual respect.

We must learn together that coming to terms with our embodied sensuous capacity for relationship—that is, our sexuality—is a condition for freeing ourselves from patterns of compulsive and controlling sex, so widespread in our churches. To come to terms with our sexuality means to reappropriate sex as a vital, delightful dimension of our sexuality, but also as a dimension without our self-control.

Since our sensuality is the ground of our transactions with the world, it is also the foundation of our creativity, our spontaneity, our power to affect and be affected by each other. A disembodied faith and a disembodied church are without sensuality, spontaneity, and creativity. A church which denies the positive reality of sexuality is dead, ponderous, boring, and unable to touch people's souls. I believe we have paid a high price for our evasions of human sexuality. I see too much banality, superficiality of feeling, and a lack of deep sensibility and emotional responsiveness in our churches. We are out of touch with the depth of life and with the concrete sufferings and vulnerability of people. Furthermore, the almost morbid fear of conflict among us, related as I believe to our denial of sensuality, endangers us far more than any specific conflict could. The price we pay for this fear of conflict is lifelessness and the impairment of our power of relation. We fear the growing "spiritual power" of the rising evangelical groups on the one hand, but stumble to ape them on the other. At the same time, we cut ourselves off from those who are experiencing new sensuous empowerment through liberative struggle. Racial and ethnic people who struggle for justice for their communities, strong women, gay people, and all those who have left sexual repression behind, do *not feel welcome in our churches*, and these are the ones who are "coming of age," critically, in our social world, no longer willing to "please" the established powers in society.

All of this also has deep implications for our theological understanding. Ours is a tradition in which the relationship between God and God's people has been understood, too often, as precluding reciprocal power-in-relation. God is too often understood in our tradition as invulnerable in relation to us. By contrast, a feminist paradigm evokes recognition that an invulnerable deity would, necessarily, be one who objectifies us, who rules us by external control. This is not the God we meet in relation.

From a liberation theology perspective, our relationship to God is intrinsically shaped through our relationships to each other. Our social relations are not separable from our God-relations. To speak of social relations is already to speak of God-relations, and any conception of God-relations already implies patterns of social relations. The normative role of justice to our theology means that we understand that in making right relations God's power is disclosed. Gustavo Gutierrez has argued that justice reveals the face of God.[14] I have learned from him to understand that when a society gives up the struggle to do justice, to make right our disordered relations, we lose a living vision of God.

I believe that this society is profoundly atheistic, precisely because we are losing concern for the struggle for justice. In such a world, we Reformed theologians may proclaim "the mighty acts of God" and "God's preeminent power" to the high heavens—and no one will believe us! For when we no longer experience the depth of our power of agency, when our longing to act toward each other in search of right relationship atrophies, *we are cut off from God's power*, which is not objectified power, separate from us, but the power of relation in our midst. This power of God draws us to each other in common commitment, and into the struggle to embody our cohumanity mutually, that is, toward shared well-being. When we cut ourselves off from those who are now engaging this struggle, we say "no" to God. And in such a situation, surrogate, disembodied, dualistic spiritualities emerge, tempting us to forms of withdrawal from the real, sensuous life that is God's gift to us. In such a situation, "love" becomes not the power to act faithfully and loyally toward another, but a sentiment, an isolated feeling, to be manipulated to secure our invulnerability to mutual relationship. To be a Christian comes to mean that one wears a plastic smile and passes out palliatives, theological and psychological, to kill the searing pain which rends our world.

By contrast to this manipulative spirituality, which purchases "spiritual security" at the price of evasion of reality, we Christians require a deep, subtle understanding of our spiritual situation. In this situation, we need a conception of our ethical responsibility that evokes our calling as God's people, not under the rubric of mere "obedience"—for "obedience" is always conformity to the *external* rule and order of another—but under the images of discernment and creative praxis.[15] We are called to find *new* patterns of relationship, fresh ways of being with and for each other, in the struggle for justice. In the past, those who have called us to join the struggle for justice have too often implied that doing justice is a stern task, a joyless demand, a requirement or obligation which must necessarily lead us to turn our back on our own well-being. But this way of viewing justice presents us with a false portrait of reality. To reach out to each other, to struggle for rich relationship, to accept our *cohumanity*, does not require us to renounce our own well-being but to begin to find its authentic ground and depth in the joyful discovery of the richness that comes through deep relation. To be sure, the human costs of the struggle for justice are high, and many are called upon to give of themselves radically, even unto death. But those who love justice, and have their passion lovingly shaped toward right relation, act not because they are enamored of sacrifice. Rather, they are moved by a love strong enough to sustain their action for right relation, even unto death.

In this regard, we Christians have, I believe, even misunderstood the praxis of him whom we name as "Lord." Jesus' paradigmatic role in the story of our salvation rests not in his willingness to sacrifice himself, but in his passionate love of right relations and his refusal to cease to embody the power of relation in the face of that which would thwart it. It was his refusal to desist from radical love, not a preoccupation with sacrifice, which makes his work irreplaceable.

We are called of God to *life abundant,* and in the struggle for justice we discover that genuine abundance of life comes from embodying a solidarity with one another that is deeply mutual, which is to say, reciprocal. We need desperately to learn that it is the struggle for justice itself which empowers us to learn to dance together, celebrating in anticipation the cohumanity into which we are called. In solidarity born of the struggle for justice, we can joyfully live, empowered, toward those right relationships in which *all* may know that abundant life is the birthright of those God brings to life. The path of justice is often costly, but it is always, also, the path to discovering, through the sharing of our cohumanity, how good and real is the sensuous, embodied life God gives.

Notes

1. Samuel Laeuchli, *Power and Sexuality* (Philadelphia: Temple University Press, 1972), 92.
2. James Nelson, *Embodiment: An Approach to Sexuality and Christian Theology* (Minneapolis: Augsburg, 1979).
3. Jerome, *Letter* 22.25–26, and *Against Jovinian* 1.9, 16, 26–31. See also J. N. D. Kelly, *Jerome: His Life, Writings, and Controversies* (Westminster, Md.: Christian Classics, 1980).
4. See Nancy Jay, "Throughout Your Generations Forever: A Sociology of Blood Sacrifice" (Ph.D. diss., Brandeis University, 1981).
5. See H. R. Trevor-Roper, *The Great Witch Craze of the Sixteenth and Seventeenth Centuries and Other Essays* (New York: Harper Torchbooks, 1967).
6. Cf. Emil Brunner, *Man in Revolt: A Christian Anthropology* (Philadelphia: Westminster Press, 1947), esp. 352ff.; and Karl Barth, *Church Dogmatics,* III/4, ed. G. W. Bromily and T. F. Torrance (Edinburgh: T. & T. Clark, 1961), 116–240.
7. See Boston Women's Health Book Collective, *Our Bodies, Ourselves* (New York: Simon & Schuster, 1973).
8. See John MacMurray, *The Self as Agent* (London: Faber & Faber, 1958); and idem, *Persons in Relation* (London: Faber & Faber, 1961).
9. This term is from Isabel Carter Heyward, *The Redemption of God: A Theology of Mutual Relation* (Washington, D.C.: University Press of America, 1982), 25ff.
10. Nelle Morton, "The Rising Woman Consciousness in a Male Language Structure," *Andover-Newton Quarterly* 12, no. 4 (March 1972), 177–190.
11. See Michael Lewis, *The Culture of Inequality* (Amherst, Mass.: University of Massachusetts Press, 1979).
12. See William Ryan, *Blaming the Victim* (New York: Random House, 1971).
13. See Johnny Greene, "The Moral Wrongs of the New Moral Right," *Playboy,* January 1981.
14. See Gustavo Gutierrez, *A Theology of Liberation* (Maryknoll, N.Y.: Orbis Books, 1973).
15. See Dorothee Soelle, *Beyond Mere Obedience* (Philadelphia: Fortress Press, 1981).

Chapter 8

Challenging Sexual Ethics
and Social Order

Interview by Jane E. Hicks

Hicks: *You've written quite a bit on the topic of sexuality over the course of your career, including your first book,* Our Right to Choose, *on abortion, and the essay "Mutuality and Sexuality," which is included in this volume. Suffice it to say, constructing a more satisfying sexual ethic is among the central tasks of a liberatory feminism. I'd like to get your sense of why that is, why our mores about sex and sexuality are important to a more just and livable society. I'd also like to explore how your thinking about sexual ethics has grown since your earlier work and how sexual ethics relates to your approach to ethics in general.*

To start, how did your interest in sexual ethics arise? Why teach and write in this area?

Harrison: As a graduate student, I had no interest in sexual ethics, but I quickly learned that I would have no choice. As long as I had the right genitals I was going to be expected to talk about the topic. It started very quickly when I became a lecturer and an assistant professor in Christian ethics. The president of Union Seminary had calls from churches to the effect that they needed someone to talk about sex and sexuality, and he looked around and sent me. And that was okay with me, but at that point I didn't have a transformative agenda, except knowing the deep discomfort women were experiencing. I had no idea how badly men were suffering. However, my first talk was to a group of laymen who wanted to hear a woman talk about sexuality. I learned a great deal that day about men's suffering around issues of sexuality and also about the ignorance in the churches. My experience with these groups jogged my thinking about doing a course in sexual ethics, and it grew from there.

Hicks: *How does your work differ from the way sexual ethics is usually considered in religious and theological studies?*

Harrison: I knew right away that I had to do it differently. In liberal tradition, discussions of sexuality always plug into psychology. The assumption is that when you are dealing with human sexuality, you're dealing with people's deepest stuff as persons. But what I hadn't seen anybody do was figure out why sexuality splinters groups and why everyone goes crazy when you talk across other lines of structural difference. The most obvious, of course, is race and sexuality. Gradually I began to see more clearly that what we have here is an overly privatized view of sexuality, which basically assumes that "sex" ends where your skin ends.

In the 1970s, I was a consultant on the United Church of Christ sexuality study with Jim Nelson and Eleanor Morrison. Eleanor Morrison, a leading sex educator at the time, did a workshop on how to teach sexuality for those of us who were consultants and staff persons. It was very transformative for me. For example, she taught us not to expect people to start talking about where they are as sexual persons in the present moment. They won't do it. Instead, ask people about when they were young, how they first began to have a sense of what it meant that they were sexual persons: "Did you talk with anybody? Did anybody say anything to you?" And then she would have students write short papers about their early experience. She said she had thousands of these papers in her files, and over 90 percent of them described painful experiences in "learning sex." They were about fear, guilt, and unpleasant learning. Few had begun to discover what it means to be a sexual being in a context where they were supported and where they felt that sex was okay.

People feel they must have done something wrong; they're so surrounded by half-truths and fears that they pick up from parents, frightened Christians, and others. People should not be asked to "talk sex" until they have talked about their pasts and what hurt when they were young. Most, by the end of the class, will have dropped their defensiveness about something "dirty." The atmosphere of fear dissipates once people communicate at the level of real pain or real insight. People all feel that they have made mistakes. In this society, nobody is taught anything about how to develop relationships, or how to negotiate with a sexual partner. We don't teach anything you need to know in order not to get hurt, so everybody gets hurt.

Hicks: *One striking difference in your approach to sexual ethics, as I see it, is your insistence that the subject be considered in relation to broader social structures, in relation* *to race, class, and political economy, for instance, and above all, be understood as historically situated. You've touched upon these ideas briefly already, but I think it is important to clarify a bit more. Over the years, you have consistently framed Christian sexual ethics in terms of "sexuality and social order," for instance. Why talk about sexual ethics this way?*

Harrison: Sexual ethics is not strictly personal and private. The "psycho babblers," as I like to call them, like to think that our deepest reality is in our relationship with Mom, Pop, and the kids. But what did "Mom, Pop, and the kids" make of this great cosmos-altering political economy and the cultures that have been shaped by it? What role have religious systems played in transmitting those cultures in relation to the political economy? That is of tremendous interest to me. The churches are stuck in the issue of sexuality not just because individuals feel so uneasy and don't know how to talk about it but because the family is the structure that has been sanctified by the liberal worldview. It is our horizon, and, in terms of how we get the way we are as sexual beings, our understanding is blocked at the boundary of the dominant concept of "family." We have dehistoricized sexuality so that it is difficult to broach a sufficiently complex understanding of sexual subjectivities and the incredible way our subjectivities are conditioned by a racialized, class location.

My subjecthood is closely tied, for example, to the way my security is structured—whether I have a safe bed to sleep in and a roof over my head and enough food. That has a lot to do with how I feel as a sexual person. It has to do with whether I can be a sexual person safely. It really is important to reimage, to revision, to see all of this in a different way, because to be sensuous and at home in my body person, whatever sex partners I decide to have or not have, comes from having safe space, the well-being and the tender loving care that all of us deserve. We must figure out this world and come to a radically different understanding of how we come to our subjectivity as sexual persons. I've reached the point where I don't think that my sexuality is "my identity" to the exclusion of everything else, or that my role in the political economy is everything. Rather, these qualities of life are integrally connected.

What we call "sex" is really just overrigidified sensuality. I have learned from collaboration with people from other cultures that we in the West genitalize sex. Current sexology textbooks recognize at least four or five different kinds or patterns of gender. Sex is a much more fluid thing than we normally grant, which is not to say that any given subjectivity will be fluid in the sense that one can wake up in the morning and choose one's gender for the day. It does mean that people don't come to the question of personal sexual identity or sexual norms with the desire to know very much about what people *really* need or how they differ. We have botched it, in my view.

Hicks: *I think your indictment of traditional sexual ethics will resonate with a lot of readers. Is there anything to be learned from traditional religious approaches?*

Harrison: If you work from the traditional Christian ethic, you talk about committed relationships, about "till death do you part" relationships. You talk about lifelong loving. Now, I'm in favor of lifelong loving. But given our world, if anybody really learns to do it, that will be quite an accomplishment. But you know this glib talk about commitment and being sexual only in marriage gives away the fact that we don't really have an ethic about sex; we don't really teach *anything* about sex. Instead we teach where you should put your genitals and when, if ever, you should hop into bed. That is an atrophied sexual ethic. It represents a kindergartener's moral thinking! I always started my classes arguing that we have never had a true Christian sexual ethic before. Let's start thinking about it and construct one, because all we have now is a series of ill-considered taboos.

What we're teaching is terrible. We're not helping people. In the local church, people are starved for a more mature conversation about how to live in self-affirming, other-affirming, nonhurtful ways. Putting forward a wider framework and identifying what else we need to learn is part of that work. The fluidity regarding gender subjectivity has to begin to come into our understandings, and we also have to stop ghettoizing our sexual talk. To begin to talk across lines of real gender and sexual difference and to learn from sexual experience is an important contribution.

Hicks: *Will you discuss how our bodies are implicated in our moral work, particularly as women? As part of your materialist feminist methodology, you root sexual ethics in the body. Would you discuss the term* embodiment *and its significance for you in addressing sexuality and social order?*

Harrison: This term *embodiment* relates to a shift in my thinking that started with an early insistence that if I were going to teach sexuality, I would teach it from a feminist perspective. At that point almost everything that passed as knowledge in the academy had been conjured by men and explained by men, including women's sexuality. The women's movement that I was a part of in the late sixties and early seventies redefined orgasm. Orgasm is a full bodily experience for women. Women are not as genitally fixated as men. When women see themselves as sexual only in relation to men, it is a disaster! The feminist perspective on sexuality goes back to *Our Bodies, Ourselves*, which was a kind of revolutionary document.[1] That book was important to me personally, but what it also made me realize was that the most important change that had to happen was that women should not be defined as sexual persons only when there was a man around. And, in fact, women are fully sexual when we are, as persons, fully embodied. We have a body. We are a body! You have to start there, and you find that as a major theme in what I have written and certainly in my speaking. Affirming women's experience as sensuous embodied human beings is the way I start talking about sexual ethics to this very day.

It should be clear that the metaphor of embodiment began first to mean being a sensuous person, being at home with yourself and your own body and taking care of your body. These things are not linear; they explode, they don't just unfold. Then I also began to think about the community more as an embodied reality. And I began to think of our culture as a form of embodiment. What is culture? Culture can be theorized as the patternings of life, not so much in large institutions, but there in the primary face-to-face institutions such as church and family. So culture is literally the embodied stuff of how we transact life in our daily world. Such insight has helped me methodologically. One should always start with where people live. Our ethic has to be *ours*. And so I began to think of communities primarily as being embodied forms of social practice, in analogy to a sensuous body. We lose the sensuous stuff of the culture when we reduce ethics to rule-making functions.

Finally, the metaphor came to fruition for me when reading Larry Rasmussen's *Earth Community, Earth Ethics*, in which he noted that the ozone layer is our collective skin.[2] All of a sudden I made the connection that our embodiment extends to this entire little planet Earth. I had always noticed ecologists' interesting earthy insights, such as "We're throwing our sewage into our living room" with our methods of consumption and disposal. An ecological perspective teaches us that we cannot separate ourselves; we can't disconnect ourselves from waste and from the harm we do to the entire biological system on which our lives are dependent. As a result, subjectivity and embodiment began to have a different reach in my thinking. In a liberal paradigm, one's psyche is the place where one's deep subjectivity ends, which is the way most people see it.

By contrast, I believe that all of us have a deep moral sense of connectedness. You see pain in people's faces, you see the consequences of actions, you get this feeling, and there's a bodily response—a bodily response which is trustworthy. When I talk about embodied feminist ethics, I image us as existing in the personal, the interpersonal (the face-to-face intimacy), the cultural community, and the political economic order. Most people can no longer see the political and economic levels of our embodiment. They are just mystified. Now we need to add the whole cosmic dimension too. Everything we produce and manufacture impacts our existence as sensual beings. We're always dumping our waste in our living rooms. Healing begins only when these connections are made.

Hicks: *Yes, sexual ethics is integrally connected to environmental ethics. Given that gender and embodiment must inform our sexual ethics, another aspect of the broad sweep of sexuality and social order has to do with political economy and the ways corporations and trade, or patterns of economic exchange, structure our intimate relations. How do you understand sexual ethics specifically in relation to economic violence and the commodification of sexuality and the body?*

Harrison: All of us who do feminist work have started with violence against women, and all of us have been overwhelmed by the pervasiveness of the violence. In the theological literature, Rita Brock and Susan Thistlethwaite's book on prostitution, which really begins to move away from what I call a victim-centered analysis, is an important resource.[3] We need to illumine victimization, but one of the real problems in feminist thought has been to illumine and lift up the perspective of the victim and to stop there. We need to come through the subject's gaze and then move out. You also have to come from the gaze of the exploitative system that teaches the violence. What is advanced global capitalism doing to sexuality? One of my favorite insights of Karl Marx, that capitalism will force the mediation of all social relations through money, comes into play here. He was pointing to the way that every system of exchange leads to the construction of not just things but people as commodities. Governments in Asia promote prostitution for the sake of dollar exchange, for instance. They promote sex-trade tourism, which flourishes around U.S. military bases. Prostitution has become the center of a new industry in Thailand and the Philippines. It is the poorest of the poor who are recruited for sex trade work because this is something that every woman can do if she has a body. The intimate connection between what we women have to do with our bodies in order to survive economically in the world is the most missed piece of this feminist historicizing of our sexual identity. Currently we have this extraordinary disruption of traditional cultures. The fact is that the exploitation and modernization of women's sexuality goes hand in hand with the breakdown of traditional roles partly because of the power of capitalist political economy to direct and redirect change. Some facets of traditional culture oppress women, but through them women have struggled and have gotten greater space and place and protections. These protections within traditional cultures all disappear under conditions of rapid economic globalization.

As feminists, we must first address the process of commodification and the erasure of traditional protections for women. Why, for example, do Islamic women often want the protections of their traditional cultures? Because they don't have any other viable options; they don't have a way to survive safely otherwise. Women in non-Western cultures always welcome opportunities for education. They always welcome the life-enhancing stuff that comes with Westernization. What they really resist is the premature demand that they be like us Western white women, that they work in a public world and thereby give up raising their children even before they have the means to raise them well. This, of course, has been a problem in feminist discourse in that we have failed to realize that for many women, children are the deepest, most fulfilling aspect of their lives, and, for many, just not having to sell their bodies is a great relief!!

Hicks: *What you're saying here is so important in an age of increasing economic globalization. We in the West are often complicit in the untenable, deplorable conditions women around the world face in what they have to do with their bodies to survive, as you say. At the same time, many would prefer to treat sexual ethics as a decontextualized, ahistorical question, in a sense denying those very connections, and to all our detriment.*

Harrison: The commodification of "sex for sale" in the present capitalist system is presently reshaping our own understanding of sexuality in the West as well. It's very hard for kids to grow up in this society and not objectify themselves. Their gaze comes from the television. Young girls objectify themselves through that external gaze. The transformative power of a late-capitalist industrial culture, particularly through image making, must be acknowledged. I agree with traditionalists who argue that children—boys and girls—should grow up slowly enough so that they can learn to make their own judgments. We have to give due credit to some of the traditional values because they are real. Think of JonBenet Ramsey.* Why does a six-year-old have to be a sex object? She wasn't able to understand what her parents were doing to her and, if she had lived, she probably would have been anorexic or bulimic by the age of twelve. Why? Taking the view of the other against oneself at such an early age creates eating disorders, I'm convinced. It's part of the process of objectification which should not happen. And we have so many girl children who think they have to be a certain way or they aren't going to be loved when they grow up. Children grow up in this society imaging themselves, objectifying themselves through the visions and dreams the culture offers, and for girl children, the images offered have gotten worse, not better. Feminism will be the longest revolution because these patterns of objectification and exploitation of women are so deeply embedded and their power hidden within the dominant culture.

Hicks: *You've said recently that you've been captured by this metaphor of being queer about everything. What do you mean by* queerness *and why is it a compelling ethic for you and potentially for others?*

Harrison: I came about this new manner of speaking with intellectual indebtedness to Carter Heyward, who has been teaching queer theology for the last several years. The postmodernist movement of language is turning to que[e]rying sex,[4] which turns queer into a good thing rather than a bad thing. As Carter understands, inviting people to become more and more queer is to question the authority and the definitions and the established truths of the society and to do this in the service of justice.

This invites people to think of "queer" not as something that applies to a specific fixed identity, but to think of queer as something we all can become. We all can become as odd as possible and question things as they are, and, especially, continue interrogating the things that are killing us. That is what a liberative ethic does. It will not settle for the mystifications, and so the que[e]rying just has to go on and on. Queer then becomes a metaphor that nonlesbians and nongays can also appropriate.

---

*Six-year-old JonBenet Ramsey was found dead in the basement of her family home in Boulder, Colorado, on December 26, 1996, after her parents had reported her missing earlier that day. The case drew national attention in part due to disturbing home video footage of JonBenet as a beauty contestant in which she appeared in makeup, dress, and poses typical of adult pageants. The Boulder Police Department focused upon JonBenet's parents, John and Patricia Ramsey, as their prime suspects in the killing, but no formal charges were filed, and the case remains unsolved.

I don't think of most of my gay-affirming friends as "straight." If you advocate for gays you are "queer." Unfortunately, we still assume that only the lines of victimization define us. We need to see that not every gay and lesbian has been threatened with death and not every nongay and nonlesbian is happy with the miseries that come with being heterosexual. If we can only stop assuming that victims and nonvictims are so easily identified, or that our identities are primarily created by victimization, we would all be much better served. We need to remember that what we passionately love is what creates growth, the cutting edge of our lives. We have to learn to let people love each other, and we all need to learn to cross these lines of victimization to find new justice-loving friends.

Notes

1. Boston Women's Health Book Collective, *Our Bodies, Ourselves: A Book by and for Women* (New York: Simon & Schuster, 1973).
2. Larry L. Rasmussen, *Earth Community, Earth Ethics* (Maryknoll, N.Y.: Orbis Books, 1996).
3. Rita Nakashima Brock and Susan B. Thistlethwaite, *Casting Stones: Prostitution and Liberation in Asia and the United States* (Minneapolis: Fortress Press, 1996). See also Rita Nakashima Brock and Rebecca Ann Parker, *Proverbs of Ashes: Violence, Redemptive Suffering, and the Search for What Saves Us* (Boston: Beacon Press, 2001).
4. The term *que[e]rying* is a play on *query,* meaning to pose a question. As indicated, the phrase *queerying sex* has gained currency in postmodernist literature, particularly in queer theory. See Carter Heyward, "We're Here, We're Queer: Teaching Sex in Seminary," in *Body and Soul: Rethinking Sexuality as Justice-Love*, ed. Marvin M. Ellison and Sylvia Thorson-Smith (Cleveland: Pilgrim Press, 2003), 78–96; and Beverly Wildung Harrison, "Christianity's Indecent Decency: Why a Holistic Vision of Justice Eludes Us," pages 25–44 in the same volume.

Part Two

WORKING WITH PROTESTANT TRADITIONS
Theological Liberalism and Feminist Transformations

Introduction
Elizabeth M. Bounds and Marilyn J. Legge

Theological fidelity never means merely obeisance to what the churches currently claim as theological "truth." Rather, it means candidly and judiciously facing our own community's complicity in those roots and structures of oppression our social analysis lays bare. Authentic spiritual maturity requires a conception of theological truthfulness as an ongoing process.
—Beverly Wildung Harrison,
Making the Connections

To forget that the feminisms and feminist theorizing that spawned and fuelled our work were generated by women's activism is suicidal. Activism with and for community and against enduring patterns of violence, resistance toward the concrete sources of life threat, the "primary emergencies" that require the daily encounter in women's lives, are our lifeblood.
—Beverly Wildung Harrison,
"Feminist Thea(o)logies at the Millennium"

Part 2 demonstrates ways in which Harrison critically and contextually appropriates particular mainstream and marginalized Protestant liberal theological voices that have shaped her both professionally and personally. Since for her, theology is an ongoing moral and religious process, she approaches tradition as praxis carried out under particular social and historical circumstances. Although she was educated in both liberal and neo-orthodox Christian theologies, Harrison has consistently reclaimed the task of the Social Gospel strand of liberal ethics through her insistence that love and justice must be lived out in responsible social action. Her sense of morality as a matter of creative constructions of better ways of living together is indebted to the Social Gospel emphasis on shaping a common good.

However, engagement with liberation voices and movements profoundly reshaped her notions of theological ethics and pluralized her understanding of common good. She has critiqued Protestant liberal theological tradition by drawing upon the voices of the justice-seeking marginalized, especially the voices of women. For her, serious engagement with these voices requires not a simple addition of their views but, rather, a methodological shift in ethical work and accountability. While the use of experience has always been central to liberal theological method, Harrison has challenged its abstract and individualistic construal, along with its implied universalized Euro-American male location. Instead, moral knowledge is generated through reflection on multiple concrete experiences, a process that can only be carried out through dialogues committed to social transformation. And while an emphasis on unmasking power has been a hallmark of Christian realism, Harrison increases the critical capacity of Christian ethics through her use of transformative (particularly Marxian or critical) social theories.

Harrison's work has always situated the task of doing ethics as simultaneously continuing and disrupting mainstream liberal Protestantism. The division of essays in this part reflects these dual strategies. Chapters 10–12 aim to situate her work more clearly in the ongoing traditions of Protestant liberal theological ethics. They include her reflections on three figures, all profound influences on her, who shaped twentieth-century Protestant social ethics—Reinhold Niebuhr, Harry Ward, and James Luther Adams. Through her attention to each of these white male ethicists, her own varied appropriation of their work emerges. In every case, she is trying to preserve the best of the progressive liberal Protestant heritage in the United States while always challenging it to move beyond the limitations, gaps, and blockages that, in her view, may close off its future.

Although Harrison has listened to feminist and womanist voices from a range of locations, the next three essays, chapters 13–15, attend more closely to the relationship of her work to white Protestant women who have been present as role models, intellectual companions, and "sisters in the struggle." These essays have been chosen in part because they make clear some of the ways feminist theologies reoriented Harrison's theological framework, in tandem with the feminist reorientation of her ethical methodologies shown in the previous section of this volume. The first essay (chapter 13), framed by engagement with foremother Nelle Morton, represents the ways Harrison has pointed to alternative women's traditions in opposition to distorting malestream accounts. The next two essays honor two sister feminist pioneers, Letty Russell and Dorothee Soelle, personal friends and collaborators with whom Harrison shares a vision of a reimagined justice-centered theology. For all three women, "the work of theology . . . was not primarily explanatory, the creation of justifications for the way things are, but rather an evocative task, a calling forth of energy and power to struggle against spiritual entrapment."[1]

Along with these six essays by Harrison are two interviews with her, one at the beginning and one at the end of part 2. These conversations will help situate Harrison's engagement with each individual in the broader context of her own theological formation and commitments.

Harrison's own theological reimagining invites persons to place the work of moral formation and discernment at the heart of religious communities, especially, in her case, Protestant churches that have not repudiated a liberal heritage. But this is not a self-preoccupied formation, done for the sake of denominational identity. For her, the purpose of Christian ethics must always be "to encourage Christians and their churches toward more adequate ethical engagement, which is always simultaneously public engagement."[2] These essays suggest some of the theological resources, past and present, that Harrison draws upon for taking up this task.

Notes

1. Beverly Wildung Harrison, "Dorothee Soelle as Pioneering Postmodernist," in *The Theology of Dorothee Soelle*, ed. Sarah K. Pinnock (Harrisburg, Pa.: Trinity Press International, 2003), 335–6 and p. 133 in this volume.
2. Beverly Wildung Harrison, "The Quest for Justice," in *The Public Vocation of Christian Ethics*, ed. Beverly Wildung Harrison, Robert L. Stivers, and Ronald H. Stone (New York: Pilgrim Press, 1986), 290. Harrison wrote these words about Roger Shinn, but they apply equally well to her project.

Chapter 9

Working with Protestant Traditions: Liberalism and Beyond

Interview by Elizabeth M. Bounds

Bounds: *Many people don't think of you as a liberal Protestant ethicist. In my view, these people fall into two groups. One are your feminist and liberationist friends, who want to believe that there is nothing redeemable in the liberal Protestant voice. The other group is mainstream Protestant ethicists, especially the ones Jeffrey Stout has recently called the "new traditionalists,"[1] who would like to exclude any of the criticisms you raise as simply belonging to another conversation which, in their view, is not a conversation within liberal Protestant traditions. Can you characterize some of the ways you actually name and locate yourself?*

Harrison: I do still think of myself as largely accountable and responsible to what I will call here liberal Protestant social ethics. Now let me say that, characteristically, I speak of this part of the liberal theological legacy very favorably—differing, I might add, from what seems to be almost everybody else's interest in trashing the liberal tradition. What Stout calls neotraditional, I call neoliberal, but to me it is really pseudoliberal. For quite some time, I have been what you could call an unapologetic postliberal liberal, committed to what I see as the best of both political and Christian liberal traditions.

79

What I mean by the best of Protestant Christian liberalism are the traditions of Christianity largely rooted in the tribes of Europe and in the practices of religious community they generated. The churches that developed as splits in the streams of European Protestantism also contributed to the positive shaping of liberalism. Here I include enhancements to Christian traditions contributed by Methodism and by the many Baptist movements in the United States. (Oh, how I wish these days that the Baptists remembered why they invented the separation of church and state!) I am talking here about what I was taught to call mainline churches. Today, though, no longer trapped within a colonized mentality, I call these churches "old-line" Protestant—indeed, by now they are only a very small sector of what has come to constitute the worldwide movements of Protestant Christianity.

In any case, my sense of liberal Protestantism has been profoundly shaped by my perception of its twentieth-century crisis in identity. I take a very different view of where liberal Protestantism went wrong than do most Christian ethicists. In my view, the theological voice of recent liberal Protestantism has been chiefly preoccupied with survival, whether it be in the academy or in the churches. In the face of the realities of declining numbers and especially of declining social and cultural influence, fixation on fantasies of a golden past has set in.

The tragically wrong response to this has been to try to reassert Christian identity by embracing one of two different strategies to "recover" presumed lost grandeur. In the first strategy, we are told we must get back to one or another great or "real" tradition and make the continuous and exclusive reading of the texts of that tradition the real stuff of what it means to do theology. In the second, we are told that by reconstructing or feverishly reproducing the ecclesial culture of one's past denominational tradition (whichever pieces you choose to reinscribe), we will be able to revive the power of our denominational ritual and culture. Only, it is claimed, if we reinscribe ritual precisely or reiterate conventional theological wisdom without deviance will we have a spiritually alive church. What these strategies are producing is not a living tradition, but, rather, a fetishized escapism. The kind of closed communities of moral formation they envision have only contempt for the public and its goods. Why focus on a public world where strangers meet, when the intimate community of Christian spirituality is so much more profound (and so closed to any challenges from others different than ourselves)?

Neoliberals give up on any effort at Christian contributions to public policy and thus on any sense of what Christian people should contribute to the wider society. Consequently, they give up on the work of Christian social ethics. In the debates in my own Presbyterian denomination, I have heard general presbyters, the leaders of my own denomination, basically say, "Justice is not a Presbyterian idea." I have been disappointed that John Calvin has not risen from the grave to challenge them!

Bounds: *In contrast to these neoliberal readings of liberal Protestant tradition, I think of the careful, critical ways you have worked with a variety of liberal theological voices, from Social Gospel to Niebuhr and Tillich, alongside, of course, liberation voices. How has this critical liberalism shaped your own ethics? Who of the liberal*

Protestant males have shaped you? How and what have you appropriated, and what have you tried to change?

Harrison: My understanding of what has most influenced me has evolved as I have gone through what I would call the "radicalizing" of my liberal stance. By the early eighties, I was very clear. Protestant liberalism in this country had failed to move toward a genuine, critical theory offering clear criteria for separating what was worth carrying forward from what must be left behind. I was able to find the source of a genuinely critical reflection only in the methods of liberation theology.

Bounds: *But when you got back to Union Theological Seminary in the sixties and began to do your doctoral work, obviously the influence of Niebuhr was omnipresent, especially since he was still alive.*

Harrison: Of course—he was the great star. But it's important to remember that there are two Niebuhrs. There is the Niebuhr created by the endless academic treatment of his work, the Niebuhr who most often was cast as consistent cold warrior Christian realist. But there is also the more multifaceted and politically active Niebuhr as understood by the people who studied with him at Union and were shaped by his teaching and by the power of his personality. He was a passionate but modest man! And he had a sense of humor! The first year I taught a seminar on Niebuhr, the class went over to his apartment several times. Once, when we were talking about Barrington Moore's *Social Origins of Dictatorship and Democracy,* he got excited and said, "I think we have been [we, being the realists] hard on these newly emerging nations. We forget how violent and bloody was our own struggle for democracy." He had by this time begun to think that the Vietnam War was a very bad idea.

Bounds: *Niebuhr was willing to change his mind because he engaged the ongoing political situation in ways that would allow him to reshape his thinking in relationship to events.*

Harrison: Yes, you could see how pragmatic and topical he was whenever he preached in the chapel. When I read some of his sermons today I think they're a little superficial and overstated, but you can't imagine the astonishment and excitement they generated. I recall Columbia senior professors who slipped into the chapel to hear him and raved about his political astuteness. Recently I reread a sermon of his on race. When he was making a point about the power of institutions in making change, he talked about a conversation with a black senior officer in the U.S. Army, who said to him, "I don't give a damn whether people like me or not. In the military I'm an officer, and I have to be treated like one." And the officer added something about how justice was better than being liked! And Reinie, the realist, thought this way of seeing the matter was the greatest thing. In many ways the rest of the sermon was not earthshaking, but when he told that story you could have heard a pin drop in the chapel. Niebuhr is much better read from his occasional writings than his books. Paul Tillich once said that Reinie doesn't tell you how he knows, he just starts knowing. I thought that was important because I'd never heard anybody else say, "Hey, this guy has no clear methodological foundation." Even back then I felt Niebuhr needed to think more carefully about some of his assumptions.

Bounds: *Did Niebuhr's influence simply eclipse any sort of concern for Social Gospel themes? Was there any self-consciousness about the Social Gospel heritage, or was that really underground at Union?*

Harrison: Well, every so often Niebuhr would get off his high horse about the failures of liberalism and stop dumping on the Social Gospel. At such times he would acknowledge that it would be terrible to lose the concern for social justice. However, Niebuhr did not teach Christian ethics historically, so he spent more time in class on how theological ideas qualified our ethical perspective than on engaging other views. What I learned in the fifties about the Social Gospel did not come from my ethics courses. There we read Brunner and Barth, and debated sources for doing ethics. I read Rauschenbusch for the first time in Bob Handy's courses in modern American religious history. In fact, the only work of Harry Ward that I ever had assigned to read in graduate school was also in one of Handy's courses. I am grateful that this exposure helped to create, or perhaps deepen, my growing suspicions that Niebuhr's criticisms of Social Gospel liberalism were overgeneralized. Yet it would be a long time until I came to fully appreciate Ward, who in my view really was the figure who brought social Christianity to Union. I still believe he is the most sophisticated artisan of Christian economic and political thinking in modern U.S. Christianity. Of course, his theology was thin and his method overly biblicist, but that is another story!

But back to your question. No, the progressive Social Gospel voices never went completely underground at Union, chiefly I think because John Bennett represented it so well. I see John as someone who over the decades stayed the course as an unapologetic social liberal who was consistently concerned about social ethics and its vocation. He always saw himself as the middle-of-the-roader in terms of any progressive critique of liberalism, but, as years went on, he more than once said to me, "I guess I'm really still a liberal" (rather than a neo-orthodox Christian realist), recognizing that he was more radical than he wanted to admit. He was the one who always said, "Realism is a boast, not a clearcut position." Yet he also was completely deferential to Niebuhr. Nevertheless, he stayed with a progressive critical position toward U.S. foreign policy and had a Social Gospel sense of politics. Bennett never sounded like a cold warrior as Niebuhr did.

Bounds: *How did you see the ways you were putting these different influences together during your doctoral work? You were not planning to join the fight over the heritage of Reinhold Niebuhr, so how did you work through the possibilities?*

Harrison: In my first semester at Union, I wrote a seventy-page paper for two courses on Reinhold Niebuhr's theory of the self and decided he had a German idealist monadic view. His assumptions about the inevitable selfish nature of the agent were, I realized, erroneous. This was an intellectual coming of age for me because I realized I had located some contradictions in Niebuhr's theory. In my research, I read practically every book he had published up until that time, certainly anything he wrote on the topic of selfhood. I also came out of this total immersion in his thought with a feeling that Niebuhr was seriously unfair to John Dewey, and that, even though he talked continually about the power of community, his view of personhood was terribly individualistic. When I read *Basic Christian Ethics*, I realized that Paul Ramsey had detected the same inconsistency in Niebuhr, a disjunction between an individualistic self and a political emphasis on the communal and collective. Unfortunately, Ramsey's response was to sharpen the split between the personal and the social! If you do this you get a false reading of Niebuhr, because Niebuhr himself was political to the core, and he was communitarian, and for better or worse, did care deeply about the impact of Christianity on society. Those who see Ramsey and Niebuhr on the same wavelength about Christianity and politics are just wrong!

Bounds: *In your dissertation you started to look at H. Richard Niebuhr's notions on self to see if there was a richer, nondualistic possibility.*

Harrison: I was attracted to the fact that H. Richard, for example, understood Troeltsch to be struggling with ways of making Christian ethics more authentically historical. However, as I say in my dissertation, he also failed in some important ways to reach a historically informed method for ethics. But his nondualistic model for relating self and society was very important to me. Still, I found H. Richard's work to fall short of its nondualistic promise because he was always limited by his notion of an absolutely transcendent and impassable Calvinist God. In order to image that God sovereign, he was finally caught between two histories, the inner history of God (revelation) and the outer history of human objectivist knowledge (especially social-scientifically generated knowledge). My research for my dissertation confirmed an already deep conviction that the so-called neo-orthodox preoccupation with protecting divine transcendence at all costs was bad news, and I found I could give up once and for all apologizing for being a theological liberal. I suppose it was this conclusion about the failure of H. Richard's theistic project that set me to reading James Luther Adams. Though, like me, he published little, I found his work was rich in concrete historical texture and detail. I think he did as well as any prefeminist Christian intellectual at situating religio-political ideas in a lived-world context. In a sense, Adams led me back to Tillich and to the socialist project. He was also unapologetic about theological liberalism, and that gave me courage not to flinch in the face of endless rhetorical criticisms of liberalism, most of which I tend to consider contentious half-truths.

Bounds: *How would you describe the kinds of constructive strategies within liberal Protestant social ethics you have tried to develop?*

Harrison: Well, since Niebuhr's day we have tried to think a little differently at Union about the tasks of Christian ethics. My work with colleagues Larry Rasmussen and Don Shriver attests to some of that shift. A brief comment on Larry's impact on me will be forthcoming in an issue of the *Union Seminary Quarterly Review* honoring him on the occasion of his retirement.[2] Both Larry and I feel a deep debt to John Bennett. I think we both learned from him that the work of social ethics in the churches is to be done chiefly in the service of developing and forming communities of Christians, and even judicatories of the denominations, into living moral communities. This means that the work of the ethicist sifts both tradition and contemporary knowledge to enable and encourage reformulations that clarify what it means to live the Christian life together, in the present. Once you get that straight, you have a *living* tradition of social ethics. The liberal Protestant churches need to know that we live in a world where Christian participation in public life is vital, and that the voices that need to be there are not merely the few voices of the old-line Protestant elite theological tradition. We have to learn what it means to be religious people, speaking from our traditions without the colonizing mentality that ours is the only *episteme* from which anything can be said in terms of morally significant teachings.

Doing Christian ethics has always been exciting for me because there is always new work to do to meet the challenges that a rapidly changing—not always for the better—world sets for us. I think we manage to keep the passion for justice alive when we do not flee from encountering the painful conflicts that the alienations of past injustice have created. That is the test of our professions of faith: Do they keep us on the journey of justice, or propel us to denial of the suffering around us?

Notes

1. See Jeffrey Stout, *Democracy and Tradition* (Princeton, N.J.: Princeton University Press, 2004).
2. Beverly Wildung Harrison, "Mediating and Deepening Union's Legacy," *Union Seminary Quarterly Review* 58:1–2 (2004): 169–177.

Chapter 10

Niebuhr: Locating the Limits

This essay was one of a series of reviews of Reinhold Niebuhr: A Biography *by Richard W. Fox (New York: Harper & Row, 1985). Fox's study was a significant contribution to the evaluation of Niebuhr (1892–1971), one of the most prominent Christian ethicists of the twentieth century. From* Christianity and Crisis *46, no. 2 (February 17, 1986): 35–39.*

The impressive prepublication endorsements of *Reinhold Niebuhr* proffered by a diverse group of U.S. historians and theologians signal the importance of Richard Fox's work for ongoing discussion of Reinhold Niebuhr's legacy. The large number of enthusiastic reviews accompanying the book's release—all appearing in prominent places—confirms and further assures its stature. It is all but certain that Fox's study will hold an authoritative place in public perception not only of Niebuhr but of mainstream Protestantism in this nation. For those who care about "the use and abuse" of Reinhold Niebuhr and about the role of religion in society, a discerning reading of *Reinhold Niebuhr* is a must.

Readers of *C&C* [*Christianity and Crisis*] are aware that something of a Niebuhr renaissance has been under way already. Theologians, ethicists, and politicians not

only invoke his name but seek a hearing for their message by linking it to a purportedly "essential" Niebuhrian teaching. Claims and counterclaims about
Niebuhr's intellectual legacy abound, testimony that in the U.S. Christian mainstream fidelity to his heritage still counts for a good deal.

Fox himself reports—with apologies to Albert Schweitzer—that his initial
desire "to probe beneath the conflicting Niebuhrs of faith" derived from the differing impacts his undergraduate teachers, Robert McAfee Brown and Michael
Novak, ascribed to Niebuhr. This explanation, offered in the book's introduction,
along with Fox's ability to provide gentle parody of familiar theological jargon,
fueled my already considerable anticipation of his book. A social historian, however gifted, could not, I recognized, catch the spirit of the man, much less his
ideas, unless some sensitivity to theological context and discourse existed.

I am pleased to report that for the most part I am willing to join the swelling
chorus of praise for *Reinhold Niebuhr: A Biography.* It *is* a mighty fine read, and
it goes a long way toward fulfilling the author's professed goal of providing the
first genuinely critical ("impartial, not negative") biography of Niebuhr. Many of
Niebuhr's close friends and former students, including several whose comments
have already appeared in *C&C*'s discussion of the book (*Christianity and Crisis*
46:1 [Feb. 3, 1986]), have testified that the Niebuhr one meets here is a trustworthy representation, one that catches nuance and subtlety in relation to this
very complex man and his even more complex life project.

To portray Niebuhr in a manner that invites enthusiasm from the many who
loved him, even when the portrait is not always flattering, surely confirms the
author's skill. Really fine biography always requires integrating the most sophisticated social/cultural historiography with the arts of narrative. That Fox has written a good biography of a controversial man, whose ideas are for some part of the
stock of conventional theological and political wisdom and for others nonsense,
is quite an accomplishment. If I also find some reasons for caution amid adula-
tion, it is not because I am unimpressed with what Fox achieves.

A RICH AND COMPLEX PORTRAIT

Of the book's many virtues, two, it seems to me, are especially important for any
ongoing evaluation of Niebuhr. Anyone versed in the vast literature on Niebuhr
will be relieved, gratified, and perhaps even surprised at the depth and complexity of the Niebuhr portrait Fox has provided. As the author himself notes, an
almost cultic reverence surrounds Niebuhr. Only an astonishing amount of historical digging could have produced so vivid, fresh, and candid a personal picture. Not only has Fox analyzed and sifted familiar data; he has also turned up
much evidence that others missed. Apparently he visited every place Niebuhr
lived in, and the structure of his narrative—a dozen chronological chapters that,
apart from the first and last chapters, focus upon relatively brief periods of
Niebuhr's busy life—enables him to probe deeply when evidence warrants it and

to move more cautiously when confident generalization is not possible. Where a reader's lack of orientation may require it, he paints a culturally rich picture.

For example, Lincoln, Illinois, at the turn of the century comes alive within U.S. social history, and the Niebuhr family's life is thereby illumined. Niebuhr's years as a pastor in Detroit, so frequently envisioned inaccurately, are subjected to genuine scrutiny. Fox culled local church records and carefully perused Detroit newspapers to enable this reconstruction. The result of his inquiry ought to end, once and for all, suggestions that Niebuhr's Detroit sojourn grew out of or expressed special sensitivity to that city's rising working class or that it greatly deepened his awareness of racial justice in this nation. Here and elsewhere, Fox documents clearly the dubiousness of Niebuhr lore often uncritically transmitted in the name of scholarship.

Fox also penetrates some of the barriers of Niebuhr family reticence, born of protectiveness on the one hand and Germanic cultural diffidence about self-expression on the other. He locates a significant number of letters that Reinhold Niebuhr wrote—to friends, obscure contacts, prominent people, and relatives. These letters enable him, from time to time, to cast dramatic new light on the life of a man who was reluctant to talk about his personal life. Fox also manages to demonstrate repeatedly that Niebuhr's memory was often faulty, and that some accounts he gave of his past were at best only partially accurate. I suspect that a major reason for much of the enthusiasm toward Fox's book is that there are a good many surprises and not a few new insights here, even for those who knew Niebuhr or his work very well.

None of this means that the personal portrait Fox draws is beyond dispute. I for one find remnants of Freudian reductionism in his account of the dynamics between Niebuhr, his parents, and his siblings. Niebuhr's mother appears here chiefly as one with neurotic attachments to her most prominent son; his brilliant sister, Hulda, is rendered more invisible than the evidence warrants; and brother H. Richard suffers a double wrong. Fox's portrayal of Richard overstates his suppressed rivalry with Reinhold and misses his characteristic generosity. In addition, Fox's interpretation of the brothers' intellectual disagreements only clarifies their early differences and is off target in several respects. Nevertheless, what emerges is a believable, affectionate picture of a much appreciated man who manifested some conspicuous limitations—of education, of style, of awareness.

It does need to be observed, however, that not all of Fox's overt valuations conform to this amiable personal portrait. Some of his judgments, in fact, suggest serious character flaws. Niebuhr, he insists, did not bear the scholarly mantle judiciously—whether in interpreting others' ideas or in formulating his own with precision. Though on other issues Fox's conclusions are often muted or hidden altogether, his devastating assessments of Niebuhr's grasp of the vocation of the intellectual in society and of his scholarly ethics stand out. Given this fact, there are points—particularly in the later sections of the book—where one wonders whether the appreciations Fox heaps on other aspects of Niebuhr's intellectual perspective aren't somewhat contrived.

READING FROM CONTEXT TO TEXT

The second contribution Fox's book makes to our understanding of Niebuhr is of even greater importance than the personal portrait he draws. Because Fox's research methods are predicated on Niebuhr's own intellectual style, his study reaches new heights in integrating Niebuhr's personal, political, and theological views. Unlike many academic interpreters, Fox understands clearly that Niebuhr was chiefly a preacher and occasional writer. Therefore, he interprets all of Niebuhr's writings through the concrete historical and sociopolitical situation out of which they were written. Often he reads Niebuhr's book-length manuscripts through his occasional writing, not the reverse.

Because Niebuhr was so prolific and because so much of the occasional writing is not readily accessible, even some quite reputable scholars have ignored his essays and editorials, and few, if any, have followed Fox's methodological lead. The result has been that many interpreters have loosed Niebuhr's already overly abstract prose from its so very concrete moorings, deepening the impression that Niebuhr's theological utterance does indeed aim at timeless, ahistorical status. Reversing the procedure, as Fox does—reading from context to text—frequently enables him to make a plausible case for a fresh revaluation of Niebuhr's ideas and books. For example, he observes what every scholar I know who follows Niebuhr's self-perceptions misses about *An Interpretation of Christian Ethics*. Following Niebuhr's own evaluation of the book, Niebuhrians relegate this work to the sidelines as the final word in Niebuhr's idealistic or liberal phase. By contrast, Fox shows how it *should* be read—as a book that prefigures Niebuhr's mature theology, stressing the radicality of sin and the nonrealizability of full human deliverance in history. Fox helps us appreciate why Niebuhr's work never overcomes the dualism of love and justice that is conditioned by his formulation, in this book, of love's marginality in history.

As the bibliographical appendix demonstrates, Fox's theological evaluation of Niebuhr relies very little on the vast secondary literature on Niebuhr's theology. This may account for its originality, but it also leads to a few lapses. For example, Fox's understanding of the intellectual influences on Niebuhr is not always accurate. He exaggerates the impact of William James and Paul Tillich. While he credits Niebuhr, in passing, with being a Kantian, he does not explain what this means. Nor does he pursue the incompatibility between certain Kantian and pragmatic elements in Niebuhr. Fox is aware of Niebuhr's penchant for having it both ways on controverted intellectual points, but he tends to credit the intellectual inconsistencies he notes to the primitive nature of Niebuhr's education rather than to the theoretical incompatibility of some of Niebuhr's, and much of mainstream theology's, intellectual roots.

Even so, Fox's methodological sophistication in reading Niebuhr's book-length studies through historical events, his shorter writings, and his political convictions also ensures that he does not interpret Niebuhr as if his theological utterance were set in stone or merely abstract. This in itself is a great gain over many academic readings. If Fox's intellectual account of Niebuhr is less than the final word, it is actually more reliable than some influential theologians' readings. Like Niebuhr, Fox is ambivalent about how theological truth fits into a political and ethical view of the world, so he is never tempted to treat Niebuhr's views as though he produced an adequate theological system or settled the question of the relationship of theology and public morality for us.

BEYOND THE MANLY GOD

Some nuances of Fox's evaluation of Niebuhr as theologian could have mischievous impact, however. For one example, while Fox draws his *political* valuations of Niebuhr from a full national ideological spectrum—placing Niebuhr's views in the context of the conservative, liberal, and radical options available in Niebuhr's lifetime—he evaluates Niebuhr's *theological* ideas differently. Like many theologians, he reads modern theology as if the only theological options were liberalism and neo-orthodoxy. On this point, Fox—himself "an unbelieving believer"—seems to veer toward uncritical conventional wisdom. He apparently assumes that the shallowness of theological liberalism rests in its hopefulness about humanity and its anthropologically based vision of God and that neo-orthodoxy escapes this latter "problem." (Most assuredly not!) He also implies that theology is profound only insofar as it successfully avoids being humanistic. Such notions will warm the hearts of Fox's neoconservative readers, but they should not persuade those concerned for a social justice-centered faith.

Fox is correct in saying that Niebuhr did not move beyond theological liberalism. What he does not grasp is that fundamentally neither did any other major theologian of Niebuhr's generation, including Karl Barth. Fox appears to understand Barth's theology and rightly defends him against some of Niebuhr's misinterpretations, though he prefers Niebuhr's greater respect for secular wisdom and his disdain for sanctimonious religiosity. (Barth, of course, opposed "religion," but his insistence on churchy theology encouraged Christian provincialism at just the time more respectful "worldliness" was needed.) Still, at some points in this book, what Fox rejects in Barth he then presents as the essence of his own "post-liberalism." Like Barth, Fox implies that a really profound theology would succeed in envisaging divine action as discrete from human action, as dramatically different and more powerful. He seems to define transcendence as over-againstness, nonrelationality, and nonvulnerability, and to understand theism as a logical contradiction to humanism. Insofar as he makes these theological assumptions, Fox joins all dominant malestream theology, including Barth and Niebuhr in different ways, in demanding that we escape "wimpy" theological liberalism by recovering the truly *manly* God. The claim that this goes "beyond" anthropomorphism is silly.

Happily for those of us who dissent from these assumptions, Fox's methodology also requires that Niebuhr's theology be closely juxtaposed with his political judgments, and it is in its account of the development and shifts in Niebuhr's political views that Fox's book should be taken as most definitive. While Fox does not identify every aspect of Niebuhr's public policy convictions, his clear account of Niebuhr's major positions is invaluable. At several points it provides an urgently needed corrective to the usual view of Niebuhr's politics.

Fox makes clear that the early Niebuhr was, in some respects, politically naive and inconsistent. He demonstrates that in spite of his analytic rhetoric, Niebuhr's political sensibilities and practice never moved further to the left than the idealist pacifist socialism of Norman Thomas. His narrative may also help younger readers appreciate the full controversy that accompanied Niebuhr's assault upon pacifism, because it enables us to grasp that Niebuhr's contemporaries heard his denunciation of pacifism *as a move toward the political right*. (It is one of the marks of Niebuhr's impact that today pacifism is often perceived as apolitical!)

Few today understand what Fox stresses: Throughout his career, Niebuhr was a political centrist; neither his views nor his activities were radical. His brief engagement with Socialist party politics was tepid, and while it agitated the board and some faculty of Union Theological Seminary, it hardly warranted Niebuhr's reputation as a consistent political radical in his earlier years.

While Fox makes all of this eminently clear, his evaluation of Niebuhr's centrism becomes muted in the later part of the book. There Fox attends only to centrist and more conservative political assessments of Niebuhr. Political radicalism disappears in his narrative just as it did in the consciousness of "respectable" U.S. academics in the years of Niebuhr's greatest prestige. As a result, Fox's evaluation of Niebuhr's politics may also finally be read as partaking of an insularity not unlike the one that afflicts his theological evaluation.

Had Fox bothered to read any of the interesting critical literature on Niebuhr from the pens of Third World, black, and feminist theologians, he might have gotten some hints on how Niebuhr and Niebuhrians should get "beyond" liberalism. He also might have spotted the deeply embedded individualism in the way Niebuhr conceives of selves and divine-human relations. Instead, Fox heralds *The Self and the Dramas of History*, with its doctrine of the transcendental ego, as among the most important of Niebuhr's mature works.

WHOSE EXPERIENCE? WHOSE NATURE?

Fox certainly presses at some of the cultural limits of liberalism in Niebuhr. He is rough on Niebuhr for his ignorance of black reality and of racism in the U.S., but not in global perspective. Early in the book, he is also rough on Niebuhr for his failure to be fair to the full spectrum of the U.S. political left. (As noted, this marvelous insight evaporates as the work unfolds.) However, in the appendix Fox criticizes Canadian Paul Merkeley for making Niebuhr too much of a cold warrior. Even the data Fox provides make one wonder why he is so hard on Merkeley, but the basic difference between Fox and Merkeley is that finally (and surprisingly)

Fox evaluates Niebuhr only in a U.S. and East-West context, while Merkeley speaks somewhat from outside of those U.S. nationalist presuppositions.

What a fully critical perspective on mid or late twentieth-century Christian liberal theological and political reconstruction—Niebuhr's, Barth's, or ours— requires is to locate its limits. But this is also to locate the limits of the worldview that Fox himself still so largely shares. Questions simply must be raised about the deep cultural provincialism and chauvinistic Eurocentrism of the dominant male theological and academic culture in which Niebuhr lived out his life. Failure to ask critical questions of this culture also flaws Fox's elegant work. U.S. theological, political, and academic liberalism continues to resist a genuine sense of limits, and is still uncritical about the preferred values of European and U.S. white male culture. There is no longer room for the sorts of generalizations about "the nature of man" Fox commends in Niebuhr, or for the expectation that everyone wants the sort of social relations "he" requires. A critical perspective must recognize liberalism's inability to deal with—or respect—difference or particularity.

Insofar as Fox is a splendid cultural historian—and he is—he gives us a profound sense of the particularities that made Reinhold Niebuhr the fascinating man that he was. Insofar as he refuses to take a deeper look at *whose* experience is reflected in the world that both celebrated and rejected Niebuhr, he too is tied to the narcissism of Western male ecclesiastical, academic, and political culture.

At the conclusion of his otherwise fascinating introduction, Fox offers a word of explanation about language. He says that Niebuhr was "untroubled" by the use of the generic *man,* though he recognized a possible slight to women in using it. In Niebuhr's day, slights to women were surely not a reason for men to be "troubled." It is true that Niebuhr "saw no alternative to the male generic, noun and pronoun." But nearly twenty-five years after Niebuhr's death it will not do simply to say, as Fox does, that he "shares his view." A small thing, you may say. Why pick a nit with so glorious a work?

Here we "marginals" must dissent strongly. The theologies and politics that will finally carry us "beyond liberalism" are those which force us to grasp that such "small" failures of empathy and imagination are serious, that we dare not make a virtue of them. On the contrary, we need precisely to note such small violations of others' well-being. They signal that *Reinhold Niebuhr* serves the interests of some more than others. Good as it is, the book is still constrained by the limits acceptable to a moderately progressive academic worldview.

You do indeed hear my voice among those who cheer Richard Fox's book. However, I am far from confident that it will press those of us who, with Niebuhr, care about justice, to move far enough or fast enough in the needed directions.

Chapter 11

On Harry Ward

Harrison has long maintained an interest in the work of Harry F. Ward (1873–1966), progressive social ethicist and Methodist activist minister who taught at Union Theological Seminary from 1918 to 1941. For many years at Union, Harrison offered a course on the work of both Reinhold Niebuhr and Harry Ward, which emphasized the greater adequacy of Ward's approach to economic justice by comparison to Niebuhr's. This review of Labor-Religion Prophet: The Times and Life of Harry F. Ward *by Eugene P. Link (Boulder, Colo.: Westview Press, 1984) was first published in the* Union Seminary Quarterly Review *39, no. 4 (1984): 316–22.*

Harry F. Ward was professor of Christian ethics at Union Theological Seminary in New York from 1918 until his retirement in 1941. Born in England in 1873, Ward began work as a Methodist lay preacher shortly after immigrating to the United States in 1890, and he died in 1966, at the age of ninety-three. His writing, research, and activism on behalf of social justice continued for over seventy years, almost until the end of his life. He published far more books than most theological teachers, including the groundbreaking *Social Creed of the Churches*, and few could match his output of Bible study materials and church-sponsored reports. Many students at Union in the 1920s and 1930s testify that he was the most dynamic intellectual presence on Union's faculty.

Although a strong case could be made that Ward was the most sophisticated economic thinker in the history of Christian traditions, historian Eugene P. Link's biography is the first book-length study of the man and his work. Prior to this book, a few articles and memoirs and several master's and doctoral theses focused upon Ward, but many theologically educated persons in mainstream Protestantism have never heard of him. Few of those who could identify him would presume that his intellectual work and life called for respectful attention. How can this be? In a word, because the reputation of Harry F. Ward remains under a cloud created by red-baiting.

Ward committed the gravest of the many unforgivable sins that American academics can commit. He was, and remained, an admirer of the Russian Revolution, and was hopeful about its long-term effects. (He also had more firsthand contact with and knowledge about that revolution than any of his attackers.) His refusal to denounce the Soviets, even after the Hitler-Stalin Pact, elicited scorn and contempt. Furthermore, Ward believed that American Communists had the same civil rights as other citizens. For reasons that will become clear, Ward was little interested in the internal life of political parties, but he recoiled at the prevailing "wisdom" that Communists should be treated as outsiders to our constitutional protections.

Ward was also a lifelong sceptic regarding the benevolence of capitalism. More than any other American Christian of his generation, he genuinely grasped Karl Marx's critique of capitalism, although it would be a half-truth to characterize his own social theory as Marxist. Nevertheless, he understood and learned from Marx's attempt to give a precise historical account of capitalist dynamics. At the point in the 1930s when others, such as Reinhold Niebuhr, believed U.S. capitalism would eventually produce more economic justice than its rivals, Ward never wavered in his belief that America was on a road that would render most of its citizens politically and economically marginal and destroy the moral soul of the people. He believed the historical directions of world capitalism threatened human survival on earth.

Before the First World War, one was permitted to hold such opinions in this country. Ward had the misfortune of living out most of his life after J. Edgar Hoover came to power and began his long, unbending, and largely successful effort—with widespread assistance from intellectuals—to discredit all radical criticism of our political economy as "anti-American." Ward held to his principles when others "recanted" their presumably "naive," anticapitalist sentiments.

Slowly but surely, suspicions about Ward took root, and, in the last decades of his life, journals that had published many of his articles refused anything from his pen. He was, Professor Link reminds us, in the racist imagery of the time, "black-listed." One cannot help but be curious about how Ward survived, much less thrived and persevered so energetically, for as long as he did.

To say that Ward was out of step with his times is, at best, an understatement. The nature and scope of his political activities may seem unbelievable to us; they were not of the sort in which "respectable" academicians usually engage. He helped found the American Civil Liberties Union and was its most uncompromising libertarian. He resigned from its board when it buckled to anticommunist hysteria and expelled Communist Elizabeth Gurley Flynn from its membership. While the ACLU publicly recanted this act in 1976, that repentance came far too late to provide comfort to Ward for his courageous protest. Ward also chaired and helped to organize numerous "front" organizations and committees on the left, including the League against War and Fascism. For Ward, to be a Christian was to be a member of a social movement, for that is what the church was for Ward. As Professor Link's title implies, Ward prided himself that the only official memberships he ever possessed were to the Christian Church and to the Labor Movement.

Placing Ward theologically is every bit as complex as placing him politically. Until the Red Scare of the 1920s, Ward's priority was to put his energy toward mobilizing the churches, and in particular, Methodism, to embodied expressions of love and justice. In this work, he was associated with most of the major figures of the progressive movement and of the Social Gospel. Yet Link stresses correctly that Ward should not be classified as a Social Gospel Christian. The reason he dissociates Ward from Social Gospel liberalism is that Ward did not believe that Christianity was a "spiritual" message to be "applied" to secular reality. It may seem to many that distinguishing Ward's views from those of Rauschenbusch and other Social Gospel liberals is mere hair splitting, yet I would press the distinction between Ward and the Social Gospel even further than Link.

To be sure, there are typical liberal theological emphases—respect for science, and even, especially in his early work, a tone of evolutionist "automatic" progress. In many respects, Ward's views also illustrated the tensions and complexities of the transition from liberal to radical sensibility. As Link stresses, he was antimilitarist and greatly admired the pacifist Gandhi, yet he was also postliberal in refusing to embrace nonviolence as the normative Christian perspective. Furthermore, he believed that class conflict was inevitable so long as economic democracy did not exist. In spite of these views, however, Ward's theology was, in a very real sense, a *premodern* theology in a way that neither neo-orthodoxy nor religious liberalism is premodern. Link's point is that there is no idealist/materialist dualism here. Ward believed neither in the idealist "spiritual" dualism that grounds liberal thought and theology, nor in the privileged position of normative dogma that neo-orthodoxy used to reformulate this liberal dualism.

It would take a book-length study simply to examine the complexities of Ward's thought in relation to the neo-orthodox accusations of superficiality aimed against his sort of social Christianity. I like to remind students that Ward is surely the best exemplification of Karl Barth's adage that Christian theology is best done with the Bible in one hand and the daily newspaper in the other. If ideological fashions were other than they are, we could praise Ward for embodying Bonhoeffer's call for the Christian to be a worldly "man come of age," because he moved with such complete aplomb between ecclesiastical and secular cultures. This exemplary Methodist was devoid of the pious posturing and cant that so many secular people, then as now, equate with practicing Christianity. Even so, Ward's theological outlook remains so completely out of fashion that it is difficult today even to reconstruct the sensibilities that give it plausibility.

I belabor all of this to underscore the immensity of the task facing one who sets out to interpret Ward. To do so, one must also restore the credibility of Harry F. Ward's life and person, for his way of being in the world and his deepest convictions are almost as despised among so-called educated and enlightened people today as they were during his lifetime. In the world that Reagan rules, it cannot be said too strongly that a sympathetic revisioning of Ward's life and work depends far more upon a willingness to question sacrosanct ideological platitudes than it does upon gaining knowledge about Ward's life and worldview. I suspect that anyone who is seeking a deepened appreciation of Ward, and who comes to this book with an expanding list of questions about his intellectual roots and the ethical resolve that marked his life, will find this "first" volume disappointing. Although I find some serious flaws in it, it also has some virtues that need to be enumerated. I will begin with some of these.

Professor Link has carefully examined the extensive writings and personal papers of his former teacher, interviewed Ward's family and numerous living friends, and identified available sources about Ward's life. This in itself is no small contribution to restoring Ward's voice to the world. Link shaped the biography by interweaving chapters that follow a linear sequence. Some of these focus upon specific periods in Ward's life, while others, inserted within that temporal frame, focus upon either his academic career or his social and political struggles. Link's way of organizing his extensive materials is effective, although the chapters are uneven in quality. Their style and clarity vary enormously, and several should have been heavily edited. The book is greatly enriched, however, by the inclusion of the powerful political sketches of Lynd Ward done during his father's lifetime, and by the use of a number of well-selected photographs.

The Harry F. Ward we meet here is a feisty, spirited, unpretentious man of uncommon energy, decency, and kindness—one whose life is marked by modesty and reticence. Link's portrayal is of a public man, an organizer, whose personal life is given little attention. There are glimpses of the loving Ward family, of the strong relationship between Ward and his wife, Daisy, of long summer retreats in the Ontario lake country, of quiet hours spent tending his New Jersey rose garden. But Ward the person stands hidden behind Ward the public man. Furthermore, the emphasis is upon the projects Ward engaged in, not upon his daily round of teaching, writing, or research (though testimonies to Ward's impact as teacher are included).

While this portrait of Ward as activist may well convey his contemporaries' sense of him, it omits a great deal. The activist picture of Ward lays only partial groundwork for a renewed appreciation of him. What is most neglected is Ward's substantial intellectual labor. A number of Ward's books are mentioned only briefly, and one short chapter describes the argument of Ward's work on Marx and Jesus that no one would publish, during his lifetime or since. A few other important unpublished (and unedited) excerpts are also included in an appendix. Nevertheless, it is possible to read *Labor-Religion Prophet* without learning anything concrete about Ward's economic analysis or his conception of the work of a teacher of the Christian moral life. It has been my experience in teaching Ward that people are most likely to give him a second hearing after they listen to his analysis of the economic conditions of life in urban America, whether in 1913, 1935, or 1950. In fact, if one does not identify the source of the quotation, listeners are likely to assume that the description is a contemporary one.

Given the blistering (and, I believe, profound) critique that liberation theologians have mounted against mainstream theology and ethics, the time may be ripe for a new evaluation of Ward's ethical, if not his theological, method. It is, in fact, the liberation theologians of Latin America who most resemble Ward and share his literal, premodern theological vision. It is perhaps not so serious that Link does not focus on these points, but it is unfortunate that he actually dismisses Latin American liberation theology summarily, much as Ward's work was dismissed. Like that of liberation theologians, Ward's activism was intrinsic to his intellectual labor. I believe a case can be made that Ward's direct, concrete, and prolific research and writing are related to a praxis epistemology basic to liberation theology. Until all of this is made clear, portraying Ward as "activist" simply plays into the hands of those who wish to dismiss him as a polemicist in order to obscure their own ideological entanglements.

My criticism of Link's failure to integrate Ward's intellectual contributions adequately may seem a transparent professorial ploy. Link could respond (and fairly) that the task I envision should be the responsibility of persons like myself who specialize in Christian ethics. That criticism aside, then, the most serious problem with *Labor-Religion Prophet* is that although the title of the book promises a treatment of Ward's life in the context of his times, it does not deliver on that promise. The events that characterized Ward's journey are rehearsed, but the ideological depths of the social conflict in which Ward's life was enmeshed are not depicted in a way that brings his struggle fully alive. Readers not already informed about Ward could, I believe, read this work without gaining a sharp sense of the unrelenting controversy and vilification that surrounded his last forty, or even fifty, years. Even by the midpoint of the volume, when several of the major organizational battle lines had been drawn, the jarring controversy breaking around Ward is not described. Moreover, only when one reaches the final three chapters is its scope hinted at.

The narrative thread, while traced in some detail, never quite whets our appetite for the sort of question we must ask if we are ever to have a renewed appreciation of Ward. Link states clearly that Ward was ill-treated by errant individuals and organizations: Ralph Roy, Roger Baldwin, Norman Thomas, the ACLU, and Beacon Press, to mention a few. But the glacial movements of anticommunist hysteria and the complex intricacies of institutional and theological fashion that supported these ill-considered acts are not described. What intellectually grounded the attacks on Ward and rendered him pathetic in the eyes of Protestant Christians is not specified.

The Harry F. Ward we meet here is commendable, not controversial. He would seem both more astonishing and more admirable were the ideology of his times the backdrop of his life. This question should nag: What made this man tick, what was it that enabled him never to miss a beat in his ongoing work in spite of the innuendo and contempt heaped upon him and in the face of *betrayal* (the term is not too strong) by friends and organizations that he loved? Ward will never get a serious hearing unless we allow ourselves to be astonished at a life so irrepressible in times like those (and these). Ward was a man whose wit and exuberance for life seemed undaunted even in an eclipse of public respect and support.

I dearly wish that Link's pioneering attempt to open a path for Ward scholarship more readily invited our wonder about how Harry F. Ward survived with so much vigor, grace, and dignity. Yet I recognize as well that Eugene Link is plowing unfurrowed ground here, and that scholarship is always hard when none have preceded you. In the case of Ward, it is even more difficult because the ideological conditions that rendered him despicable still prevail so strongly. Professor Link's work, for all its constraints, is an important beginning, one that challenges us not to forget the little professor who pioneered the work of Christian ethics in this place.

It is certainly a time for nonfascist Christians to pay new heed to Ward. He was a man who believed that transcendent hope is to be found *in the struggle for justice*, not beyond it. Link includes an unpublished excerpt from Ward entitled "Winning but Never Won" that puts this point precisely:

> So those of us who are working to get life changed intelligently and in the direction of ideals, instead of blindly and brutally, are left only with the future. And with no knowledge at the last, but only faith. And is that not enough?

Ward quotes Cyrano, "But I have never fought with hope to win," and adds that even God struggles without sure knowledge of victory: "If that is good enough for God, it ought to be good enough for us."

Chapter 12

On James Luther Adams

James Luther Adams (1901–1994) was a Unitarian social ethicist and minister who taught at the University of Chicago, Harvard University, and Andover-Newton Seminary. Harrison uses this review of Adams's books The Prophethood of All Believers *(ed. George K. Beach [Boston: Beacon Press, 1986]) and* Voluntary Associations *(ed J. Ron Engel [Chicago: Exploration Press, 1986]), as an opportunity to insist upon the centrality of the analysis of political economy and ideology in the doing of Christian ethics. Adams was a gifted historian of Christian ethics who was himself a committed socialist, but his U.S. heirs generally have ignored or obscured this emphasis, identifying him only with the study of civil society and voluntary associations rather than critical assessment of political and economic institutions. The review shows the difference between the reasons Harrison admires Adams and the reasons he is more conventionally appreciated. A much abbreviated version of this review was published in* The World *(January/ February 1988), a magazine of the Unitarian Universalist Association.*

News on the publishing front is good for serious religious liberals and others attentive to intellectually stimulating religious thought. The year past has seen the publication of not one but two well-selected collections of essays by James Luther Adams, arguably the most learned and artful defender of the vocation of liberal

theology writing in the twentieth century. Adams also is incontestably a prominent member of that too small circle of really first-rate social thinkers spawned by
the Euro-North American theological community in the twentieth century.

A productive scholar throughout his long career, octogenarian Adams has
devoted much energy to editing, translating, and interpreting the work of other
major theological spokesmen—notably among them Paul Tillich, Ernst Troeltsch,
and Karl Holl. He has been afflicted with excessive modesty regarding the importance of his own constructive work, and a scholarly perfectionism that assures
that all he writes will be worth reading. The result, though, has been a slower pace
of publication than his admirers, myself included, wish for. And it has taken a
fair bit of digging in theological libraries to get hold of substantial portions of his
corpus, which has been published in a myriad of places. Two collections of these
rich sources have reached book form previously.

Only three important essays in the Beach volume and one in the Engel collection were published in the earlier volumes. Happily, there is no duplication
between these new collections. *The Prophethood of All Believers* includes several
essays, sermons, and statements not previously published at all, including many
quite recent ones, each splendidly edited, that are vintage Adams, venerable in wit
and cultural sagacity. Beach's introduction to Adams's intellectual significance and
professional impact is informative and focuses his theological contributions
extremely well. His organization of and introductions to the major subsections,
though brief, are also, to my mind, absolutely on target. For example, he selects
key essays in the theological materials to illustrate Adams's conception of and
address to liberalism's most troublesome theological issues—the reality of evil, the
mediation of judgment and grace, and the religious necessity of community. In so
doing, he provides an extremely reliable orientation to Adams's constructive work,
one that will be invaluable in introducing Adams's theory systematically. His volume rightly highlights the essentially justice-oriented and communitarian nature
of Adams's theology and ethics.

All of the entries in Engel's collection have been published previously, and the
book is a photo-offset compilation of the originals, making for some variation in
readability. This format also precluded changes to emend the male gender exclu-
siveness of the language of these early essays, which both Adams and Engel regret.
Like Beach, Engel included some inaccessible gems from Adams's writings that
are essential to appreciating the breadth and subtlety of his work, including several from the 1970s which have not received the attention they deserve. For example, his "Use of Symbols" is of perduring importance to those concerned for
method in religious ethics. The concluding piece on "God and Economics,"
authored in 1978, reminds us that Adams, unlike so many contemporary religious ethicists, does not neglect economic reality nor ignore the constraints of
capitalist economic structure on genuine political democracy.

Both volumes contain important testimonies to Adams's consistently candid
approach toward the evils of this society, especially its racism, resistance to dissent, and lack of genuine democracy. Both attest his aversion to monopolies of

power. Both also demonstrate that Adams has always been a walking refutation of the neo-orthodox thesis that theological liberalism is fated to be intrinsically and uncritically identified with modern society. We must hope that the near simultaneous publication of the two works will detract from neither. There is no such thing as too much Adams, and at a time when many theologians and ethicists are wrapping themselves in the label "neoliberal" and formulating some rather eccentric modern versions of doctrines expounded by the right wing of early liberal political economy, we need Adams more than ever. His is a voice of genuinely critical social liberalism undeformed by subtle identification with privilege and of a theological liberalism unthreatened by the historical and contingent character of all religio-cultural forms.

If there is a quibble that needs registering here it is about Engel's decision to publish his selection under the title *Voluntary Associations*. Admittedly, he has academic precedent on his side. Most discussions of Adams's work take it as axiomatic that his distinctive contribution is as a theorist of voluntary associations. Certainly he has taught religious ethicists to view the cultural impact of the churches and their relation to public policy from this paradigm. However, my own view is that the academic consensus that makes this theme the central one in his work is misguided, and has tended to lead to Adams's marginalization in the theological enterprise by portraying him chiefly as a sociological thinker and sociologist of religion. The reason I like the volume Beach has edited so much is that it challenges this sort of interpretation. To be sure, voluntarism in Adams's thought is basic, but chiefly as a normative theological and moral principle rather than as a sociological thesis. Beach is wise to group the fourth and last section of the essays under the always yoked (to Adams) themes of "Vocation and Voluntary Association" only after dealing with theology and culture. In the present ideological climate, what needs to be said is that Adams values voluntary associations *insofar* as they are *authentically* mediating structures that both constrain and distribute power in society. The long theoretical essay contained in Engel's collection, "Mediating Structures and the Separation of Powers," though published by the capitalist think tank the American Enterprise Institute, should be read as an irenic—to my taste, too irenic—argument with theorists such as Michael Novak, Peter Berger, and Richard Neuhaus, who have abstracted voluntarism from the rich historical moorings and power analysis in which Adams places it. Adams repeatedly insists that participation is the necessary condition for genuine voluntarism, and notes here the obloquy that falls upon those who support the cause of blacks, or women, or gays, or the poor. Such movements are, to the neoliberal theorists cited, concrete exemplifications of the antichrist, while "voluntary associations" are a euphemism for all that is good about capitalist societies and all that is evil, by their absence, about socialist ones. Nothing should be allowed to obscure the fact that Adams's passion for voluntary associations is rooted in his theological conviction regarding the movement of the Spirit toward openness to change and greater democracy and in his moral preference for justice and noncoercive community. In this respect, he is worlds apart from the "neoliberals."

Adams is also atypically a theological ethicist whom one reads for the pleasure of encountering literary richness and depth. And the new collections make clearer than did the earlier ones why this is so. The inclusion of more informal writings gives us a deeper glimpse of the graciousness of the man whose learning may otherwise intimidate. Here it is the unapologetic, even joyful, voice of critical theological and ethical liberalism at its very best that we encounter. Though never formally his student, I have long considered Jim Adams to be my teacher. As an equally unapologetic liberation theologian, I rely on Adams's work to measure the legacy of liberalism that must be cherished and sustained even as liberation theology challenges and reconstructs liberal tradition. This is not to say that there are no critical questions to be posed.

Rereading revered essays and discovering new ones made me aware of the limits of aspects of the liberal theory of religion Adams at times employs. Religion here is frequently more about "the search for meaning" than about the bonds of relationship and loyalty we acknowledge or the character of healing power to which we relate. And for all his historical sensitivity, Adams's thought still occasionally betrays the tendency of German idealism to bifurcate "nature" and "history" and to place sex and family within the order of nature. The essay in Beach's volume entitled "Thou Shalt Not Commit Adultery" attests to his devotion to marriage, but its claim that "marriage is rooted in the Covenant of being itself" is a rare example of ahistorical theological cant and does not answer to the urgent need we have for fresh critical reflection in sexual ethics. One can find here no hint of why feminism and gay liberation movements insist that sexuality and gender are as thoroughly historical as every other dimension of human culture and why "compulsory heterosexuality" is an institutional and ideological construction of dominant male-hierarchical history, culture, and imagination. Nor does Adams's work (or any other liberal theology impacted by German idealism, American pragmatism, or process thought) seriously address the structural realities of class, now rending every society and forging implacable barriers between and within nations.

It is because James Luther Adams is the best of the liberals that these questions must be pressed. He has always demonstrated that to acknowledge the limits of a perspective does not mean lack of appreciation for it. I rejoice that these new compilations of his work have enhanced, if that is possible, my appreciation and respect for his work. Their publication should, rightly, widen the circle of his admirers.

Chapter 13

Restoring the Tapestry of Life:
The Vocation of
Feminist Theology

Harrison delivered the Nelle Morton Lecture at Drew Divinity School on March 8, 1984, during Women's History Week. It was later published in the Drew Gateway *54, no. 1 (1983): 39–48. Nelle Morton (1905–1987), longtime faculty member at Drew, was a personal friend of Harrison's and until the 1980s the only woman teaching full-time in a theological school in the Northeast. She was also a pioneer Christian feminist and social activist, widely know for her collection of essays,* The Journey Is Home. *In this essay, Harrison explores the twin tasks of feminist liberation theology–to deconstruct dominant dualistic theologies (particularly by reconstructing transcendence as radical immanence) and to construct new ways of knowing that are mediated by imagery and sensual relation.*

I wrote the first draft of this lecture before I had learned that on this occasion an honorary doctorate would be bestowed upon the remarkable woman for whom this lectureship was named. (It is doubtful whether I am going to make it through this lecture without tears; in fact, I hope I do not! It would not be fitting for a *feminist* theologian to make it through such a moving and important event tearless!) What I want to note at the outset is how adequate my original lecture plan looked after I reassessed it knowing that Nelle Morton would be right here for it, and that this would be, even more than in other years, a distinctive celebration of her. The reason for its adequacy was, I assure you, not Beverly Harrison's prescience, but rather the remarkably formative and central impact that Nelle Morton has had upon the development of feminist theology.

This lecture occurs not only during Women's History Week, but on International Women's Day itself. Need I say that the demands upon the time of feminist scholars during Women's History Week and on International Women's Day are considerable? Nevertheless, I considered the invitation to do the Nelle Morton Lecture a "command performance," an inestimable privilege, and the best business to be about on this day; and I can testify that the three other women scholars to precede me in giving this lecture share my feelings. Feminist scholars in theology do not decline when an invitation to do the Nelle Morton Lecture comes!

The committee that invited me suggested that what would be welcomed on this occasion was a lecture introducing the role of feminist theology and reviewing its assumptions. We feminists are realists enough to know that within theological education specifically, and academia in general, it is well to use our few genuinely public occasions to reiterate the simplest lessons we have to teach! So I agreed to offer such an overview and turned my mind to a title. Knowing that it was the Nelle Morton Lecture, I said to myself, "Oh, we must have an image!" (Why this was my response will become clear in due course.) Feminist theology begins with the image, and the image that suggested itself to me was tapestry. No doubt tapestry came to mind because it conveys an image of handwork and of the domestic arts, much celebrated among feminist theologians. A tapestry is woven–by hand. It is work, a careful, minute work of artful human hands. So without thinking too deeply, I suggested the title "Restoring the Tapestry of Life: The Vocation of Feminist Theology."[1]

After learning about the gloriously celebrative nature of this occasion, I reviewed my manuscript out of fear that I had not done full justice to this beloved woman we honor so emphatically on this occasion. Only then did it occur to me that "restoration" is much too static an image for the likes of Nelle Morton! It is neither a Mortonesque image nor a notion characteristic of her way of relating to the world. Nelle is the theologian who many years ago defined the task of theology–and especially of that wholistic theology to emerge when women's experience is taken seriously–to be "creating the path by journeying."[2] To "create the path by journeying" and to respect the sort of imagery appropriate to Nelle, I should have adopted the image represented in the hymn we sang this morning. It contained images characteristic of one of Nelle's favorite theologians, Mary Daly: "Spinning . . . spinning . . . the Creation." "Spinning the Creation: The Vocation of Feminist Theology" is a title that would have better captured the spirit of Nelle Morton. With this forewarning, let us consider how feminist theology functions, not so much to restore, but rather to spin "the tapestry of life."

THE SOURCES AND CRITIQUE OF
FEMINIST THEOLOGY

What I want to do here, in rather general and perhaps overly superficial terms, is to identify what I take to be several of the most important, constructive base-points or criteria for a theology that deserves to be designated "feminist." I want to stress the *constructive* task of feminist theology because aspects of its *critical* task are more familiar, and are occasionally discussed and debated in seminaries today. The way in which we feminists view the constructive task and positive contribution of feminist theology is, for the most part, neglected, however. Even so, I cannot get to the constructive task without saying a word about the deconstruction so far developed against the dominant theologies of Christianity.

The critical task of feminist theology has been developing now for nearly two decades. It is an enterprise with a vast literature, and those who do this critical work are identified as the "professional" feminist theologians. But feminist theology cannot be equated with a few academics. It arose in its modern incarnation—that is, its late twentieth-century incarnation—with the second women's movement. This second wave of feminism can be viewed as the media view it and invite us to view it. It is portrayed by dominant forces as "untypical," the fruit of a few discontented women. Dominant groups need and want to discredit the women's movement, want us to view it as the rising of a small minority of women within this culture. In point of fact, however, the locus of feminist theology is a broad-based and global *rising of women*.

Not surprisingly, Nelle Morton was the first feminist theologian to address an international conference under the rubric of feminist theology. I remember the occasion well. It was over a decade ago. I recall vividly how I felt when one of my students, in tears, described the attacks that had been launched on Nelle Morton at this first Christian international women's conference when she lectured on the subject of feminist theology. The student, who had been present and who described the event, was distraught as she recounted how women from Europe and from the Third World stood up and angrily challenged the validity of what Nelle had said about theology from a feminist perspective. The student reported that Nelle Morton had been "ill treated" and "brutalized." I phoned Nelle to commiserate. Her response stunned me. She laughed and said, "It was wonderful! Wonderful! Oh, they were angry. But now I am getting letters from all over the world, some from the very women who attacked me. They have taken my manuscript home and have studied it and reflected on it, and they are *beginning to see*." And so it is that the multifaceted character and future of feminist theology is rooted in this rising of women, a rising that is "catching" because it represents a movement between women grounded for the first time in our taking each other and ourselves seriously. This is why feminist theology has emerged.

In our critique, which has been the first level of our work, our deconstruction, we have challenged the monopoly of male-gender symbolism in the established religious traditions. We have zeroed in on the monopoly of male symbols in theological language, a monopoly in the dominant traditions that dictates that only what is male can be associated with holiness or sacred power. We have had to make a continuous effort, pointing out again and again and again, that however divergent are the concepts of theology among the various streams of Christian tradition, or other religious traditions, women essentially are invisible in all of them. Our experience is devalued; that which is associated with the feminine or with the female is seen to be weak and trivial, certainly as lacking genuine sacral significance and power. This critical task, one that admittedly has made so many uncomfortable, has also received what I believe to be a well-orchestrated and carefully timed backlash, a massive and none too subtle effort to discount the validity of our deconstruction. Nevertheless, this critique of male supremacy is morally critical work. It must be done for the spiritual health of Christianity and religion. Both degenerate into social pathology without self-critical capacity. No one should doubt that such work will be ongoing; it already has reached astonishing proportions. It is reported that 50 percent of the scholarly works in religion sold in America today are the fruit of feminist scholarship. There is not a reputable scholarly journal in theology or religion that has not finally been forced to follow other disciplines and focus upon the work of feminist scholarship. And all of this has been accomplished in less than twenty years.

THE CONSTRUCTIVE TASK OF FEMINIST THEOLOGY

Beneath and with this critical work, there also has been bubbling up, slowly emerging, gradually breaking open, a reconstructive, alternative understanding of the positive work of Christian theology. What I want to do in the time remaining is to identify some of the presumptions of this constructive task. It is not easy to do this in brief compass, because feminist theology represents such a deep "epistemological rupture" (to borrow a phrase from another liberation theology) with dominant ways of understanding what theological discourse is about. No one has had greater awareness of the depth of the epistemological rupture that feminist theology requires than the woman we honor today, Nelle Morton. When I reviewed my outline for this lecture in light of this celebration, I pulled from my files those many well-worn folders containing her articles, published here and there, in this or that minor journal, long since out of print. (We feminists often do that to each other—modestly publishing, if we publish at all, in sources that make it hard to locate our things.) Going through these articles, I found over and over many of the phrases and exactly the same points that I had decided to discuss in this lecture. Over a decade ago, Nelle Morton described the epistemological rupture of feminist theology by insisting that spirituality—the work of spirit—is to be discovered in *that which is breaking up from below.* "Breaking up from down under" was her phrase.[3] Nelle has argued—rightly, I believe—that the needed epistemological rupture will not be accomplished if we merely "balance" Western religious tradition in terms of gender imagery. The deepest challenge of feminist theology rests in recognizing that our entire conceptual heritage must be reoriented, so that we come to feminist theology as "a new way of seeing." Long ago, Nelle Morton reminded us of what all feminist theologians, most of us learning from her, have come to treat as axiomatic: that the Western Christian tradition, and in fact our whole Western sense of reality, is blinded fundamentally by ruptures or dualisms that have made it impossible for us to recover a wholistic and healing relationship to all that is.[4]

The basic dualism of the Western theological tradition is one in which the subject/object split is primary. In Western patriarchal religion, God has been understood as the One who is truly objectified, is truly Object. God is as distant from and as unlike those of us who are subjects as possible. Objective otherness and discontinuity with the lives of historical subjects have been the dominant features of our theism, of how we represent holy power and sacredness to ourselves in Western Christian tradition. Objectivity—the Objectivity of God—here means that which has no vulnerability to subjective relation.

For me—this is Beverly Harrison speaking now, not Nelle Morton—Karl Barth is the theological symbol par excellence of this sharp object/subject split in theology. He is celebrated, on the one hand, as the theologian who proclaimed God as wholly Other, but he is equally renowned, in the second half of his career, for insisting on concrete incarnation and the fundamental character of relation in theology. Wholly Other *and* utterly relational. Oh, the seeming deep *awareness* that that which is wholly other is that to which *one cannot be related!* To feminists this divided consciousness in dominant theologians is astonishing. The notion that there is no Holy Power, no real godliness, except by standing "beyond" relationship shapes the dominant theological imagination about "God" *and* "Man."

We feminists have challenged this subject/object split with a vengeance. We have said that that which is Holy Power could not be, cannot be, and is not, related to us under the image of that which is Object. What is totally objective to us, Object to our subject, without vulnerability to and immersion in our subjectivity, is unknowable, and, above all, unlovable.

Our primary form of feminist protest against the subject/object split has often gone unnoticed, however. It is exemplified in our challenge to the notion that the basic category of theological envisagement is the concept. Concepts function to explain reality. Theological language evokes reality. No one among feminist theologians has been as insistent on this point as Nelle Morton. She has contended for many years, largely to deaf ears, that *the primal and irreplaceable mode of theological discourse is the image,* and relatedly, *the metaphor.* The fundamental language of theology is the metaphorical image. Nelle has insisted that our spirituality is rooted most basically in energy, in the flow, spontaneity, and creativity of the aesthetic experience itself. "Not creation," she once said, "not even new creation . . . but creativity, ongoing creativity."[5] The statically rationalized Western religious tradition envisages the Holy One chiefly as Logos, as Word, a metaphorical image born of listening and reading written texts. The "Word" holds an image monopoly that conditions an overwhelming bias in terms of how we learn to experience the Holy. To walk with the Holy One, to be related in faith and practice to the power of God, means chiefly to *take in*, to express the receptivity of hearing, or to "understand," to *comprehend a fixed message*. Static and passive images predominate.

All feminist theologians have been quick to recognize the importance of image and metaphor to theology, but not all have perceived how dramatically the enterprise of systematic theology must be affected by this shift. Here too, Nelle Morton has been the one to remind us that feminist theologians dare not move too quickly to correlate our insights about image and metaphor with established theology. To assume, as some have, that the metaphorical image basic to our perception and experience of God can be reduced to traditional theological concepts is dangerous. Nelle has objected, albeit gently, when feminist theologians correlate metaphor and analogy in a way that legitimates a move in feminist theology back to male-stream discussions of "foundational" theology. To do so is to return to an epistemology predicated on the subject/object split. Metaphors are not analogies. Images and metaphors relate and express relationship; they move, they enable us to "see," but they cannot be pinned down to "essence." Max Black is one of the few linguistic philosophers who seems to me (and to Nelle) to have aptly noted this characteristic of metaphors. Metaphors are precisionally suggestive, but they cannot be contained by connotation or definition.

It is a basic presumption of feminist theology, then, that we will not recover the immediacy of our experience of the Holy, nor perceive the awesomeness of our relationship to all things, until we pay attention to, look and see, those fundamental images that put us in touch with life through vision. The point here is not that the images of hearing and listening need to be abandoned. But we must come to recognize the impoverishment of our theology that has resulted from aural-imagery primacy combined with fixed-text mediation. The result has been our incapacity to "locate" God in what is alive, moving, growing, and changing, or in chaos (which is filled with potential) rather than in stasis and order.

The epistemological rupture of feminist theology stakes out a new path to constructive theological work at a second point as well. Not only do we target and challenge the ultimacy of the object/subject split, but we also insist that our mode of knowing God/dess/Godding—our mode of knowing that which is Holy—is the same as our mode of knowing all things. And that mode is sensuality! Feminist theologians are challenging the Western theological tradition at its core by insisting that spirituality, and with it, all knowledge, emerges from and is expressed as a form of *radical embodiment*. Spirituality is the capacity to live deeply into the concrete, creative order of things as cocreative participants. The dualisms of dominant theology set material and spiritual reality in contradistinction, and equate the spiritual with mind or intellect and the material with "mere" body. Not only does such imagery reiterate the ancient disvaluation of women so often rehearsed among feminists—the real, physical world as fallen, evil, "feminine," "mere" nature—but it also reveals how dissociated and disembodied is our sense of what is Sacred and Holy and what can mediate Healing Power. And so we feminists, led here as elsewhere by Nelle Morton, have said that our spirituality is a *spirituality of the body*, of our bodies, ourselves. Vision and energy and sensuous engagement are invoked as the ground of our knowledge, in recognition that to restore the role of authentic hearing—if we are to be hearers of the Godly Word—there must be someone there to hear. To put the point bluntly, ours is a theology and epistemology of *passion*.[6] For us, it is by living deeply into our world, which includes living deeply into our own subjectivity, selfhood, feeling, and passion, that we come to be human—which is to say, truly spiritual beings, those who meet God's love in our own, in and with each other, and whose lives bear up God in the world.

For those who challenge us, claiming that our vision lacks a tragic sense of life, that it idealizes mutuality and shared power, our reply must be clear. Evil is a real and active force in our world, and we are indeed caught up in a web of life in ways that often make us agents of that evil. All that ruptures, all that distorts and cuts and tears the tapestry—the interconnecting threads of life—is evil. For feminists, the core dynamic of evil is located in the uses and abuses of the power we share with God. Power that is not reciprocal is *always* violent power, abusive power. It destroys our capacity for, and cuts us off from, embodied, sensuous relationships with one another. Power that does that—alienated power—is evil. No one knows better than feminists that our capacity for sensuously imaging life as blessed and beautiful ceases when we treat each other's bodies as objects, as things. Whether through the institution of chattel slavery, or institutional racism, or through the pornography and domestic violence so widespread in this culture; whether through the torture that has come to characterize the treatment of political prisoners in almost every state that we, the United States, support in this world, evil is the sensuous assault upon our concrete body-selves, the violation of the body-space and body-self of another. It is the violation of others' spontaneity, their capacity to be present and to express power *over against us*. In feminist theology we do evil when we deny another's presence and another's power to affect us, and when we cut off possible mutual relation between us.

Ours is a society and a world in which control of some human beings by others is taken for granted, presumed to be the way things are or should be. It is a world in which human control of the environment, of the natural world, is taken for granted. It follows that it is a world in which repression of true feelings and manipulation of sentiment (body-response) characterize much of our public life. The pain we feel in the violation we experience must be contained and manipulated. In the face of growing repression, we feminists insist that there is a reason, a very clear reason, why our communities and lives are so disordered, so ruptured, so torn apart. *We do not respect relation or reverence it as Holy.* Our problem is theological. It is rooted deeply in the way in which we envisage and experience what is sacred. Mary Daly has characterized ours as a culture of necrophilia—a death-loving, death-sick, culture.[7] There is a clear feminist consensus that violence and violation are as American as apple pie, that S & M—sadism and masochism—are becoming our most fundamental ways of relating to each other.

Because this is what we see, we do *not* intend to cease our complaint against dominant theologies. We are serious in our conviction that the dominant spiritualities within Christianity or Judaism, Islam, or Hinduism are themselves a fundamental part of our spiritual malaise. We are indeed straw men, empty men. This is true to a large extent of all of us in the dominant culture or of these identified with it, because we have presumed that we are most holy when most empty of concern for one another or most unengaged by our passion for relation. Since in reality God comes as Holy Power only when we are most present to ourselves and simultaneously (always both) most present to and related to each other, we are now *functionally* atheists, whatever "faith" we profess. By contrast, God/ess is the power of Presence-in-relation. The power of God/ess comes through my/our presence and capacity to mediate Holy Power. The presence and power between us when we are reciprocally related to each other in mutual dependence, *and* in the capacity to affect one another, is the distinctly human experience of God.

So when we feminist theologians finally resort to concepts (and all of us do eventually, even though such concepts are not the *primary* language of theology), we say that God/ess or Godding is the *Power of Relation*—not "being itself." God is one who comes *through us and between us,* one we must recognize and acknowledge as beyond our manipulation and control, but who also does not aspire to control us or to require our obeisance. This sort of revisionism of divine-human relations is fundamental to the shape that feminist theology is taking, a form that lays claim to being a serious, unapologetically reconstructive theological envisagement.

What does the mainstream of the theological establishment make of these admittedly controversial, and in the view of some, outrageous claims about our relation to God/ess, our experience of Holy Power, about the nature of human spirituality and of faith? As I have already suggested, for the most part, the theological establishment has pretended not to notice the full logical import of what we are saying. Our critical claim that patriarchal religion negates women has registered and received some response, albeit highly defensive, and often characterized by contempt or even rage. The chief condemnation of our constructive work that one hears among theological neoconservatives is that feminists are bringing back the Baal cults and reintroducing nature religion or other heresies long since purged from Christianity by the spiritually perceptive. We are, they say, doing away with transcendence—the transcendence of God—and reintroducing pantheism and theological immanence. They say that all of this results in a theology that cannot strongly and seriously address our violent world with a *clear and decisive word*. It is true, of course, that we feminists have a respect for the nature religions and the heretics that the dominant tradition does not share. What we have learned from feminist historians is that in male-dominant theology, the nature religions got a very bad press. We have learned that part of the polemic of the ancient Hebrew community against the Baal cult was related to the effort to put down the female images that were central to other communities of faith. And we are resolved to look again at *all* of the heretics with sympathetic eyes. I happen to believe we need a criterion of orthopraxis in theology, but not a fixed concept of truth. For us, however, orthodoxy is always, at least retrospectively, what Simone Weil and Elisabeth Schüssler Fiorenza have dubbed it: the accounts the victors give of those they have vanquished.[8]

We feminists also have had to resurrect the term *pagan*. While doing historical research for my recent book on abortion, it took me months to realize the significance of the fact that most early Christian theologians who condemned abortion ridiculed and denounced it as wrong either because it was a "pagan practice" or because it was a confession of adultery! What I learned confirmed what other feminists have documented in other research, namely, that the imagery of *paganism*— which originally meant "country person" and has come to mean not only "outsider" but "unbeliever"—is *always* associated in Christianity with women and with what is female.

Nevertheless, we feminists reject the charge that what we are about is merely putting immanence at the center of our spirituality and pushing transcendence aside. What we are demanding is that our awareness of both immanence and transcendence be dialectically reconnected, and that both be fundamentally reenvisaged as modes of relationship. The most powerful single response to this unimaginative charge that feminists are "eroding" divine transcendence (and is anyone *persuaded* by what male-dominant theologians say about God's transcendence today?) is succinctly expressed by Carter Heyward:

> [T]he complaint voiced frequently against "feminist theology" is that we have no "place" in our theology for "the transcendent." It is time we respond to this charge, and we can begin by suggesting that, by "the transcendent," these critics mean "God"—and most surely not the power of mutual relation but rather a power of hierarchical relation, a god at the top, He who has been imaged in christian tradition as Father, Son, and Holy Spirit, who before the worlds began, before the curtain had been raised on the drama of salvation history (creation/fall/redemption), knew the plot, how it would begin, how it would end. An Almighty God, the essence of whose power is control. This is the "transcendent" god whom many of us reject, not in the first instance because He is portrayed as male, but rather because He—reflecting that which generations of religious men have venerated—represents a use of power which neither we in our own lives today, nor Western history itself from our perspective, can testify to as creative or redemptive. . . .
>
> The problem with this patriarchal view of transcendence and the god who is said to be its essence is that it really has very little to do with actual transcendence, that fundamental relational power which moves to cross over from people to people, race to race, gender to gender, class to class, binding us into one Body of human and created beings, healing our wounds, breaking down the assumptions and structures which keep us divided, and, through it all, empowering us, each and all, to know and love ourselves and one another as participants in this transcendence. . . . Many of us are ready to proclaim, gladly and gratefully, that we, in our daily lives, experience a

wonderfully mysterious power truly crossing over into and through and from our lives into the lives of all created beings—and that this power is indeed God, transcendent precisely in the fullness and radicality of her immanence among us.[9]

Transcendence is radical immanence, and radical immanence—a living in relation, with and toward all creative beings—is transcendence. This, I submit, is the only response we feminists should make to the charge that it is *we* who have jettisoned the transcendence of God: No more of a God no one actually experiences!

On this wonderful day, we celebrate the prospects of the transformations feminist theology may bring, and we do so to honor a remarkable woman who has marched shoulder to shoulder with us to bring about these transformations. Please note that I speak of marching in *sisterly* fashion—shoulder to shoulder! Years ago I had the occasion to introduce Nelle Morton, and I did so by speaking of her as the feminist theologian who is "the mother of us all." She chastised me roundly and charged me with cruelty, reminding me that she wanted only to be my *sister*. So on this day we honor a sister, but I must also press her tolerance to say that shoulder to shoulder, this woman, nevertheless, has marched in the front rank. What we owe her, we sister feminists, is the pledge that we shall continue to march with her, insisting that we be taken seriously in our claim that the spiritual problematic of our culture often has been fundamentally misconstrued because of male supremacy. To understand it aright, we must reenvision it through the passion and power of all those who have been invisible, who have been treated with contempt and trivialized. Until that day, the work of feminist theology must continue, and to that end many of us are ready to stand as sisters, shoulder to shoulder, pressing our agenda. For the vision and power of sisterhood you have bequeathed, we thank you, dear Nelle.

Notes

1. I need also to acknowledge that that day my imagination was impacted—without appropriate awareness—by the wonderful title of the essays collected by Pam McAllister, and published as *Reweaving the Web of Life: Feminism and Nonviolence* (Philadelphia: New Society Publishers, 1982).
2. Nelle Morton, "Toward a Whole Theology: A Working Paper," presented to the Task Force on Women of the World Council of Churches (n.d.), 1.
3. See Nelle Morton, "The Dilemma of Celebration," in *Women in a Strange Land*, ed. Clare Fischer, et al. (Philadelphia: Fortress Press, 1975).
4. See Morton, "Toward a Whole Theology."
5. This quotation is from Nelle Morton, "The Goddess as Metaphorical Image," in *Weaving the Visions: New Patterns in Feminist Spirituality*, ed. Carol P. Christ and Judith Plaskow (San Francisco: Harper & Row, 1989), 111–18.
6. For a feminist perspective on passion and relationship, see Carter Heyward, *The Redemption of God* (Washington, D.C.: University Press of America, 1982); and Alice Walker, *The Color Purple* (New York: Harcourt Brace Jovanovich, 1982).
7. See Mary Daly, *Gyn/Ecology: The Metaethics of Radical Feminism* (Boston: Beacon Press, 1978). See also Starhawk, *Dreaming the Dark* (Boston: Beacon Press, 1982).

8. Elisabeth Schüssler Fiorenza quotes Weil on this point frequently and documents the thesis in her important study *In Memory of Her: A Feminist Reconstruction of Christian Origins* (New York: Crossroad, 1983).

9. Carter Heyward, "Crossing Over, On Transcendence," in *Our Passion for Justice* (New York: Pilgrim Press, 1984).

Chapter 14

Feminist Thea(o)logies at the Millennium: "Messy" Continued Resistance or Surrender to Postmodern Academic Culture?

This essay was Harrison's contribution to the Festschrift honoring Letty Russell, a leading feminist theologian, on her retirement from the Yale Divinity School. Here Harrison takes up some concerns about keeping liberationist methodological assumptions alive in the midst of nationalistic academic construals of postmodernism and neoliberalism. She considers elements of a feminist legacy that held internationalism and cultural inclusion as normative and judges them on the basis of their contribution toward a "less violent and more cordial common life." From Liberating Eschatology: Essays in Honor of Letty M. Russell, *edited by Margaret A. Farley and Serene Jones (Louisville, Ky.: Westminster John Knox Press, 1999), 156–71.*

I write on the verge of retirement, a senior academic pondering the current condition of feminist the*a*- (or the*o*-) ethical work and musing on its future.[1] The occasion, writing an essay for a collection honoring an esteemed colleague, Professor Letty Russell, as her seventieth birthday nears, stirs joy. But the fast-approaching terminus to my own formal academic career encourages reminiscence and even a few nostalgic fears about an emerging academic scene that will be going on with far less input from us in the near future. Such moments surely tempt to romanticized memory and even to nostalgic rereadings of the past. So

I pause, concerned that voicing worries about the directions of feminist reli-gious/thea(o)logical work as women's religious and ethical scholarship burgeons may reveal nothing more than an anxiety generated by aging. How self-serving and defensive of my own generation's efforts may such an essay seem? I have decided to express my worries, confident that my readers can perfectly well judge for themselves.

In spite of our often-noted similarities of social location, feminist theologians now in our sixties to seventies were, in fact, quite a divergent group, differing in our styles of work, the sources we used, and our accountabilities. Seen now as rather homogeneous and chiefly as "reformers,"[2] what should be at least as notable is this diversity of our voices and of the communities on which we impacted. Even though we mostly engaged existing religious traditions and communities from within and were mostly white and surely not as insightful about white racism, class, or the depth and tenacity of male sex/gender power as we needed to be, we did our work with persistence. When our thea(o)logical and ethical naming overgeneralized our own cultural worlds in ways costly to other women's well-being, we sought to correct our myopias on these matters while we got on with an extraordinary range of constructive work. In retrospect, the rather remarkable array of women who responded is noteworthy, especially given the power of "feminist backlash."[3]

Let it be noted as well that, on the whole, we avoided acrimonious infighting about our disagreements and points of tension. If, in the eyes of many who were to follow, we spoke in styles reminiscent of some of our male academic mentors, we nevertheless forged critical perspectives that fueled rising expectations among women and drew diverse groups of women into the enterprise of thea(o)logical reconstruction.

WERE WE SENIOR FEMINIST SCHOLARS MODERNISTS?

Pondering the relationship of Letty Russell's early work and mine is instructive to me in light of current criticisms of our generation's work. We are both Pres-byterians of a rebellious sort, both passionately committed to a continuously reforming theological stance that was, at best, our tradition's rhetorical ideal, even when honored more in the breach than in the practice. Both our efforts have been faulted, not without justification, for language insufficiently reflective of the chasms of difference among women. Neither of us, I am confident, has the least interest in denying the charge that *difference* was not the first word in our early theorizing of women's oppressions, and that we did, at times, speak of women's "experience" in the singular, without sufficient caution. What is not always rec-ognized, however, is that our assumptions, if not the style of voice we employed, were already *explicitly and substantively postmodernist* at the methodological level. As I reread the work of my age coterie (with the exception of the most influential and evocative of us, Mary Daly[4]), the past-sixty crowd of feminist theologians, without exception, *assumed* that theological categories as such are not, nor could they be, ontological in the manner presumed in classical philosophy. To the contrary, all of us began on this side of historicism recognizing that the foundations of theological claims were not transcendental but were situated *historical-cultural constructs*. Catholic and Protestant alike among us explicitly avoided classical ontological theological approaches. Today, I find that few younger feminist religious theorists recall that Daly's early use of Paul Tillich actually *reinserted* an ontological option into feminist theological discussion, which others of us avoided.

There was, of course, another source of "foundationalist" feminism invoked by those who used a Whiteheadean process approach.[5] Alfred North Whitehead's thought, popular among some feminists, was, if properly understood, a postmodern style of metaphysics—that is, it was scientifically grounded and "speculative" or conjectural, and it did not yield firm or unequivocal knowledge. Nor did most feminists really use Whitehead's cosmological, scientifically based speculation as a source of theological knowledge. Historicist perspectives took primacy in feminist work over speculative ones.

Much more could be said about the status of Tillichian and Whiteheadean methods in early feminist theologies in relation to postmodern criticisms of essentialism. Here my point is simple: No theologians in our over-sixty group (nor, as I read the record, any of the now fifty-to-sixty crowd) purported to ground theological claims in philosophically transcendentalist-essentialist categories or in Enlightenment theories of transcendental reason. Yet the rhetoric of some younger feminist scholars often seems to imply that we worked from such assumptions and that our work is, for that reason, at best deeply flawed, at worst no longer tenable. Though some questions can be raised about what our appeals to "experience" as a source of knowledge really meant, it is far from clear that the most general complaints of postmodernist critique apply. I read our theological anthropologies as rooted basically in historical and cultural claims. Our occasional uses of "ontic categories" that presumed some homogeneity in human identity or constancy of need were derivations from natural or social-science assumptions that are far from being discredited today.

Gender, race, and class were for us "durable inequalities"[6] created through time. The "death of metaphysics" message so dear to current younger feminist theorists had long since reached us, because liberal theology itself had already widely taken a shift toward nonfoundationalism. If we had not been presuming historical malleability, we would not have adopted the theories of social change we embraced. None of us really imagined that the male gender-supremacy mode of quaint and charming nineteenth-century discourse, with its always inadequate abstract term *woman*, was a wise way to talk. If women's experiences were, for us, often analogous and parallel, that was because perduring patterns of male supremacy had taken some definite historical forms.

KEEPING LIBERATIONIST METHODOLOGICAL ASSUMPTIONS ALIVE IN POSTMODERNIST DISCOURSES: PRACTICE AS POLITICS

Today more than ever before, it needs to be remembered that those of us who adopted the term *feminist liberation theology* for our work did so because we shared the epistemic conviction that theory is a moment *within* praxis, and that theory is to be judged by the practice it engenders. We came to recognize in an urgent way that what was needed was an *academic-political practice of inclusion* that would bring other voices to the academic table as a condition of more adequate knowledge. Our goal was not so much to perfect *our* theories individualistically but to broaden concrete participation in the work of constructing and expanding women's theological "knowledge." In retrospect, I believe this is the important legacy by which subsequent work among us should be assessed. But I am bound to ask, "Is this really the lesson that current academic women, like us still too largely from the tribes of Europe, will carry forward?" Will calls for greater political risk taking and more "messy diversity" continuously emerge in religious studies and theological faculties, or will the heavy hand of an ideological consensus that is quietly at home with the academic status quo replace it?

Continuing reflection on the relation of my own work with Letty Russell's is instructive on this point as well. I read (and have always read) Letty's work as rooted in a passionate embrace of human freedom and the continuous need for ecclesial renewal. Most of her readers did not know or appreciate enough of Karl Barth's aim and agenda to understand that his goal was rooted precisely in a militantly anti-essentialist historical political agenda.[7] Some have dismissed Letty's work as "not radical" or "male-dominated" because the innovations of Protestant male voices were sometimes lost on feminists because of *their* gender monism. Because I rejected Barth, I came off better initially among those who were critical. I was unpersuaded that he had found either a satisfactory way beyond liberalism's limitations or a theological method that would make Christian theology genuinely critical enough to escape cultural provincialism. I thought then, and still think, that none of us can afford so wholesale a jettisoning of liberal social, political, and moral theory as Barth attempted, or as postmodernists sometimes call for. So Letty Russell, not Beverly Harrison, deserves credit for taking a path most consistent with postmodernist claims.

Were Letty Russell and I to have an occasion to compare notes on the matter, I expect we would both be amused at the range and convergences of the learnings and unlearnings that each of us has passed through. The solidarity I have with her as a theologian is the havoc we have mutually inflicted on the norm of "decency and order" so valued in our shared Reformed or Calvinist theological tradition. Both of us have frequently referred to our sad little denomination as "God's frozen people,"[8] and we have gotten on with the tasks of encouraging heterodoxy, not for its own sake but because we both find any orthodoxy to function as a subtle patriarchal norm. For us, the practice of feminist thea(o)logy aims to give all women the power of their own voices in the naming of diverse visions of sacred power, relations, and healing community. Feminist work envisages no formalized, "fixed" starting point and no final resting place. Such a perspective makes the need for ongoing reformation not a ponderous platitude but a continuing source of theological energy and excitement. It is Letty Russell and Shannon Clarkson, on the occasion of the publication party for the *Dictionary of Feminist Theologies* that they so lovingly edited, whom I quote here: Our ongoing work is "the wonderfully messy business of encouraging women's theologies."[9] Are younger feminist theologians as clear as they need to be that this, not the production of "correct" theory, remains the ongoing task?

THE NEW SITUATION IN ACADEMIC CULTURE: NEOLIBERAL ANTIPOLITICS

Unflagging effort to sustain the desire for more messiness is critical in a time when style has replaced depth in academic discernment. Continuous learning of uncompromising moral-political practices that encourage and enable alternative lines of departure not aiming at homogeneity will be far from easy. Not only the diversity of sources used and the rhetorical styles and genre to be developed but the constituencies that women in theology and religious studies work among must continue to increase. What "united" us in the past were broadly shared *political* goals—that is, to enhance concretely the range of voices participating in the project of theo(a)logical and moral reconstruction. The cultures and institutional sites that need religious transformation if "women are to count" are innumerable and unending.[10] The currently fashionable "trashes" of "liberationist" approaches to theology, rooted in sometimes subtle and sometimes crass deconstructions of what is and is not possible in our appeals to historicity and our efforts for change, can be dangerous if they celebrate resistance without the determination to *struggle* for such change continuously. Our now-older generation of liberation theologians learned the dialogical style respectful of disagreement, which we practiced in part because we knew the change we sought required a wide range of support systems for diverse constituencies. Our *theories* may not always have borne the stamp of our diversity concretely enough, but our *practices* encouraging diversity fueled our theoretical learnings directly. Much of the work that we did therefore encouraged a dialogical, not a competitive, ethos.

Today we are living in a hostile, neoliberal climate.[11] The chilling hand of this neoliberalism is contemptuous of any political commitment as "political correctness."[12] This discourages *any practice norm* for defining truthfulness. Neoliberalism is currently working its way into the academic bloodstream so deeply that this point cannot be too much stressed: The lifeblood of feminist religious thought in the late twentieth century has been *resistance* to any *episteme* of "correctness." Here, as in our pragmatic practice, rather than "foundationalist" justifications for religious truth, most feminist theologies have been *appropriately postmodernist*, and in my view far less dogmatic than some current feminist theories that describe any truth claim as "violence."[13]

OTHER ELEMENTS OF OUR LEGACY

In retrospect, the impact of feminist liberation work in the(a)ology has been as dramatic as, from one point of view, it was unexpected. Feminist voices became numerous and posed questions that had to be heard and addressed even in some highly traditional academic and religious circles. The much-remarked massive backlash against feminism is to a considerable extent a measure of the groundedness of our sometimes less-than-elegant theory in a practice consistent with our intention to *do* "liberating theology." Will setting aside the rhetoric of "doing liberating theology," a prospect that some now celebrate, assure that practices of inclusion remain *the* criterion for whether speech acts may be said to be "truth bearing?" As one who is not prepared to give up the ongoing search for more or less adequacy in truth claims, I am not optimistic. While it is clear that our task is to accelerate religious and moral movement away from canonical readings of religious traditions, treating all theological traditions as at best "works in progress" and as completely contestable, we need not eschew the middle ground of "feminist standpoint" theory.[14] Positioning ourselves spiritually for an unending struggle to realign theo-moral resources away from the truth-as-given, most of our work must aim at *creating* "the truths needed" to bring us to a less violent and more cordial common life.

In sum, then, I believe that an important epistemic shift has already occurred, along with the development of the practice of "networking" toward ever new and shifting solidarities. It is a legacy no one should challenge. Networking has been and must continue to be our the(a)ological mode of practice par excellence.[15]

This legacy, especially powerful in light of Letty Russell's work, was also accompanied in our generation by a singular scepticism never much enamoured of the standards of pedagogy prevailing in the academy, including academies of theological education. Truth to tell, most of us shared with Letty a willingness to spend perhaps an inordinate amount of our time and energies seeking even *minor* revisions in the curricular, teaching, and institutional practices of the schools where we worked. Few of us gained kudos for the multidimensional involvements we took on. Our research and publications sometimes suffered from our wider investments in academic change, but none of us was or could have been a theorist for theory's sake—if only because all of us understood how much change was needed and knew that *only as we struggled for it* would our theories come closer to adequacy.

In the theological schools where we worked, exploding populations of women presented us with demands that none of us could ignore. In fact, women students, who would often tolerate suffering at the hands of men, invariably expected us, their beloved feminist teachers, "to walk on water."[16] For most of us the workload was unbelievable, and in the face of it we largely proved astonishingly and wonderfully resistant to trying to pull off miracles! Perhaps Letty Russell, better than any of us, modeled a realism in the search for change, all the while being completely persistent in its pursuit. She worked for a revolution of "small changes."[17] It was clear to us that the deconstruction of patriarchy (or "demonarchy," as my womanist colleague Delores Williams has recently taught me to prefer)[18] allowed no superficial commitments to change. If a "liberal" cultural ideology had taught us an overly simple hopefulness that change was possible, our lives as lived out taught us another lesson altogether—a clarity that *nothing* deeply serious for women would happen easily or once and for all, much less in our lifetimes.

Years ago, when Phyllis Trible and I shared an inaugural event celebrating our respective professorships, we received an inspiring reminder of the long-term nature of liberation struggle. Phyllis had come to Union Theological Seminary's faculty as a distinguished scholar from another institution, while I had finally gained promotion from within, after endless battles over my scholarly competence. Because our respective accessions to Union's senior faculty had not been easy, we created an event to mark and celebrate *two* feminist professorial inaugurations. On the occasion, a number of women from Boston Theological Institute faculties made a banner for our respective professorial processions. The banner depicted small drops of water falling on a huge rock and carried the well-known words of a Holly Near song: "The rock will wear away." In the twenty ensuing years, even with all our collective accomplishments, the image of water working ever so slowly, so slowly wearing away stone, remains an apt metaphor for the work women must continue to do.

ONGOING SOURCES OF BACKLASH

It is all too obvious to me that, as we near the millennium, the Christian Right commands near-monopoly power of interpretation as the sole organized public voice of Christianity. Among us, the wearying organized and systematic discrediting of feminism is taking a toll of ideological fragmentation. Audre Lorde's cautions regarding "the master's tools" of ideological divisiveness are more relevant than ever before.[19] Daily among us, even some of the best insights of postcolonial theories and gender- and sex-transgressing theories are now appealed to *in order to legitimate* newly "objectivistic" theological strategies. Revival of patriarchal assumptions today takes the form of appeals to Christian cultural particularity and postmodernist communal identity.[20] Now as never before, reaction is able to present itself using the intellectually respectable face and creative style that the postliberal apolitical aestheticism enables. At times I wonder if younger feminists see the dangers of this situation. Personal brilliance, I fear, can sometimes obscure subtle retreats from an uncompromising political practice of advocacy for women.

Given this situation, it is not surprising that there is little clarity or sustained conversation among the growing numbers of women in the academy about the ongoing directions that our feminist religious studies, the(a)ology, and public policy initiatives should take. In the face of this situation, the good news is that our diversity is growing, and as noted, the "messiness" of our lives and work is on the increase. Even in the most traditionalist academic enclaves there is now recognition that, whatever the future portends, it should not be shaped exclusively by white, Eurocentric knowledge perspectives. But elitism is also alive and well, and with the growing homogeneity of the antipolitical and aesthetic neoliberal voice, only a few non-Western cultural critiques are given a genuine hearing.[21] These are selected by male Western elites and often feature only elite voices from other cultures. Popular voices, and above all popular and grassroots political movements for change, are invariably excluded.[22] The real virus of Eurocentrism will never be challenged simply by incorporating other cultural elites.

GENUINE CULTURAL DECENTERING:
SOME SURPRISES FOR ALL OF US

The full range of the deep epistemic shifts required to accomplish a needed European and North American decentering is bound to require a respectful overturning of many of our attitudes of contempt toward lived-world cultural realities and spiritualities that have sustained those marginalized by dominant Western sensibilities. This includes the religio-political views rejected by most cultural elites and the spiritual practices that sustain the actual resistance of concrete communities. These frequently include cosmological and religious claims that Western and non-Western elites alike frown upon. Even the axioms of postmodernism that I have celebrated here may need to be reviewed.[23]

In a vehemently antipolitical world (the heart of neoliberal polemic), the *practice* of a serious religious feminism is sure to be ever more difficult, postmodernist jargon to the contrary notwithstanding. If concrete practices of resistance flag, the critical consciousness generated by those practices will also wane. For most of my generation, the heart of feminist religio-moral work was lived out and worked out actively between our concrete religious communities and actual ecumenical (that is, planetary) and interreligious networks of women. We measured a postcolonial "decentering" of our Eurocentrism by ongoing involvement in global projects and perspectives. Postcolonialism was far more than an endless set of sceptical questions about problematic truth claims and suspect "manners of speaking." It was through these practical involvements that we discovered the insularity of our own cultures and the need for retheorizing our own cultural understandings and certitudes. Yet, at the moment, trumpet calls to postmodernist feminism seem to me to lead more often to enunciations of what one *cannot* do, say, or mean than to interesting revisioning of what we *can* mean religiously, morally, or even descriptively.

THE COMPLICITY OF ACADEMIC INSTITUTIONS
IN NEOLIBERALISM

The cultural crisis through which little planet Earth and its dependents are passing also requires all who espouse any version of feminist work to recognize that our academic institutions themselves are deeply complicit in that crisis, and that they are deeply and profoundly aligned with dominant political and economic systems. Those who gain self-esteem through academic achievements are particularly vulnerable to hubris on this point, as Mary Fulkerson has frequently reminded us.[24] The successes of academic feminism in religious studies programs and in theological schools could well lead feminist concern for diversity to be erased by elitist cultural identifications that catch many off guard in the face of an ongoing, grinding pressure for academic conformity. *Nothing that can be "learned" in the present academy can teach any of us what we need to know about political activism.* Grassroots activism together with the rough-and-tumble of actual global networking are the only sources of the knowledge we need. These are the two sites—the only two—where the lessons most needed can be learned. If I am right about this, the taste for the messiness and complexity so much needed to expand the tiny beachheads women in theology and religious studies have gained over the past thirty years depends on concretely maintaining global and local activist contacts. Without them, complacency about a static notion of an already achieved multicultural sophistication may occur.

All around us, in the midst of turmoil, the newer global political-economic institutions are continuously sponsoring powerful new neoliberal theoretical constructions that legitimate their control.[25] Let no one miss the point that avant-garde feminist literary theory and queer literary theory in particular are at risk for a new captivity because of their overreliance on French philosophical sources and their reaction against the vicious positivism of formerly structuralist historical perspectives. Crass neoliberal calls for the "recovery of cultural values" do not take feminist and queer theorists in, but harder to detect neomodern reinscriptions of postliberal stylistic "traditions of excellence" have an impact on them because style and creativity have become so important in themselves. How will so-far-achieved commitments to diversity continue to propel us to new coalitions under such circumstances? May we not find ourselves moving down a different road, the one where clever expressionism of fractured subjectivities is ever more cleverly articulated? Emerging feminist theories now being generated in the academy may produce moral and spiritual wisdom sufficient to keep us in touch with concrete longings and yearnings for the changes we need, but they may also deliver us to new games of academic upmanship, poetically expressed.

Current calls for ever more critical and postliberal theory are no substitute for clarification of assumptions and carefully formulated conversations about the possibilities of ongoing feminist theorizing. Too much recent feminist discourse has been dismissive of questions needing ongoing work rather than satirical rejection.[26] To put the point bluntly, too many of us are accepting "the rhetorics of postmodernity" without the depth of textual engagement needed to understand what appeals to postmodernity really propose and reject. Sweeping generalizations about a necessary postmodernity do not suffice. Postmodernist theorizing is "in" for theology and ethics, but postmodernist critics are diverse and varied. Their theses, in my view, have led many to embrace some "misplaced prohibitions" about what thea(o)logians can and cannot claim in our work.

URGENT QUESTIONS, NOT GLIB ANSWERS

Several topics only touched on here need far more careful discussion in current feminist religio-moral theory than they have so far received. Three in particular deserve at least brief further comment here. First, the immense but subtle power of the neoliberal ethos escalates daily in academia, and it is not well diagnosed by most religionists, who imagine that claims of objectivity in knowledge are weakening. To the contrary, ours is a time of unparalleled metaphysical control—albeit a control by neoclassical economic theory, with its withering contempt for "political correctness." In the face of this, it is disastrous for religio-cultural studies to rule out any sources of social-political-theoretical voice, much less to embrace escalating elitism born of the dismantling of opportunities for broad-based participation in higher education. Increasingly, only economic elites who can learn the expressionism of stylistically defined "meritocratic" achievers find their way into places where the most-admired religious studies occur. In the universities where elites gather, the economists teach the true metaphysics and everyone else practices poetic deconstruction of truth claims. As noted, some globally recognized elite intellectuals from outside the "colonial center" are occasionally heard and sometimes even lionized in these elite bastions, but fewer and fewer grassroots voices are being heard there. To forget that the feminisms and feminist theorizings that spawned and fueled our work were generated by women's activism is suicidal. Activism with and for community and against enduring patterns of violence, resistance toward the concrete sources of life threat, the "primary emergencies" that require daily encounter in women's lives, are our lifeblood. These movements, grounded in the discourse of justice and human rights, do not share the total moral and religious scepticism characteristic of Western epistemic scepticism. Certainly, the demand for decentering Enlightenment and Western hegemonic theorizings will require a careful revisiting of epistemic perspectives. This will no doubt include a newly serious interreligious dialogue that involves interrogation of Western knowledge binaries of (among others) spiritual/material and religious/secular.

Second, those of us (myself included) who feel at home in postmodern feminist discourse in North America may be required to recognize that our nearly a priori rejections include the convictions that other cultures value—that is, cosmologies, metaphysics, or inclusive narratives of valuation. The "spiritualities" and the "materialities" (always both) of many non-Western cultures are, by our Western standards, "premodern." And the radical *desacralization* of "reality" underlying our Western binary—secular (or profane) and religious—seems only to grow stronger as enthusiasm for difference and avoidance of any and all essentialisms increase among us. Many of our calls for decentering involve deep and growing scepticism precisely about the sorts of affirmations that are the heart of non-Western worldviews. Nor dare feminists fail to note that it is a Eurocentered male nihilism that has erupted to declare the death of most Western theoretical traditions. Articulating scepticism about the meaningfulness and adequacy of any and all presumably objectifying discourses does not open the way to the necessary new dialogue. While some of these lines of neopatriarchal analysis have more salience among feminist theorists in other fields of study than they do in religious studies, there is evidence that a new postmodernist religious dogmatism is on the increase. Surely we must ask, Can we celebrate multiculturalism while proclaiming the impossibility of certitudes that are an epistemic bedrock for many non-Western cultural traditions?

In my networking, I have often heard religious women of other cultures express astonishment at the corrosive attitudes toward knowledge that they believe they encounter in Western intellectual traditions. On one occasion, a woman religious educator put the point succinctly: "Your culture seems to look at knowledge as you look at the world economically—knowledge, like all other resources you image, is to be understood within the *conditions of scarcity.* You seem to believe that only a few can really possess it. By contrast, in my culture we believe that knowledge is everywhere, that everyone can learn and everyone can share what they know. Truth is inexhaustible. When everyone teaches and everyone learns, only then will we approximate the range of truth we need."[27] I think of this woman when I hear the ever-growing lists of things that the academically sophisticated tell us we cannot claim to know or have no warrant to say. We have, it seems, forgotten even the simpler wisdom of a great postmodernist male philosopher of this century, Ludwig Wittgenstein, who dethroned logical positivism by contending, "It is not the business of the philosopher to tell people what they can and cannot claim."[28]

It is also not for the feminist to replace specific arguments with categorical constraints against certain philosophical claims. So many such a priori constraints have, as I have already noted, derived from French intellectual traditions, above all those bordering on neoliberalisms that have proclaimed the "death" of Marxism. The highly ambiguous legacy of positivist structuralism is obvious, but the "fate" of Marxism in the collapse of French social theory needs a book-length study. Here it can only be observed that the legacy of the "decline" of Marxism in French thought has been a tendency to challenge or dismiss any generalizations regarding the historical character of political economy, labelling all social theory as "master narrative" and "grand theory," though only certain forms of French social theory deserved that characterization. However, the decentering of a few of the worst positivisms created by those Frenchmen who invoked Karl Marx's name has hardly ruled out the growing creativity and persuasiveness of numerous neo-Marxist streams of theory, particularly those addressing cultural formation through a careful analysis of concrete political-economic change. Such theories are gaining even greater attention in the newer global networks of sociopolitical analysis, and those who seek theoretical insights adequate to analyze ongoing events should not ignore this work.[29]

Finally, just as criticisms of grand theory have not discredited sociohistorical perspectives on political economy, so challenges to experience as a suspect concept have not eroded empiricist or pragmatic truth claims. Many of us did not begin with *transcendental* philosophical notions of human identity or *privatized* views of individuated personhood as the appropriate starting points for human self-understanding or so-called human rationality. "Experience" was never "in" a private arena. In my own view, it is important to continue to invoke experience in order to specify more clearly the *interrelational character* and the *perspectival limits* of what we can claim. Contrary to some, my contention that experience is the crucible from which knowledge claims should be made is rooted in a commitment to perspectival rather than abstract knowledge.

Experiential claims, of course, are not only perspectival but always situated and finite. Whether or how they relate to other subjectivities comes to be known only through the discernments of those "others" who will invoke their own particular horizons of experience. *All testing of truth claims is dialogical,* and, important for most of us, narrativity as such is not what we appeal to when we speak of experiential truthfulness. Narrativity plays an important role in "coming to awareness of truth," but while some male theologians appear to have suggested that narrativity produces truth, I have never heard a woman theologian say precisely this. In my view, narrativity feeds the formation of reflexive awareness as an ongoing source of self-knowledge. It is not, however, *the* source of our knowledge per se. Without exception, knowledge is relational and grows out of intersubjective confirmations of a variety of sorts. We narrate—that is, we order our experience as subjects—in order to situate our agency, shape it in relationship to others, and to become *subjects to ourselves*. This is a process that is possible only because our subjectivity itself is a continuous pulling together or gathering in (as Whitehead noted) of the blooming, buzzing, and potentially infinite flux, the continuous process in which such subjectivity as we may come to possess is embedded. We do not "need" to become fixed or definite subjects, and the subjects we may become are changing, multilayered, and always potentially inexhaustible. Multiple identities indeed!

Like any good postmodernist, however, I (and a lot of feminist liberation thea(o)logians with me) will not readily surrender our rights to claim, albeit relatively, that *through experience we meet endless otherness*, which we come to "know" through the lenses of our theories and their ongoing uses. We will continue to revise those theories as we go, changing them as we encounter dissent to their adequacy, aptness, or applicability. Thereby we learn the limits of what we know—when others tell us that their experience is different or our account does not work for them. Thereby our experience teaches us who we are at the moment, and thereby we gain further data for reformulating our theory in order to move to another identity. As in the past, I will frequently overstate the meaning, significance, and generalizability of what I know, and happily, I will learn from my mistakes. But I will not deny, not now, not ever, that my experience mediates truth, and that my ongoing search for truthfulness is more than a manner of speaking. Nor will I assume that the truth telling I do out of my life experience will be of no interest or help to another unless that person is like me in most respects. Some very different others have told me that I have helped them understand, and some very different others have enhanced my understanding. I have learned often that others welcome the truth I have to share, just as they evoke learnings in me that I did not expect but need.

Even though all this highly proximate truth seeking and truth telling must go on endlessly, I will not give up the conviction that there are numerous, if partial, procedures for adjudicating between "better" and "worse" claims about what is, what is good, and what is worthy of reverence and devotion. If all this makes me sound "premodern" or "modernist," so be it. It surely makes me believe that feminist thea(o)logical work remains a lovely thing to do, and that my longing to stay on the journey home to liberation is no colonial impulse or desire for control. Should all talk of liberation thea(o)logies wane as the outmoded dreams of older bourgeoisie like myself? I have been pondering this question for some time now, but the more I do, the more I muse that Letty, following old Karl, had it right, and that I—and yes, everybody else—do best when we live toward freedom, refusing to settle for anything less. This implies that we can discern some dimensions of what authentic freedom is, and we can rule out some pseudoclaims as specious.

Notes

1. Editor's note: Harrison here contrasts the Greek male root "theo" and the female root "thea" to bring women's experience back to the term "theology," which literally means "talk about a *male* god."
2. The term *reformist* was first applied to Letty Russell's and Rosemary Radford Ruether's work in the introduction to *Woman-Spirit Rising: A Feminist Reader in Religion*, ed. Carol Christ and Judith Plaskow (New York: Harper & Row, 1979). The term was frequently used to designate any of us who did not characterize our work as post-Christian. I have long protested applying political terms to how feminists position ourselves vis-à-vis our religious communities, noting, for example, that in subsequent discussion Russell, Ruether, and I, among others, have been much more critical of capitalist political economy than many religious feminists who are "post-Christian" and are regularly characterized as "radical."
3. This term became feminist currency with the publication of Susan Faludi's *Backlash: The Undeclared War against American Women* (New York: Doubleday, 1991). See also Carter Heyward, Beverly W. Harrison, Mary E. Hunt, Emilie M. Townes, Starhawk, Anne L. Barstow, and Paula M. Cooey, "Roundtable Discussion: Backlash," in *Journal of Feminist Studies in Religion* 10 (Spring 1994): 91–111.
4. Mary Daly's important work has had impact beyond the field of religious studies. Many who have been influenced by her, however, miss the differences between her original, rather more traditional starting point and the starting points of those of us who did not presume we needed foundational warrants for

theology resting on a philosophy of Being. Daly's most recent work is *Quintessence . . . Realizing the Archaic Future: A Radical Elemental Feminist Manifesto* (Boston: Beacon Press, 1998).

5. Early feminist discussions of Alfred North Whitehead's work can be found in Sheila G. Daveney, ed., *Feminism and Process Thought* (Lewiston, N.Y.: Edwin Mellen Press, 1981). What needs to be remembered about Whitehead's work is that he did not aspire to do metaphysics as a foundational philosophical enterprise. His was a postmodernist project—to show that scientific knowledge did not preclude some reflection on general theory. Metaphysics was not for him "first knowledge," but rather speculation based on extending empirical knowledges to greater levels of generality.

6. This term is from Charles Tilly, *Durable Inequalities* (Berkeley, Calif.: University of California Press, 1997). Tilly's notion, which translates "structural inequality" in a less static direction, is helpful in reconceptualizing "structure" in ways more congenial to social constructionist assumptions.

7. Most followers of Karl Barth in the United States misread his political intent because they overlooked his situatedness in European political debates among left, center, and right. Letty Russell always understood the political-economic significance of Barth's theology.

8. References to liberal Protestants as God's "frozen people" originated with Robert McAfee Brown in his "St. Hereticus" columns in the journal *Christianity and Crisis.*

9. Remarks by Letty M. Russell and J. Shannon Clarkson at the publication party for *The Dictionary of Feminist Theologies* (Louisville, Ky.: Westminster John Knox Press, 1996) at the American Academy of Religion meeting, San Francisco, 1997.

10. The phrase "if women are to count" is drawn from an important feminist study in economic ethics by Pamela K. Brubaker, *Women Don't Count: The Challenge of Women's Poverty to Christian Ethics* (Atlanta: Scholars Press, 1994).

11. The term *neoliberal* was self-selected by Reagan-Bush-era theorists whose liberal worldview was reconstituted under the strictures of recent neoclassical economic ideology. Neoliberals accept the defenses of market capitalism generated in the 1980s and consider market capitalism the best possible political economy, given the abstract mathematical theories of choice that were generated during that period. Neoliberals accept, usually without historical defense, the thesis that markets are the most "efficient" way to achieve "solutions" to social problems. Neoliberals believe that "politics" can (and should) be rendered obsolete by the successes of an unfettered economy.

12. For an important analysis of the right-wing origins of the term *political correctness*, see Richard Feldstein, *Political Correctness: A Response from the Cultural Left* (Minneapolis: University of Minnesota Press, 1997).

13. The most emphatic theoretical denunciation of "objectivity" claims as "violent" is found in Judith Butler, *Excitable Speech* (Berkeley: University of California Press, 1998).

14. " Feminist standpoint theory" is the epistemic alternative to the sort of antiobjectivism in feminist theory generated by theorists such as Judith Butler and others often closely aligned with French feminist theorists. Standpoint theorists are frequently aligned more with feminist critiques of science than with literary theory. See, for example, Donna Haraway, *Cyborgs, Simians, and Women* (London: Routledge & Kegan Paul, 1991), 183–201; and Sandra Harding, *Whose Science? Whose Knowledge? Thinking from Women's Lives* (Ithaca, N.Y.: Cornell University Press, 1991).

15. An excellent theoretical treatment of networking as a goal of feminist political agency appears in Janet R. Jakobsen, *Working Alliances and the Politics of Difference: Diversity and Feminist Ethics* (Bloomington, Ind.: University Press, 1998).

16. The phrase is from an important early essay by Jo Freeman in her *Politics of Women's Liberation: A Case Study of an Emerging Social Movement and Its Relation to the Policy Press* (New York: David McKay Co., 1975).

17. The phrase is from Marge Piercy. It was Mary Pellauer, however, who reminded feminist religious thinkers that the needed women's revolution must be "a revolution of small changes."

18. See Delores S. Williams, "Black Women's Literature and the Task of Feminist Theology," in *Immaculate and Powerful: The Female in Sacred Image and Social Reality*, ed. Clarissa W. Atkinson, Constance Buchanan, and Margaret R. Miles (Boston: Beacon Press, 1985), 5–10; and Delores S. Williams, *Sisters in the Wilderness: The Challenge of Womanist God-Talk* (Maryknoll, N.Y.: Orbis Books, 1993).

19. Audre Lorde's canonical essay "The Master's Tools" appears in at least four books. See her famous collection *Sister Outsider* (Trumansburg, N.Y.: Crossing Press, 1984), 110–13.

20. See, for example, the works of John Milbank and Stanley Hauerwas, both of whom celebrate the particularity and uniqueness of Christian theological claims but reclaim the notion of only one, "classical," standard Christian truth as right or "orthodox" (read: patriarchal). Denying the ongoing and continuous contentions among Christians is evidence of premodern "postmodernism."

21. Anticolonial thinkers such as Gayatri Spivak and Edward Said often ruthlessly satirize Western colonizing truth claims but also treat the intellectual traditions of anticolonialists like themselves as clear-cut, noncontestable. Many non-Western intellectuals seem to have secularized antireligious biases, rather characteristic of the Western counterparts whom they criticize.

22. The divide between feminist intellectuals who theorize in academic isolation and those who do their work in solidarity and collaboration with grassroots movements of various sorts runs through and across national and global-cultural alignments. Not all critics of Eurocentrism are deeply engaged with concrete communities of struggle.

23. It should be clear that my own theological bias is in sympathy with the assumption of social-constructive historical theory, and that I am skeptical of the sort of metaphysics that characterized "classical" Western philosophy. This makes me comfortable with the consensual Western assumption regarding postmodernity, that metaphysics is suspect as a source of knowledge. However, all of us need to be clear that a genuine cross-cultural global dialogue will require the careful revisiting of even our own most cherished "postmodernist" certitudes. I also want to dissent in the strongest possible way from any readings of postmodernism that do not make a connection between late capitalism and the suppression of normative political and moral categories.

24. Mary McClintock Fulkerson has made this point in several essays and in *Changing the Subject: Women's Discourses and Feminist Theology* (Minneapolis: Fortress Press, 1994); see esp. 133–82 and 355–95 for an excellent depiction of the work of feminist theologies.

25. I believe one of the less desirable consequences of the numerous and not always carefully constructed lines of postmodernist criticism is already becoming visible in the religious studies literature—that is, the "blending" of scientific, religious, moral, and political claims, treating each of these as an "equal claimant" to knowledge. The result has been some new interdisciplinary speculations that combine astonishing sense and nonsense. See, for example, Nancy Murphy and George F. R. Ellis, *On the Moral Nature of the Universe: Why Theologians Should Pay Attention to Science* (Minneapolis: Fortress Press, 1996). Murphy and Ellis bring together debatable scientific claims with even more contestable theological

assumptions about Christianity. The total erasure of "middle ground" consensus about truth and falsity in historically developed arenas of inquiry hardly constitutes a great gain amid the new dogmatisms of neoliberalism, with its sequestered metaphysic of neoclassical economy.

26. Feminist discussions of the limitations of appeals to experience frequently puzzle me. Some seem to challenge such appeals altogether and to rule out any reference to identity, but then move back to something approaching a "standpoint theory" position. See, for example, Sheila Greeve Davaney, "Continuing the Story, but Departing the Text: A Historicist Interpretation of Feminist Norms in Theology," in *Horizons in Feminist Theology: Identity, Tradition, and Norms*, ed. R. S. Chopp and S. G. Davaney (Minneapolis: Fortress Press, 1997), 198–214; as well as her contribution to "Round Table Discussion," *Journal of Feminist Studies in Religion* 11 (Spring 1995): 119–23. I agree with much that Davaney says but long for greater specificity as to what methods and claims really meet her criteria for adequacy. I also worry about her following Richard Rorty on epistemic matters.

27. This conversation occurred at a meeting at the University of Zimbabwe in Harare in 1991. Sadly, I never learned the name of the remarkable woman who engaged me in this revelatory exchange about the limitations of Western views of knowledge.

28. Ludwig Wittgenstein, *Philosophical Investigations*, trans. by G. E. M. Anscombe, 2d ed. (New York: Macmillan, 1958).

29. See Ellen Meiksins Wood, *Democracy against Capitalism: Renewing Historical Materialism* (Cambridge: Cambridge University Press, 1995); and Frederic Jameson, ed., *The Cultures of Globalization* (Durham, N.C.: Duke University Press, 1998).

Chapter 15

Dorothee Soelle as
Pioneering Postmodernist

Harrison wrote this essay for a collection honoring German feminist theologian Dorothee Soelle (1929–2003), who was frequently a visiting professor at Union Theological Seminary. Besides celebrating Soelle's work, Harrison here endorses as a genuinely critical postmodernism Soelle's radical reorientation of theology toward concretely meaningful spiritual and ecclesial practice. From The Theology of Dorothee Soelle, *edited by Sarah K. Pinnock (Harrisburg, Pa.: Trinity Press International, 2003), 239–255.*

THE ROOTS OF SOELLE'S POLITICAL THEOLOGY

Nearly fifty years ago, H. Richard Niebuhr, probably the Christian theologian most admired by peers in the United States during his lifetime and in the decades that followed, assessed his work in the *Christian Century* series "How My Mind Has Changed."[1] Musing on what perhaps he could have done differently, he observed that he might well have chosen to travel more with the poets than with the philosophers. To my knowledge, no academic theologian has ever inquired as to what difference it might have made had Niebuhr, in fact, followed this intimation of an

129

alternative path to a theological voice. Nor have I read any serious discussion of how such a methodological move might have affected the subsequent doing of theology within the confines of the American academy.

Ironically, since the era of the two Niebuhrs, it is difficult to name a Christian male academic theologian in this country who actually has joined the poets in actively reimaging the contemporary meaning of Christian faith. To some extent, the ever more insular character of male-generated Protestant and Catholic theology in the United States during the second half of the twentieth century is foreshadowed in the reluctance of male theologians to seriously engage the possibility of genres of theological speech that embrace the creative and recreative dimensions of spiritual knowing. Since the late 1960s, the voices of most established theologians have been directed at asking whether and for whom theological reflection can be done. In fact, it may be said that if the work of those holding theological professorships in divinity schools is taken as the measure, Christian theology in the United States could be said to be much talked about but little done by professionals!

Most theological tomes written by university-based theological professors in the latter half of the twentieth century addressed questions of what if any justifications for theological discourse exist, whether there really are legitimate forms of theological utterance or any discursive substance to Christian theology. Methodological preoccupations have been the center of university-based discourses, and some have claimed that constructive statements as to what the meaning of the Christian theological message in our time and place might be, are possible. However, the truth is that in the corridors of institutions where professional theologians were being shaped, little reinterpretation emerged and practicing Christians ignored professional theology done in the academy. By the last decades of the century, practitioners of Christian theology seemed even to abandon dialogues with the philosophers, and few teaching in university-based institutions hazarded fresh ways of speaking of faith or conjuring its practice. Slowly but surely, attention turned to reiterating teaching familiar and comforting to the already convicted and ecclesially loyal Christian, and interest in public impact of any sort was lost.

All of this took place at a historical moment when, for many within the academy, Christian faith claims were losing plausibility and becoming increasingly suspect on epistemic grounds. Frequently, the well educated, including those raised in liberal Christian traditions, ceased the practice of Christianity, and within the churches, denominational piety became increasingly cut off from public culture. As the churches became more privatized, the focus within that public world shifted toward a culture-wide preoccupation with enhancing human material existence. Ardor for constructing a post-World War II liberal society came to the center of political and economic life. H. Richard Niebuhr's musings notwithstanding, what Martin Rumscheidt describes in *The Theology of Dorothee Soelle* as "theo-poetics" did not emerge among male academic theologians. That methodological development had to await the advent of the powerful theo-poetics of the woman whom Rumscheidt elegantly celebrates.

It is not too much to say that Dorothee Soelle was the earliest and most distinctive reconstructive voice to emerge in an era in which European culture began to experience a profound sense of displacement and cultural decentering. As the twentieth century entered its sixth decade and debates over the "death of God" were taking shape in Europe and North America, Soelle emerged as the first of what would become a panoply of new liberationist voices. As a European voice, she acknowledged the huge cultural shift that these discussions about God-talk signaled, but she used this cultural rupture to reimage and restate the meaning of Christ for our time, thereby proposing a fresh conception of the theological task in a world in which traditionalist theism had become problematic for some very legitimate reasons.

Few have recognized the significance of Soelle's work methodologically, especially her pioneering reconception of the way theology must now be done in this deeply changed world, one where no single cultural *episteme* can serve to ground truths that can be abstracted from specific histories and cultures. Making a profound theological shift, Soelle voiced Christian memory and hope in concrete and nonimperialistic terms. Christian theology in the present moment can profit by revisiting her theoretical assumptions because she found ways of affirming wisdom out of Christian tradition, not by treating tradition as fixed and established treasure but rather as memory of origin and awareness of human vocation, on the one hand, and as source of an indestructible dream of possibilities not yet realized, on the other. What Soelle did parallels exactly what the Jewish lesbian feminist poet Adrienne Rich has described as the role spiritual tradition plays in orienting us to the source of our strength and the direction in which we elect to move into the future. The similarity between Soelle's moves and the manner specified by Rich for reclaiming her own religious tradition should not surprise us, for Rich, one of the greatest poets of the American cultural tradition, embraced the power of poetic imagination as a challenge to imperial and dominant modes of patriotism. In Rich's words, spiritual identity enables awareness of "from whence our strength comes" and "with whom our lot is cast."[2] But of course, for Soelle to find her way to a form of liberative religious speech was far more difficult than for Rich, because for Soelle, the powerful history of the Christian-legitimated triumphalism of German Christianity had intervened. For her, any reclaiming of Christian ways of speaking could have integrity only after a blunt facing of ongoing Christian complicity in evil and a radical reorientation of one's current political practice as a clear evidence of genuine repentance. Among German political theologians, Soelle was singularly insistent in demanding a new form of ecclesial practice. The "political night prayer" movement, which she helped to found and continuously participated in, was testimony that a different practice was a nonnegotiable condition of truthful religious speech. Theology that conjures hope when there is no hope, positive aspiration when that is called for, and steely critique and resistance to "what is" when that is what is needed, is possible only as part of an active public practice of resistance.

Soelle was, then, the first of many to give voice to a genuinely praxis-oriented theology, what she called Christian "*Phantasie.*" But *Phantasie* for her is not merely an imaginative act but rather a fully political and publicly engaged way to live one's life. That what the latter affirmed turned out to be very much akin to the way Rich later reenvisaged the meaning of Jewish tradition as she reembraced it as her own living spirituality should not surprise us. Both of these superb poets place a biblical moral tradition of right relationship and justice making at the center of what any memory of origin requires. And both stand in adamant opposition to all established power that resists inclusive visions of justice.

The constructive Christian theology done in the late twentieth century by Soelle, other radical feminists, and other liberation theologians was authored by those whose spiritual concerns stand in deep variance to traditional ones, and whose interests are not focused on the justificatory preoccupations so central to theology done for the churches or within the academy. Soelle's books were sold not to professional peers but to an educated and politically concerned lay readership. Hers was a public theological voice, perhaps the first genuinely public theologian in the postmodern era.

My colleague at Union, Professor Christopher Morse, once remarked, after a research trip to Germany, that he had heard a young German graduate student say that he and his peers read Soelle for the same reason that earlier young Germans had read Martin Luther. Like Luther, this student remarked, Soelle was reshaping German language and culture even as she spoke. Her small books were found not only in academic bookstores but wherever a reading public shopped. How unlike her male theological contemporaries!

What is noteworthy is that the movement of Christian theology into this work of *Phantasie*, or what some others called utopian envisagement, would not have occurred without a deep discontent with the way the various Christian traditions had been articulating contemporary theological claims. It was their varied rejection of established theological norms that won a fresh hearing for liberative theologies, including the German movement of "political theology" with which Soelle is associated and in which she stands out in terms of cultural impact.[3] Within conventional theological institutions, the lack of excitement I have already alluded to was fed by the fact that those in charge were deeply aligned with the directions in which dominant social, political, and cultural life was moving. By contrast, Soelle's work was distinctive in the lucidity of its articulation of the dangers of the established religious landscape.

SOELLE'S IMPACT ON MY OWN WORK

I remember very clearly the impact of Soelle's early work on me. It may be difficult for contemporary readers to imagine the scene as the 1950s receded and to sense the despair that began to pervade professional theological faculties at the time. The immediate postwar period had been a time of heady optimism for liberal Protestantism, then widely celebrated as contributing wisdom to the public culture that had made the "good war" against fascism successful. Faced in the

1960s with sudden awareness that all was not well in Protestantism, and that something like a collective depression had descended, I picked up Soelle's work more out of curiosity than expectation. I was astonished at the fresh energy that reading her evoked. It is not too much to say that it rekindled anew my own intellectual pilgrimage. Having only recently committed to traveling the path of professional theology, I felt both relief and elation when I read, and then reread, both *Christ the Representative* and *Political Theology*.

Truth to tell, my decision two years earlier to concentrate my work in Christian ethics, rather than on what we at Union Seminary call systematic theology, had been made self-consciously out of a growing sense that the entire theological project was in crisis. By the end of my first year of graduate study, it had become clear to me that the theological guild I had expected to join was in very deep trouble indeed. Listening to ongoing discussions of a number of books on the "death of God" made me aware of the deep defensiveness, even resentment, toward critical challenge felt by academic theologians, including a number of my own teachers and their peers in sister institutions. Sensing the urgent need for new critical perspectives, I embraced social ethics and opted to give priority to ongoing social analysis, thereby shifting the focus of my work away from theology as such. My own interest in critical social analysis, I realized, would enable me to address living social ills in ways that would not depend on the persuasiveness of particular theological claims about God-talk. It became ever more obvious to me that the need to address the tangible and growing social suffering and growing social problems deserved priority. My own vocation to the continuing moral formation of communities that called themselves Christian was work that had to be done, whatever happened within Christian theology.

It was reading Soelle, then, that restored my confidence that there was a constructive role for Christian God-talk in the present. There was, I realized, a vital function for Christian theology in the deeply changing and shifting intellectual landscape of the 1960s. Even more important for my own agenda, I came to see that there was a genuinely critical role for Christian intellectuals to play, a role that no established male voice was proffering. These early years of my doctoral study had created a rather deeply felt distress in me about how often liberal theologians reiterated calls for "critical thinking," and yet how infrequently they actually said anything that really was critical of reigning social convention. By contrast, Soelle's work resonated in my hearing, with new insight about the spiritual malaise of the culture of which I was a part. As it subsequently turned out, it would be Dorothee Soelle and other "unnatural" speakers from the cultural worlds that constituted the "underside of history"[4] who collectively moved the theological task onto a new path of reimaging a not yet realized *Phantasie* of hope and resistance, not out of a traditionalist certitude but rather out of the fragments of faith remembered by those who had struggled for new possibilities in the past. The work of theology, it became clear, was not primarily explanatory, the creation of justifications for the way things are, but rather an evocative task, a calling forth of energy and power to struggle against spiritual entrapment. This revisioning of the world aimed to equip us with the courage and passion to struggle toward what is not yet and resist what is death dealing. Such a reorientation to what is the proper work of the theologian was indeed good news to my ears!

For me, learning to actually participate in the fuller unfolding of this way of doing theology, of moving beyond theological reflection as a "mere" effort to uncover positive knowledge, took some time. When my own students asked me why I did not give more constructive attention to theology itself, I often said, with some truthfulness, that I was insufficiently the poet and left the invocations of hope to the Soelles, the Heywards, the Williamses, the Gutierrezes, and others whose poetic conjuring abilities exceeded my own.[5] Yet in time, my own theological voice was reshaped by the breaking open of imagination that these colleagues elicited. I am not speaking with hyperbole when I say that Soelle's voice was primal in my own recovery of theological hope and helped me understand that theological utterance is a form that courage takes in situations in which despair is the easier course.

THE IMPORTANCE OF READING SOELLE THROUGH POSTMODERNIST EYES

I have reiterated my reasons for celebrating Soelle's place in contemporary theology to make clear her methodological discontinuity with the generation of Protestant theologians who preceded her. This seems important to me, in part, because for some, including some contemporary feminist theologians in the academy, Soelle's work is sometimes perceived as standing more in continuity with the cultural traditions of German male-generated theology than with postmodernist sensibilities. While many Roman Catholic feminists have engaged her work seriously, perhaps because of the impact of political theology in Catholic circles, too few Protestant feminists have focused attention on her work. By contrast, I believe that it is essential to interpret Soelle's theological stance so that she can be seen clearly as a groundbreaker within the development of postmodernist theological discourses. She pioneered in finding a way to articulate Christian meaning concretely, in a climate in which there was no abstract, "scientific," or privileged epistemic standpoint. She should be credited as one who found her way by doing the work of faithful speaking when the very possibility of affirmative theological utterances was very much in doubt. As she herself has stressed, and as her earliest published works attested, Soelle understood and accepted from the outset that traditionalist transcendentalist epistemic claims were passé, and that any direct access to theistic transcendentalism was no longer intellectually tenable. For her, Christian integrity required surrendering noetically privileged claims to truth. The contestability of theological ways of construing life is presumed, and moral practice is the measure of the integrity of theological speech. It is the power of theological utterance to illumine the depth dimensions of life that commend it to listeners, not the power of Christian cultural tradition per se.

For her, as I have already stressed, the cultural domination of Christianity is a problem to faithfulness, not an advantage to those who desire a living faith.

This surely was the import of her way of reformulating Christology. Her way of making sense of Jesus as Christ-bearer situates his significance in the fully human life-world, and in a way that is spiritually immanent in that world, a point that Carter Heyward makes clear.[6] Christ "the representative" is one who holds open a place in time and history that enables historical movement toward human fulfillment, especially of those who have not counted in the dominant historical scripts. What is essential to appreciate is Soelle's unqualified acceptance of the necessity of indirect address to transcendence through immanent spirituality. Hers is a transcendence found in radical humanism and in embrace of the concrete particularity of the created order of things. There is no pie in the sky for Soelle. Faith is the ability to see divine presence with us in a way that deepens our communal struggles for life. Faith enables a godly, reverent humanism. At the same time, Soelle shaped a powerful critique of reigning theological liberalism, a critique hardly noticed by her contemporaries.

SOELLE'S CRITIQUE OF LIBERALISM

In evaluating Soelle's theological contribution, it is also of particular importance not only to observe but especially to emphasize how distinctive this criticism is and how it differs from the endless accusations made against liberalism in the current academy. The current assault on liberalism bears the stamp of the present reactionary climate of neoliberalism. Liberalism is chastised ad nauseam for its failure to repeat Christian teaching in a sufficiently pristine traditionalist guise.

Soelle, by comparison, noted the privatizing and personalistic subjectivism in the way liberals specified the arena in which faith operated. Contrary to the endless charges that liberalism compromised dangerously with modernity, Soelle located the problem in acquiescence to power and privilege and capitulation to spiritual privatization. This limiting of the spheres of spirituality to inwardness was itself a massive form of acquiescence to domination. Locating theological meaning only in the psychological dimension was the form that obeisance to existing power took.

Her brilliant critique of her own teacher, Rudolf Bultmann, makes clear that the way forward for a progressive spirituality must avoid the subjectivism of interpreting Christian truth exclusively as a matter of personal transformation. To my mind, her analysis of the limits of Bultmann's psychologizing of theology deserves to stand as one of the most important constructive theological texts of the twentieth century.[7] And it must be conceded that just such spiritual subjectivism has continued to characterize mainline liberal theology over most of the intervening years. Political theology, in Soelle's rendering of it, must always be interpreted as a protest against personalistic reductionism and as a way of construing the irreducibly public meaning of faith.

As post-World War II attention began to shift toward a radical interdependence of nation-states created by the political-economic hegemony of postwar capitalism, Soelle remained mindful of the dangers of these privatizing tendencies. She saw them as parallel to the failures of German Christianity under Nazism. Any embrace of a statist authoritarian theology, she believed, extended anti-Judaism and what Soelle never ceased to name as "Christofascism," a reality she believed is alive and well in our present theological scene. She resisted more deeply than any of her contemporaries the strong tendencies of churchly Christianity to embrace the status quo in our current context.

An unapologetic leftist, she rejected the Cold War ideology that increasingly came to pervade Christian teaching, a tendency to conflate spirituality with matters deeper and higher than politics, a reading that made postwar theological liberalism congenial to and welcomed by cold warriors. At a time when personal piety rather than the address of public issues supported the reigning anticommunist stance, Soelle's work cut against the grain and began to offer a genuine alternative to the Eurocentrism of the dominant worldview.

No doubt it was her intense and searing awareness of the German Christians' earlier complicity in Nazism that sharpened her hermeneutical suspicions of any form of triumphalism in theology and also provided her with an especially clear and critical awareness of the role Christian intellectuals should play. No one should miss this point crucial to Soelle's political theology—any methodology that addresses personal well-being apart from the transformation of historically based communal well-being reinforces the dominant and dominating patterns of existing reality.

It is essential, then, to situate Soelle's work in the contestations that began in the Vietnam era and that continue until today. Vietnam represented the first occasion when the signs of resistance to Eurocentric cultural hegemony began to take definite political shape. Looked at in this light, it becomes clear that the "death of God" discussions emergent in Europe and in the United States were, in fact, initial cultural responses that foreshadowed and manifested a response to this decentering of the Western, Eurocentric worldview.

Since the death-of-God discussions of the late 1950s and 1960s have been more caricatured than analyzed in the interim, it is important to revisit them, not as a symptom of "liberal theological superficiality," as they are often construed in today's neoliberal theological climate, but rather as a sign that the wider social dislocations caused by Euro-American economic and political imperialisms were beginning to register.[8] Such resistance to these powerful imperializing changes has only increased, not ceased, in the meanwhile. As we assess developments in the interim, it is especially necessary to see the connection between such resistance and all that is specified by the virulent anti-Americanism that we now designate as "terrorism." Failure to see this point may make discerning and honest Christian reading of the current political scene not only difficult but actually impossible. I have long agreed with my former colleague Tom Driver that the 1960s must be remembered as a genuine cultural watershed, when the first signs of the blindness to other cultures that Euro-American intellectual hegemony was generating began to become visible on a global scale.[9] Since then, Euro-American cultures have shown many signs of internal struggle, including tensions between those who seek to reassert an uncritical Western cultural supremacy and those willing to learn what it means to reimage European and North American traditions as but one strand of a far more complex and inclusive planetary cultural diversity.

It is this awareness, with its openness to discover and employ less imperialistic modes of communal self-understanding, that should be foremost in our minds when we ask what constitutes the best in those developments we term "postmodernism." The death-of-God conversations signaled the need to acknowledge this cultural shift, and those like Soelle who searched for more modest and more concrete forms of theological speech created a "testimonial voice" in which Christian theology called us to and evoked a deeper humanity and an ongoing solidarity with real suffering in our actual historical moment.

KEEPING A GENUINELY CRITICAL POSTMODERNIST OPTION ALIVE AMID REACTIONARY POLITICS

The reason it is vitally important to situate alternative liberationist voices, including Soelle's, on the postmodernist side of the modern/postmodern continuum is precisely because of the growing reactionary trend already alluded to within Western and non-Western cultures—that trend I have referred to here as neoliberalism. When references are made, as they frequently are these days, to growing political conservatism, it is really the triumph of neoliberalism to which people refer. But neoliberalism is neither conservatism in the concrete form that conservatism took in the Western past, nor is it in any serious sense a reassertion of traditionalism, though a nostalgic embrace of traditionalism may make frightened religious folk feel safe in light of the deep and massive changes occurring. The triumph of neoliberalism is due to the massive and successful redefining of the terms of public debate accomplished in the Reagan-Bush-Bush2 era. Even the ethos of centrist and chastened liberalism that the Clinton political interim created must not be read as anything more than a temporary interlude, a slowing down rather than a reversal of the triumph of the new ideology.

Its intellectual trump card has been its success in convincing intellectual elites that the need for ideology is, in fact, dead. Ironically, the deadliest of Western political ideologies has turned out to be the one that proclaims that ideology is no longer necessary, that we have transcended the vagaries of politics through the triumph of capitalist modes of production, unleashed from the interference of the contentious debates that political interests interject. What politicians cannot accomplish can be left to the wisdom of "free" market exchange, in which mechanisms of efficiency and rationality prevail. The new neoliberal reaction—proclaiming a triumph of markets over politics as the way forward in human problem solving—has mounted an extraordinarily successful reinterpretation of history in which the intrinsic good of capitalist political economy can now be seen by all who possess a responsible concern for human well-being. Even more astonishing is neoliberal success in dramatically reorienting public dialogue and debate so as to erase public awareness of the existence of any genuinely left-wing dissent about the future of political economy and public policy. Alternatives to capitalism have become truly unthinkable.

In addition, the New Right has launched a remarkably effective disinformation campaign against any remaining liberation movements, a campaign that depicts progressive political agendas for change as passé or even as misguided efforts at social engineering. A continuous assault is being made on groups that propose strategies for social justice. Those who want social change are characterized as self-righteous "do-gooders" who traffic in moralistic attempts to enforce "political correctness."[10] These attacks have worked well in silencing liberals. Neoliberals have succeeded, to a distressing degree, in creating a widespread contempt for prodemocratic politics, especially in academic contexts. An atmosphere of thinly veiled intolerance prevails in the academy whenever the subject of politics is up, but most important, any criticism of capitalist political economy, as such, is taken as a symptom of an outdated worldview forged by the ideologies of the Cold War era. The end of ideology, we should be aware, is really the elimination of discourses seriously critical of capitalism.

It is because of this intellectual climate, itself the result of the new conditions of "masked ideology," that we may well characterize the contemporary political scene as what, two decades ago, Bertram Gross termed "friendly fascism."[11] We must recover the capacity to read liberation theologies, including especially Soelle's political theology, as "first wave" postmodernist Christian theological reflection, which we must continue to hone and craft in ever new, constructive directions. To do so makes it obvious that the road ahead permits no abandonment of the concrete justice agendas that have engaged activist Christians in the immediate past. Any destabilizing of the agendas of anti-white-racist work, sexual and gender justice, or resistance to poverty and class oppression is capitulation to neoliberalism. Refusal of these critical agendas is never the result of greater awareness of complexity and cultural sophistication. It is capitulation to the powers that are in place.

All of this is difficult to see, in part, because in the last decade of the twentieth century, the enthusiasm for being a postmodernist has gained standing in the various academic guilds while historical amnesia has eroded awareness of why postmodernism matters from a moral point of view. In short, the rhetoric about postmodernism has become thoroughly academized and far too fashionable for our own good. Those who can remember what historical amnesia is about should be deeply concerned about the losses of critical consciousness that all such amnesia entails.

As a result, in some contemporary literary hermeneutical circles, rhetorical cleverness has become a substitute for serious moral-political analysis. And a rather thin and clever, and largely apolitical, sort of "modernist" postmodernism has appeared, generating its own highly technical style accessible only to academic in-groups. Because postmodernism presumes a social constructionist awareness that our history is created by us even as it is being named, the creative power of the activity of human speech has sometimes been embraced as though radical ways of speaking were themselves the heart of political change. The result is precisely the loss of the intrinsically social character of human species-being that radical social theory was shaped to protect.

The entire European radical social theoretical tradition, what is known as *critical theory*, aimed to correct bourgeois misrepresentation of human species-being as possible apart from forms of political life and social cooperation. All of the movements of critical theory that arose in Europe in resistance to the earlier rise of fascism were born out of respect for the moral value of human political construction, but the conception of politics was fulsome, involving the creation of new alliances and forms of community. Today, among the new literati, the sense of the political has become attenuated. Human speech-acts, important as an aspect of social change, now sometimes become the central metaphor for all historical action. It sometimes seems, in reading youthful postmodernism, that the authors actually believe that revolutions take place in classrooms and that acts of verbal violence are of the same moral magnitude as long-standing, institutionally embodied injustice.[12] Ironically, today, the most elegant postmodernist discourses can participate in the privatizing, subjectivizing, and depoliticizing of all truth claims in precisely the way Soelle's work specified as one of the dangers of liberalism. Furthermore, the reduction of politics to verbal performance goes hand in hand with an increasing cynicism about morality itself, a cynicism that leads to a subjective rereading of and dismissal of the significance of morality. The result is a new quietism about political and economic reconstruction that exquisitely serves a triumphant neoliberalism.

Even so, for most spiritually engaged postmodernists, the fact that the social world is a human moral construction still continues to deepen the moral seriousness and carefulness of our actions and choices. Social constructionism enables us to see what is at stake in the way we enact our social morality because it is now clear historically that, over time, we will be stuck with the sort of world that we, in fact, embody or conjure. From this viewpoint, the morality we shape is the true measure of our spirituality. However, as noted, when creativity for its own sake displaces moral seriousness, enthusiasm for postmodernism can lead to the sort of moral relativism that sees morality merely as taste or arbitrary personal preference.[13] It has become fashionable among younger academics to pooh-pooh any moral seriousness or any attempt to ground morality in shared values. Among a few postmodernist cultural critics, any effort at reconstructive religious and moral discourse has come to be suspect simply as such.

It is this moral relativism, even moral myopia, which Soelle and her husband, Fulbert Steffensky, criticized in their recent discussion of postmodernism.[14] It would be a serious mistake, however, to read this essay as any sort of indication that Soelle was moving into a more traditionalist theological voice. Her recent concerns about an uncritical postmodernism must be situated not in a traditionalist voice but in her growing worries about the success of neoliberal cultural reformation and about the increasing power of the dominant political economy to erase concrete historical memories and to desensitize us both to the reality of social sin and to the need to actively resist social evil.

THE IMPORTANCE OF REREADING POLITICAL THEOLOGY IN THE CONCRETE CONTEXT OF GERMAN CRITICAL THEORY

What many young intellectuals on this side of the Atlantic seem to have forgotten, or perhaps, given the current cultural preferences for French intellectual guidance rather than German, have never fully grasped, is the continued relevance of the intellectual project that the critical theory tradition addressed. Its efforts aimed at the failures of the political left itself and at the need to find more creative cultural strategies for change, and in particular to discern better, more humane ways to shape a genuinely democratic culture. The German experience of fascism exposed the terrible failures of processes of personal identity formation within that society. What sort of cultural life, the critical theorists asked, would sustain a community in the process of struggling toward genuine social equality? In particular, German critical thinkers searched for a social theory that not only illumined class formation through the workings of political economy—long the goal of Marxist and neo-Marxist work—but also sought to make greater sense of the political apathy and preferences for the status quo that characterized those who lived and labored in capitalist culture. It was chiefly the lack of political resistance to destructive practices within capitalist societies that needed to be better understood. Trying to account for the political and cultural complacency of Germans and their willingness to endure socially generated inequality was what led German critical thinkers to begin their reexamination of religion.

A few, including the younger Tillich and several Jewish philosophers, set out to develop a genuinely critical religion that addressed these concerns and that aimed at discernment of the spiritual depth of their culture and the unmasking of its social untruths. However, the first generation of German critical theorists survived, if they did so, only by going into exile in the United States.[15] Soelle was among a very few in the subsequent generation who survived the demise of Nazism to place her work on the path staked out by critical theory. It is remarkable that she resumed the path of struggle toward a newly critical religious perspective, given that those best known on this side of the Atlantic for extending critical theory were German social philosophers who not only remained hostile to religion but greatly reduced the explicit political commitments that had informed the earlier theory.[16]

Neither Soelle nor liberation theologians who emerged elsewhere have followed German or U.S. academics in abandoning the quest for a critical religion or spirituality that would play a role in unmasking social mystification and create culturally potent religious rituals and practices that would make truthful political consciousness possible. Today, in advanced capitalist societies, there exists the same reluctance to reject political leadership that disparages their interests. Political quietism abounds, making any struggle for alternatives seem futile. The same refusal to enhance conditions for their own personal and communal well-being that stunned the first generation of critical theorists in Germany prevails here as well. And the serious failures of political progressives to create spiritual enthusiasm for genuinely democratic changes continues among us also.

It was the power of capitalist culture to mesmerize, to create uncritical loyalty, that German intellectuals observed through the rising power of Nazism. Their entire intellectual project was shaped by a passion to effectually address the spiritual value of democracy. Their suspicions of the power of capitalism to disempower resistance and to mystify its antidemocratic directions during economic crisis are what led German critical theorists to make religious critical reflection central in the work of social reconstruction. Can a seriously postmodernist perspective, one that accepts the decentering of Eurocentric abstract rationalism, afford to abandon these concerns so central to critical theory?

Perhaps it was the utter crassness of the Nazi-generated Eurocentric fantasy of the so-called Aryan myth, a version of racial supremacy vulgar to the more highly educated gaze of U.S. intellectuals, that makes it hard to read the parallels between our situation and earlier German fascism. As the quest for a genuinely critical theory gave way to the more muted academic, and less politically urgent, voice of Jürgen Habermas, the urgency of the task of demystifying social reaction has receded.

The truth is that the present spiritual hegemony of what economic historians sometimes designate as late/transnational capitalist political economy has actually been even more successful at obscuring growing social injustice than earlier German critical social theory feared that capitalism would be. We live today in a situation in which we can readily observe the social construction of apolitical human identity, and the spiritual malaise of social forgetfulness manifests itself all around us. The death of politics is proclaimed as the advent of harmony and the automatic progress of market wealth production, a wealth production that assures the triumph of cultural harmony and the nearly inevitable improvement of the human condition. Never mind that many voices warn of impending catastrophe in environmental degradation, that the scope and scale of human suffering created by the way the political economy itself functions is documented daily. There probably has never been a time in U.S. history when dissent from loyalty to existing political order would be met with more violent, or at least vituperative, reaction.

Dorothee Soelle's life work eloquently attests that participation in and collusion with any form of social amnesia is a most devastating form of evil. She lived her life in adamant refusal of any triumphalist rereading of Christian doctrinal supremacy, letting no one who bears the self-designation "Christian" forget the genocidal consequences of the self-satisfied and self-assured theological voice. But it is not only the rereading of Soelle's personal work that is at stake in the way we position her legacy. Even more importantly, all of the ongoing work of constructive Christian theology will suffer if we fail to see the concrete shape that her work and that of others have laid out as the proper direction of authentic postmodernism. We need urgently to interpret all of the recent theological labor done in the service of suffering and silenced communities as the best exemplifications of postmodernist Christian discourses. Black, Latin American, African, and Asian male theologians; feminist and womanist voices from every community; gay, lesbian, and transgendered truth tellers of every culture; and indigenous voices everywhere must be counted as important expressions of Christian postmodernist theological speech.

Whatever criticisms can be made of liberation theologies of the first wave—and in my view, much needs to be criticized—all liberation theologians are engaged thinkers for whom theological discourse is unapologetically a species of contestable and contextual language. And all such speech aims not chiefly at understanding that world but at reshaping that world spiritually.

Though old habits of definitive authoritative voice die hard, especially among male liberation theology speakers, liberation vocalizations have aimed not at positive knowledges legitimated through Eurocentric cultural hegemony but at the critical knowledge of understanding the "lies, secrets, and silences" that keep power in place. This can enable us to imagine a future, to avoid being locked into the naturalized "scripts" contained in the dominant prescriptions of what our futures must be. The point is important precisely because among far too many academics in major theological centers, liberation theologies have been treated with something bordering on contempt, as fads, or more recently, as "overly ideological" perspectives lacking in appropriate intellectual elegance and creativity. Far too many contemporary U.S. theologians seem unaware of the maldistribution of intellectual tools and resources that support the "elegance" of the work that we are able to do at the center of the global system as opposed to those working in poverty, without those resources.

While liberation theologies have deeply reshaped some seminary programs and a few other arenas of pastoral education, university-based discourses have become increasingly oriented to critique or deconstruction of ecclesial claims. In many religious studies contexts, theology itself has come to be viewed exclusively as a form of ideological mystification, and the role of the intellectual who studies religion has been cast, more and more, merely as deconstructive. There is no problem, per se, with deconstructive work, but the political currents outlined here make such fixations on critique dangerous to our public spiritual health, although deconstructive critique is a safe course in universities and colleges being pressured to move in a neoliberal direction. The directions of the theological work that we are called to do in the future requires that we continue to walk the road of justice makers who are also truth tellers. Like Dorothee, we must be unapologetically in love with life and angry at all that inhibits creatures from experiencing the joys and pleasures of abundant life, or living as godly lovers who know the ecstasy of being with the Divine Companion.

Notes

1. H. Richard Niebuhr, "How My Mind Has Changed," in *How My Mind Has Changed*, ed. Harold Fey (New York: Vantage Books, 1962), 69–80.
2. Adrienne Rich, *Your Native Land, Your Life: Poems* (New York: W. W. Norton & Co., 1986), 3–6; see also Rich, *On Lies, Secrets, and Silence: Selected Prose, 1966–1978* (New York: W. W. Norton & Co., 1979).
3. Dorothee Soelle, *Christ the Representative: An Essay in Theology after the "Death of God"* (Philadelphia: Fortress Press, 1967); see also her *Political Theology* (Philadelphia: Fortress Press, 1974).
4. The phrase is widely used in liberation theologies rooted in Latin America. It originated first in the writing of extraordinary Peruvian theologian Gustavo Gutierrez in his *A Theology of Liberation* (Maryknoll, N.Y.: Orbis Books, 1971).
5. I cite those theological writers whose work has been most influential in helping me understand the importance of the methodological shift I am celebrating here: Dorothee Soelle, Carter Heyward, Delores Williams, Gustavo Gutierrez.
6. See Carter Heyward, "Crossing Over: Dorothee Soelle and the Transcendence of God," in *The Theology of Dorothee Soelle*, ed. Sarah K. Pinnock (Harrisburg, Pa.: Trinity Press International, 2003), 221–38.
7. See Soelle, *Political Theology*, 83–98.
8. The term *neoliberal* here denotes social theorists who endorse the claim that "free markets" actually exist and constitute the "essence" of capitalism. Furthermore, they contend that government interference and state intervention in "the economy" should be avoided. It is a post-Keynsian version of laissez-faire theory, which claims a positivist status as the only true "objectivist social science."
9. Tom Faw Driver, Paul Tillich Professor Emeritus at Union Theological Seminary in New York, was the first Christian theologian in the United States to identify the importance of this cultural decentering. It is also relevant to notice that Soelle was perhaps the first theologian to regularly do her theological work cross-culturally, writing in two languages and working and teaching not only in Europe and North America but from time to time in Latin America.
10. See the important study by Richard Feldstein, *Political Correctness: A Response to the Cultural Left* (Minneapolis: University of Minnesota Press, 1997).
11. See Bertram Gross, *Friendly Fascism: The New Face of Power in America* (New York: M. Evans, 1980).
12. I detect a tendency toward such depoliticizing in the recent work of feminist philosopher Judith Butler. She sometimes seems to me to reduce human activity to creative speech-acts. She also seems to me to distinguish insufficiently between personal violence in the form of hostile and demeaning speech-acts and violence of a collective and institutionalized sort. Bombs and weapons are, morally, even more heinous than verbal abuse. See Judith Butler, *Excitable Speech* (New York: Routledge, 1997).
13. Notions about the social construction of morality do not necessarily lead to the conclusion that morality is capricious and lacking in any intersubjective objectivity. Cultural relativism, while requiring us to develop more sophisticated ways of legitimating moral claims, does not vitiate the validity of well-formed moral claims. Moral relativism is not the same as scientific or cultural relativity.
14. See Dorothee Soelle and Fulbert Steffensky, *Zwietracht in Eintracht: ein Religionsgespräch* (Zurich: Pendo Verlag, 1996).
15. Tillich's collaboration with other critical theorists is reflected in his earliest work, for example, *The Socialist Decision*, trans. Franklin Sherman (New York: Harper & Row, 1977). It is important to remember that Tillich became more reluctant to engage political and economic issues directly after he emigrated to this country. It

should be noted that Soelle's encounter with critical theory came through the influence of Ernst Bloch and Hannah Arendt. See the preface of Soelle's *Against the Wind: A Memoir of a Radical Christian* (Minneapolis: Fortress Press, 1999), xi.

16. In the United States, German critical theory is understood through the contemporary work of Jürgen Habermas. To some extent, reading critical theory through Habermas also results in a depoliticizing of that tradition. Habermas became far less focused on praxis and more oriented toward reconstructing theory after the 1960s. He also is far less interested in religion and cultural change than some of the earlier critical theorists. For a reliable account of critical theory, see Trent Schroyer, *The Critique of Domination: The Origins and Development of Critical Theory* (New York: George Braziller, 1973). A further reliable source on the implications of critical theory in relation to feminist theology is Marsha Hewitt, *Critical Theory of Religion* (Minneapolis: Fortress Press, 1995).

Chapter 16

Working with Protestant Traditions: Feminist Transformations

Interview by Marilyn J. Legge

Legge: *You have long insisted that the significance of women's praxis (reflection and action) in theological education and in wider social struggles must be carefully situated in the historical context in which women have needed to act. You have also insisted that the vision and courage of these women should not be forgotten, even where their situations differ greatly from our own.*

Harrison: We have now what I call the thirty-five-year tradition of feminist and womanist contributions to theology and to social ethics. I think what has been accomplished is astonishing.

Alas, however, this tradition still hasn't made its way into the syllabi in most doctoral programs, although it's everywhere studied in the seminaries, I'm happy to say. This tradition is a remarkable development, standing at the intersection of liberation and liberal Christian theology and ethics. The loss of these new and creative ideas, if the Bushwhackers (as I call the present leadership of the United States)[1] have their way, will be tragic. They will have killed something of incredible spiritual power.

Legge: *Three essays in part 2 draw on your work of recasting Protestant theo-ethical traditions with explicit acknowledgment of foremothers and sisters, such as Nelle*

Morton, Letty Russell, and Dorothee Soelle. Do you have further comments to make on how the work and struggles of any of these women have particularly informed your own feminist transformations of religious social ethics?

Harrison: Before I answer that question, I have one concern that I want readers to keep in mind as they proceed. Because of the way we have organized this book, my work here could be read as done only in a highly self-conscious Protestant denominational context. In the twenty-first century, with the well-orchestrated takeover of the United States by right-wing Christianity, we have become deeply re-denominationalized. Today Protestants, especially, are clinging to their little denominational tribes in fiercely fearful and somewhat arrogant ways. Younger readers probably won't even know that older women, postretirement age or even a decade younger, were, like me, raised and educated in a very ecumenical environment. Back in the 1950s, the professor who would become my beloved friend and mentor, John Bennett, would show up in his "intro" course carrying a new book by a Catholic scholar, and John would wax eloquent on the new day dawning in ecumenical theology. And one of my major research projects in my early graduate residency was a careful tracing of disputes within nineteenth-century Roman Catholicism over papal infallibility. To this day, my view of Roman Catholicism is informed by the theological views of its leading theologians of the nineteenth century, nearly all of whom rejected papal infallibility as a crass political power play by the Vatican.

I hope every reader of this book will remember that, from the beginning, feminist theology was ecumenical, and that I, like most Protestants, read Catholic feminists such as Mary Daly, Rosemary Ruether, and Elisabeth Schüssler Fiorenza as sisters in struggle. Feminist theologies were not, for us, denominational theologies, even though we accepted that we sometimes had historically traditional reasons for staying or leaving our traditions of origin. For example, I continue to embrace the Reformed Protestant tradition in some specific and important ways. To me the hallmark of that tradition is that "reformation" can never be once and for all. *Continuous reformation* is the proper work of theology. Nothing else is!

So, finally, in response to your question, let me say that the three Protestant sisters I have written about here should not be viewed as the only feminist theological voices I engaged, but rather as influential sisters with whom I traveled the hard road of feminist praxis, women who were deep sources of inspiration and courage. I never rank the people I love! Nelle Morton is a case in point. When I joined the Union Theological Seminary faculty, she was the only other female teaching in a seminary in the Northeast. I sought her out for that reason, and we became friends who occasionally talked on the phone, and as I recall it now, mostly when there was a crisis in our professional lives. (We gave each other hope by reminding each other of what turkeys men could be.) Nelle taught me patience about and awareness of how much resistance one would meet and also hope about how rapidly that resistance could turn into enthusiastic support. Thanks to her, I became much more relaxed about criticism from women; she helped me learn that strong opposition was often the first step in conversion. After Nelle retired, she and Anne McGrew Bennett, John's wondrous wife, became friends and collaborators. Anne was the first woman I ever knew who was a proud, unapologetic feminist, and my debt to her is inestimable.

Dorothee Soelle is distinctive in this group of Protestant sisters, because she was an intellectual influence through her books before she became a colleague and a friend. I say a lot about how her work influenced me in the preceding essay, so I won't say much more here except to observe that, like myself, she was an unqualified leftist who believed in economic democracy (i.e., socialism) and who had an active commitment, a praxis commitment toward that end. We both came to this understanding through the critical theory of the Frankfurt School, which continued Marx's critique of capitalism but also tried to go beyond the limitations of the objectivist, abstract worldview of orthodox Marxism and to grasp the psychology of oppression.

Also, as younger women, both Dorothee and I encountered the problem of how you rethink divine transcendence in an Einsteinian conception of the universe which exploded assumptions about separation and hierarchy. At this time, I was also influenced by Tom Driver's and Carter Heyward's reinterpretation of transcendence. Dorothee, Tom, and Carter all went beyond the idea of transcendence as any kind of supernaturalism. Instead, in their work you get to transcendence by going radically *into* the creative world, as Tom put it, or as Carter later expounded it by seeing that "transcendence is radical immanence."[2] The point is how to live in history in a way that includes a genuine spiritual connection with God and has real intellectual integrity. I think you can do that without assuming that you must start with God and move down to the human. I reject that old kind of revelational positivism which uncritically understands the Bible as revealed truth that you can then just apply as human truth. That door was long ago closed for me.

The other thing I appreciated about Dorothee was that she was prepared to embrace the humanistic perspective on Jesus, Jesus the man for others. She argued that you could make claims christologically, that is, about what is transhuman in Christ, only by going through the concrete, the historical, the human. I see Dorothee as, in many ways, the first postmodernist influence on my theology—that is, she helped me to rethink what it would mean to stay within broadly humanistic categories and not, if you will, reference a theological order that lets you escape the material world through hierarchical language about transcendence.

Letty Russell's impact on me was, like Nelle Morton's and Anne Bennett's, in the first instance, personal. Letty was the first functioning Presbyterian clergywoman whom I encountered. When I was in my first year in seminary, she was a staff member of the East Harlem Protestant Parish, and I am fairly sure that she was the first woman I heard preach or enact the sacraments. Her justice commitments and pastoral gifts touched me deeply. Our ways of doing theology differed, and I was always a bit amused that she, a Harvard graduate, and I, from Union, seemed to reverse roles—she was the transformative Barthian, while I was a more philosophical theologian. But from the beginning, I felt a deep rapport with her global political commitments concerning racism and economic justice. I thought of her as my mentor in global activism, and I still do. She is still busy doing international theological education, and in my opinion, no feminist has done more to spread the liberating passion of feminist transformation around the globe than Letty has!

Legge: *You've spoken often about opening up the kinds of discourse that count as "proper" theology and about your impatience with static and repetitious abstractions of much traditional theology. Often the imaginative alternatives you suggest are found in the work of feminist women. Say more about your abiding sense that all good theology is poetic.*

Harrison: The great poets often show us the justice imaginable, and women theologians are often poets. Three of the women who have been the most important feminist influences on my theology—Delores Williams, Carter Heyward, and Dorothee Soelle—are all poets *first of all*. They taught me to see theology as the poetry of the Christian life, the space where we articulate our pain and dreams. For me, theology doesn't begin by positing doctrinal truth from which you can deduce fixed intellectual conclusions. You don't begin with "true" language for God that is discursive and deductive and has all of the logical capacities of the languages of science. Rather theology is a kind of *bricolage*, where you patch together laments, visions, possibilities, dreams, hopes, and prayers. Theology gives us beliefs to be lived, connections that you must bet your life on. You find the speech, the words, that you dare to utter. It's very much that kind of impressionistic naming of what's possible that inspires us, that lures us and leads us on. There's always this suggestibility with theology; it is not a static or fixed form of truth.

I've always read Adrienne Rich's poetry as theology. She's taught me what I take to be the three most fundamental theological questions: With whom do I cast my lot? From where does my strength come? What must be changed?[3]

Legge: *Would you elaborate on the choice that you made to do Christian social ethics rather than theology? Are there significant differences in the ways you approach them?*

Harrison: Yes, I believe there is. Doing theology is a process of evaluating, healing, and perceiving. Doing ethics is orienting my actions to be effectual and graceful. Yet they shape and re-shape one another. In some ways, my focus on ethics rather than theology occurred for accidental and pragmatic reasons. Folks need to remember that I lived my whole professional career at Union, where there was already a division of labor established between the theologians and the ethicists. Teaching ethics shaped my priorities. Yet the truth is that I actually did most of my graduate residency, and the majority of my reading and work, in theology and theological ethics, though fortunately my reading in philosophy and the social sciences was extensive and enabled me to turn to social ethical analysis without strain. Happily, teaching graduate seminars helped me keep up and catch up in several areas. And after several years, I was able to teach feminist theology courses occasionally, which enabled me to keep up with the theological voices that had come to make the most sense to me—increasingly, of course, the voices of women.

This way of reconnecting, reengaging theology, and rethinking from the standpoint of actual practice doesn't happen very much. In social ethics one does better, I think, to work from the problem back to the theory, but you also have to keep the dialectic there—you have to reread the tradition continuously. So theological ethics is an ongoing process.

I think a lot of the problems that academic theologians have worried about are simply not real problems. For example, there's a lot of effort devoted to worrying about the authority of scripture. I found out what it means to write scripture when I gave my inaugural lecture at Union on the power of anger and the work of love. That piece took on authority. By the time I finished editing it for submission to the *Union Seminary Quarterly Review*, my original draft had already been translated into seven languages and I learned it was being quoted all over the world.[4] I realized that I had had *nothing* to do with how this text functioned, yet it literally *became scripture* in people's lives. My little essay had become a community-creating piece—that is, it created connections with others. So I came to understand that the so-called authority of scripture really was a *relationship*, a connection between the text and those persons who encounter in what the text conveys something that gives life, that uncovers a mystery that was hidden before, something that says "Aha, *this* is who I am; now I see my life differently." Scripture *becomes* sacred text to us by putting us in touch with stories of transformative sacred power.[5] This is a very different way of looking at what it is that makes a text spiritually authoritative and thus is also a very different way of looking at the so-called problem of scriptural authority. It sounds pretentious, but I have been in several countries, listening to groups of women explaining to others in their language who I am, and I will hear someone say the words in English—"anger" and "love" together—and I'll realize that I've become known as the "anger-love lady." I've written holy writ!

I have a similar sense about pseudoproblems when listening to the traditionalist's concerns about justifying God's existence. I have never understood why Christians are so threatened by disbelief and atheism. A long time ago I remember wondering, given all the enthusiasm for Whitehead's thought in recent Christian theology, why self-professed Whiteheadeans did not learn more from him and start where he started by situating knowledge in practices that produce that knowledge. To me, *Science and the Modern World* is his most transformative book. He helps us to see that we don't get knowledge from processes of proof. Mathematics and science are products of human creativity. When I read his *Process and Reality* I also noted a clear insistence that the purpose of the book was to do a thought experiment, to show that it was possible to "think God" in an Einsteinian world. We *can* think God. It's possible to imagine a constant, concrete universal. But that wasn't what Whitehead was interested in proving. He wanted to show theism was thinkable, rather than prove God exists. Like him, I am interested in life and the processes of life. He helped me suspend the problem of divine existence and get on with all the astonishing questions about what we, within the cosmic whole, are up to in our interactions with the universe. I decided I would just see where such openness led me. From these early musings on Whitehead's writings, and with the support of my favorite Whiteheadian theologian, and one of my most beloved teachers, Daniel Day Williams, I lost interest in questions about divine existence! God ceased to be a problem for me, and ever so slowly I became a *practicing* religious person, one who learned to love God, regardless. The Whiteheadian horizon I embraced put doctrine on the back burner and experiential adoration at the heart of my theology. Feminism as free-flowing spiritual envisioning and naming of divine disclosure as I experienced it provided the way forward in theological speaking.

Legge: *Let's keep talking about your work as a moral theologian. Can you comment more about your feminist theological work in relation to feminist ethics as, among other things, creative constructions of better ways of living together?*

Harrison: What I think I've learned is that there are quite different coteries of people interested in feminist ethics and in feminist theology. For example, there are a lot of religious studies faculty members within women's studies programs who are basically post-Christian in their spirituality. Many women's studies faculty don't know anything about what's happened in feminist theology within the various theological communities and they really couldn't care less. I think this is sad because the transformations that feminists have made in *all* religious traditions are worth knowing about, and feminist ritual practice is truly astonishing in almost every tradition, including transformations wrought in feminist Wiccan and other feminist earth religious movements. My hope is that feminist work in religious studies will come to model a new way of respecting and learning from each other religiously. Perhaps I am hopelessly utopian, but I would also like to see feminists address the dualistic split between the sacred and the secular. I am grateful to the Marxian tradition for teaching me to be sceptical and critical of any spirituality that lacks a historically oriented passion for political transformation, but my roots in religious tradition also make me aware of how thin and culturally barren are politics without mysticism. It has been one of the joys of my life that many once-secular feminist scholar-activists with whom I have worked over the years have returned to their spiritual roots through authentic immersion in the struggle for women's well-being. I am even surprised that I am surprised about this, since I have always taught that spiritual hope is born of struggle. But it is always a joy when something you have claimed as theological truth turns out to be true in your own life!

Legge: *How would you encourage us to continue working in feminist liberative theologies?*

Harrison: As I have already made clear here, I think more and more women work at theology as if it was the poetry of the Christian or other religious life and perceive it not so much as giving normative cognitive content about God, but as helping us to image a world in which the power of God is present and active. So I see theology not as "Let's get it right and then we can apply it to the earth in order to find out what to do" question, but rather as an ongoing process in which we name our hope, we celebrate it, we give praise for it, we sing it, and we move on. We name our way of imaging the world, but then we have to buckle down to the hard work of discerning and working for change. My bias is always on the side of organizing for change, and I sometimes suspect that forms of spirituality that shun the hard work of ethics are merely feminine, not feminist.

I should add that there are aspects of my own theology that are somewhat traditionalist. For example, I still do believe in sin and in divine grace as deliverance from sin. Why? Because I believe in radical evil. I also think we're very naive not to recognize and fear the kinds of dangers our own spiritual machinations create. I have a kind of Calvinist sense that evil is too serious to be laughed at or taken out of the picture. This means, therefore, that we also need the deepest, most profound notion of health, of deliverance, of well-being, that we can possibly get. Theological discourse is a serious way of talking about what's at stake in the cosmos, which concerns not only our life and our death but also the life and death of everything. There is something in much secularism that for me has the feel of "Let's pretend." Leaving out religious discourse omits a rich way of talking about the meaning and possibilities of our life. When I listen carefully to people I hear them returning to somewhat basic theological categories. I think there's something in the practice of the theological life which is persuasive to people who want to live life to the fullest. There's something about the love of God which generates the love of God, and there's something about doing the practice of the love of God that is really right on target for all of us. So we are called to do theology, but it is never a substitute for good socio-moral analysis. Mature spirituality requires both. Always both!

Notes

1. See also Molly Ivins and Lou Dubose, *Bushwhacked: Life in George W. Bush's America* (New York: Random House, 2003).
2. Tom F. Driver, *Patterns of Grace: Word of God as Human Experience* (New York: Harper & Row, 1971); Carter Heyward, "On Transcendence" in *Our Passion for Justice: Images of Power, Sexuality, and Liberation* (Cleveland: Pilgrim Press, 1984).
3. Adrienne Rich, *Your Native Land, Your Life: Poems* (New York: W. W. Norton & Co., 1986), 6.
4. This essay appears in Beverly Wildung Harrison, *Making the Connections: Essays in Feminist Social Ethics* (Boston: Beacon Press, 1985), 1–21. An earlier version was published in the *Union Seminary Quarterly Review* 36, Supplementary (1981).
5. See Carter Heyward, *Touching Our Strength: The Erotic as Power and the Love of God* (San Francisco: HarperCollins, 1989). Heyward is the only theologian I know who explicitly characterizes scriptural authority relationally.

Part Three

CHRISTIAN ETHICAL PRAXIS AND POLITICAL ECONOMY

Introduction

Pamela K. Brubaker and Rebecca Todd Peters

The final part of this collection offers the opportunity to examine Harrison's methodological approaches to Christian social ethics as she engages in a variety of conversations regarding issues of economic justice. What is evident in these pieces is her unwavering commitment to the theoretical task of challenging prevailing ideological positions that create injustice and her persistent participation in justice in the making. Harrison's dedication to balancing these two obligations exemplifies her own understanding of the tasks of the social ethicist as well as her own identification as a liberation theologian. For Harrison, the job of Christian social ethicists is not just to theorize about the problems of society but also to be actively engaged in our communities, our churches, and our world as we seek justice by working with and for those in the world who are the most marginalized. The essays in part 3 reflect Harrison's engagement in ongoing debates about political economy and her deep commitment to economic justice, which she envisions as genuine economic democracy. Her analysis has been particularly concerned about the mystification of economics and class reality in contemporary U.S. society as well as the erasure of the meaning of democracy as communal participation and inclusion in setting social priorities.[1]

In examining the theoretical basis of Harrison's work, we can see that she integrates several streams of intellectual theory: theological theories of historical Christian communities, moral theories of both Christian communities and the cultural and intellectual traditions integrated into them, and various streams of social theory. While it has already been noted that Harrison stands firmly within the traditions of feminism, Protestantism, and Christian realism, in this section she also engages Roman Catholic social teaching. She is unusual among Protestant Christian ethicists in her critical appreciation for both Catholic natural law tradition and social thought as sources of theological-ethical theory. Harrison has written that her own moral theology has more in common with a Catholic approach than with neo-orthodox ethics.[2] Although she is very critical of current Catholic social teaching on procreation and abortion, she thinks that the Catholic tradition is often "more substantive, morally serious, and less imbued with the dominant economic ideology" than the type of Protestant theological ethics "that claims biblical warrants for its moral norms."[3]

Harrison's engagement with social theory—the disciplines of human self-understanding perceived as separate from Christian theological-ethical theory—is of particular importance in these essays. She finds social theory to be crucial to accurately diagnose why problems exist and to evaluate "the seriousness of the moral dilemmas at hand." Her attention to the material reality of people's lives has generated a heightened awareness to the social problems of racism, classism, sexism, homophobia, and cultural imperialism that now mark much work in feminist social ethics.

Harrison's intellectual indebtedness to the Marxian tradition of social theory is evident in her political economic analysis throughout this section. It was her reading of class from the perspective of Marxian social theory that left Harrison feeling "like an outsider in the field." While Reinhold Niebuhr's critique of Marx has ruled within the guild of Christian ethics for several decades, Harrison challenges Niebuhr's negative evaluation of Marx. She claims that Niebuhr crucially misread Marx by interpreting his position as a critique of private property and not of private ownership and control of the means of production.[4] Harrison contends that Marx provided a political critique of capitalism, which enables us to challenge and demystify the wealth control system "that we're not supposed to know about." What she has taken from the broad Marxian tradition is the way in which it teaches us to look for historical contradictions, to start there, the sources of where mystification is. She also learned from Marx the gap between the rhetoric and the practice of democracy.

The fact that many of these essays are addressed to church-based audiences demonstrates her active participation in the life and struggle of Christian communities, but in each she is also speaking to a larger audience—to all those concerned about socioeconomic inequality and exclusion. Her interest is to conscientize people so that they may more effectively struggle together for social and economic justice. As she turns her attention to local congregations, Harrison's concern for their struggles is evident in her attention to the process of identifying and exploring family class histories and other personal connections to political-economic dynamics. In attempting to address the way in which our class histories and social location shape our identities, Harrison demonstrates her concern for the healing and well-being of communities that must always be part of the work of justice.

Notes

1. For further discussion of Harrison's concern for democracy, see her essay "Christianity's Indecent Decency: Why a Holistic Vision of Justice Eludes Us," in *Body and Soul: Rethinking Sexuality as Justice-Love*, ed. Marvin M. Ellison and Sylvia Thorson-Smith (Cleveland: Pilgrim Press, 2003), 25–44.
2. Beverly Wildung Harrison, "Theology and Morality of Procreative Choice," in *Making the Connections: Essays in Feminist Social Ethics*, ed. Carol S. Robb (Boston: Beacon Press, 1985), 115.
3. Ibid., 116.
4. Harrison develops this critique in depth in her essay "The Role of Social Theory in Religious Ethics: Reconsidering the Case for Marxian Political Economy," in *Making the Connections: Essays in Feminist Social Ethics*, ed. Carol S. Robb (Boston: Beacon Press, 1985).

Chapter 17

Reflecting on the Relationship between Politics and Economics

Interview by Rebecca Todd Peters

Peters: *Many people think of your work as addressing economics rather than politics. How would you respond?*

Harrison: This suggestion always surprises me because my primary interests have always been in examining how politics and economics interact. I never speak of economics in abstraction from the political context in which economic activity and economic life is set, and I can not think about economics except as an aspect of the way in which political life is organized. In a fundamental sense, I see my primary interest as the ethics of political economy. At the same time, I am particularly aware that, as a Christian ethicist, I am standing in a discipline where interest in economics is always situated within the existing economic order and abstracted from politics.

For example, I consider business ethics to be a somewhat futile effort to make capitalist life noncapitalist, because the kind of responsibility that business ethicists talk about presumes a resistance to the "iron laws of capitalism," as Marx sardonically called Adam Smith's efforts to theorize capitalism. If markets must be "free"—not obstructed politically in any way—then profit will remain the bottom line and all decisions will be made on that basis. So while business ethics may ameliorate the worst practices of existing capitalism, I've never been able to understand how you could do anything to improve the moral quality of capitalist enterprises unless you critique the way economic power shapes political power and vice versa. At best, business ethics only seeks a kind of adjustment of the internal logic of the system itself.

To me, the point of all critical social theorizing of society is to enable more movement in the direction of participation in shaping social policy. We need more movement in the direction of shaping communities so they are habitable for human beings and our cohabitants in the environment and on planet Earth. I simply don't trust the separation of politics and economics.

I have also been aware since I was a young Christian ethicist that since the early work of Reinhold Niebuhr, there has been almost *no* hermeneutic of suspicion of any sort toward the U.S. political economy, with the notable exception of John Bennett's *Radical Imperative.* I was very aware at the time he wrote that book and very grateful to him for pointing out the obvious, which was that serious questions of economic injustice in this society and in the wider world had really not been raised much by a whole generation of Protestant or Catholic academic ethicists.

So, in a sense, my constant talk about economic justice was an effort to bring up the subject that I felt was being neglected, not because economics can be separated from politics but because you do not get an adequate political ethic unless you have a highly explicit critique of political economy as a functioning system underlying our thinking about politics. You cannot abstract politics from the wider context of material production and the direction in which wealth is created and used in our society.

Peters: *Many scholars and public intellectuals argue that the "fall of communism" has exposed communism and socialism as hopelessly flawed models of political economy. How would you respond?*

Harrison: First, we must recognize that communism is a "vanguard of the party" theory, which is a *terrible* theory of politics. It is a flawed, totalitarian theory of politics that should be discredited, and it has been. But let's not forget that the historic assumption of the Russian Revolution was that you couldn't get to communism without growing through a period of socialism.

Politics and markets are two different ways to coordinate a productive system.[1] Markets are not the distinguishing characteristic of a capitalist system, but are in fact one way of coordinating activities. The problem with so much of this discourse is that the defense of capitalism is based upon a characterization of capitalism that is only a half-truth at best. Of course, market coordination is highly efficient in some situations and highly inefficient in others, and political processes are inefficient in some situations and not in others. But one of the things that you've got to do is to work toward a model of economic democracy that allows for the needs of production to be shaped both by people's wishes and desires as well as political necessity. In other words, you do not have abstract coordination of the way in which goods and services should be allocated. So a good state system is one that combines political planning and market coordination, and how you do this is not an a priori question, because it depends in part upon what you're trying to do and in what historical context. Good socialists, those committed to economic democracy, will argue that in an economic crisis, when scarcity is severe and people are hungry, you should produce, you should use political processes to effect markets as rapidly and as efficiently as possible to stimulate production.

So I know when people say, "Well, there's no viable model of socialism," I suppose that's true, but let's be clear about why there is no viable model. How can a socialist state survive as a socialist state within a capitalist world economy? It can't happen. Capitalism requires that you go with the existing global capitalist system of market exchange. And because current elites insist upon market-centered decision making, political considerations always get short shrift, so the "economy" does not produce for people's well-being. That is what happened to the so-called second or socialist world; they went under because they were the weakest sector of the global capitalist market system. They could not compete successfully not only because they had commitments to feed their people but because they were politically and economically isolated from the capitalist global political economy. There was no global socialist system in which they could procure needed resources available only in the capitalist system. The Russians had commitments to give Castro ten cents more a pound for sugar than the world market paid the Cubans. So they had to pay that ten cents when others could get sugar for next to nothing. There are always problems of survival, and the problem now is that there is only one system of production and exchange. There was no ameliorating political constraint to buffer the effects of the market. I don't think communism was an *economic* failure at all. I think it was a failure of political democracy. We're in the midst of a huge moral dilemma because everybody tells us that there is only one way to go and that capitalism will do what the impoverished globe needs. We who love democracy need to begin to create alternative political constraints on a now global economic productive system that does not have to give a damn bit of attention to what people need.

Peters: *How do you respond to those who strongly question or seek to discredit the theoretical value of including Marx in work by those of us who still locate ourselves within the tradition of social radicalism?*

Harrison: I'm not much interested in Marx's reputation for the sake of Marx. My sense about the erasure of Marx from the history of Western social thought is that it is an important part of the erasure of a truthful history that looks honestly at the human price of what we have done. Marx was obsessively preoccupied with studying the history of the development of capitalism. He had only one interest, to have a critical reading of capitalism. He didn't care about anything else. We still need critical readings of capitalism. I don't give a damn where we get them. I think the important point is that we have a radical tradition that does not project capitalist assumptions into its critical rereading. It basically argues that with no political constraint on the directing and amassing of wealth, there will be no democracy. That is the primary point of the Marxian tradition. It brings a profound scepticism to our beautiful life of admiring the rich and famous and having all the junk we've ever dreamed of. It brings a hermeneutic of suspicion that this is not what the kingdom of God is really about. Where do we get the tools for a critical reading of the past if we lose the radical social theory tradition which socialism generated? Where will we get the critical questions about what we are doing here if academics continue to show contempt for Marxism? The radical theory tradition helps us examine the past with an eye toward how it produces violence and how it produces social antagonism and antagonistic social relations. Read it that way; don't read it as though it were a utopian fairy tale about everyone having everything they need.

So I've never understood attacks on communism to have much to do with Marx. In the French Marxian tradition there was a tendency to merge a critical theory of society and a desire for a "science" of society with communist politics. I have never been able to figure out why all those French philosophers and radicals never got the sense that I have always taken from Marx that you weren't supposed to be looking for positive truths but were supposed to be unmasking falsehood. Falsification, that is what a social scientist does—s/he shows what is not the case about conventional wisdom. I understood Marx to be pushing science, not as a system of verifiability, but science as falsification. You could show what was false about the way things operate, but Marx didn't believe that social theory could produce a positive model of society. Only in acting together could we create the new patterns of social order we need. He was very much of a social constructionist.

When Marx said philosophers understand the world but our task is to change it, he meant that you cannot get theory out of nonparticipation. So the task is to enact an alternative rather than to think up an abstract model of society that will enable you to intervene. That is a Newtonian not a critical model of science. I think many religious people's discomfort with Marx derives from their fear of atheism. And I really think that, especially for theological people, it's scary to believe that people can be sincerely atheist and not believe what we believe.

Peters: *But it is not just theologians and religious communities that feel that Marx has been discredited; it is also economists.*

Harrison: Yes, but why economists ignore Marx is a different story. I think younger economists thought that Marx was trying to operationalize his analysis in the same way that the neoclassical economists were and that he failed somehow. Since in *Capital* Marx was trying to abstract the formulas of capitalist exploitation and wealth accumulation, later scholars thought he was trying to do what Adam

Smith did. He does sometimes appear to be trying to regularize empirical methods into his inquiry, but his question was, "Why is there always crisis?" For Marx, this question meant, "Why is there social antagonism or violence between groups?" Well, crisis comes from the fact that you can't make people do things against their will and self-interest. So it's the degree of human resistance that is the imponderable in the Marxian world. Did he really think he was going to objectify this so that you could predict the extent to which workers would strike? Obviously, he didn't. Many contemporary economists ignore Marx because they have misunderstood the intention and value of his work.

The chief failure of the Marxian system, according to some of his followers, the German critical theorists, was that he didn't take into account the capacity of people to be held captive by psychology that capitalist culture creates. That's what the professors of the Frankfurt school of philosophy tried to figure out; why do people objectify themselves by internalizing powerlessness? That's what the critical theorists were trying to figure out; how do we get so subjectively taken in by this system that we give it our all, our loyalty? Why do we split ourselves off from our own deepest needs for a gentle, beautiful world in which we and others play and work together and live out real well-being? So what was Marx's biggest failure? He never tried to image a socialist system; he was doing a critique of capitalism, and he did not make it concrete enough.

Notes

1. I am always amazed that economists read so little of their colleagues' work. Did anyone notice Charles Edward Lindblom, *Politics and Markets: The World's Political Economic Systems* (New York: Basic Books, 1977)?

Chapter 18

Socialism-Capitalism

This essay serves as an introduction to Harrison's approach to political economy by pointing out the way in which any definition of terms is influenced by one's ideological assumptions (that is, one's political and economic biases). It also clarifies her understanding of socialism as economic democracy not state capitalism (the USSR system). From Dictionary of Feminist Theologies, *edited by Letty M. Russell and J. Shannon Clarkson (Louisville, Ky.: Westminster John Knox Press, 1996), 264–66.*

Feminist theological, ethical, and pastoral work requires a historically grounded and nuanced awareness of political-economic discourses as well as religio-cultural concepts. Yet clarity about the meaning of terms central to the more-than-a-century-old debate about political-economic systems has never been more difficult. Defining terms such as *capitalism* and *socialism* has always exposed one's political commitments. This is because proponents and critics of both capitalism and socialism use their own, not their opponents', assumptions to define the other. They use favorable characteristics to define their own positions but stress negative realities in naming the others.

For example, the vast majority of socialists define socialism as economic democracy or as a political-economic system in which economic decisions are shaped by a society's broader political democracy—processes open to all, not merely to the rich. Capitalism, from a socialist perspective, is a specific historical arrangement in which those who have economic power demand and set limits on political options for the sake of perpetuating existing economic patterns. According to socialists, wealth, not people's democratically determined preferences, has the last say in setting priorities in capitalist societies. Conversely, capitalists define capitalism as a system that maximizes "free-market" economic activity and delimits political activity to specified "spheres." Political policies must, in particular, be prevented from unduly discouraging the presumed enhancement of economic wealth. Socialism is usually defined by capitalists as state-centered interference in so-called spontaneous economic activity or so-called free markets. Economies, they argue, prosper only when relatively unfettered. Politics should broker only those matters not central to economic growth. Conversely, socialists deny that capitalism is, in fact, characterized by free-market exchange. For them, monopoly and refusal to give needs a place, even if ventures are not profitable, are capitalism's central tendencies. Capitalists deny that socialism is democratic precisely because economic liberty is constrained by political decisions.

In discussions of political economy prior to the 1980s, all European-based progressives acknowledged that a national political economy required some political checks on the owners or controllers of wealth. Western European nations that used greater degrees of state economic planning to shape some sectors of their economy came to be known as "mixed economies" tending toward socialism. These societies developed multiparty political systems in which "workers' parties" or "labor parties" achieved some power and a considerable success in translating certain economic provisions into political "rights."

By contrast, in those nations that were more completely identified with capitalist ideology, especially the United States, efforts to build a labor-based political movement floundered for complex historical reasons, and a "mixed economy" was rejected adamantly. The powerful antilabor polemic of business and Christian churches was more effectual in the United States than in Europe, in part because of the deeply grounded belief of immigrants that the "New World" held out the promise of divinely sanctioned economic prosperity. To challenge capitalism in the United States always appeared in popular ideology to be an assault on opportunity or the American dream.

The definition of political economy is also more difficult today because of the current historical situation, which is also read differently by socialists and capitalists. In all the so-called developed countries, ideological control of public discussion has increased, so that a socialist interpretation is rarely presented by competent interpreters. The current capitalist line is that socialist "second-world" political economies have utterly failed. Some capitalist ideologists have even declared the "historically untranscendable" character of capitalist political economy. In their view, we should give up the search for alternatives to capitalism, which, it is presumed, has completely triumphed. Both the demise of the Soviet Union and the Chinese political economy's accommodation to global capitalist economic relations are construed by these ideologists as a sure sign of "the death of socialism." The new polemic against socialism is harsh and sows confusion in feminism, whose history, except in the twentieth century in the United States among white feminists, was closely intertwined with socialist movements and politics.

Socialist theorists, including most socialist feminists, perceive the recent dissolution of several major postcapitalist political economies to be the result of a twofold dynamic. The first is the ever more obvious global crisis of late twentieth-century capitalism itself. To socialists, a capitalist "crisis" is a reduction in an economy's ability to accumulate wealth. (What is called "failing profitability" or "inefficiency" by capitalists is called "labor exploitation" by socialists.) In such a crisis, existing economic forces dictate a politics aimed at unfettering economic power, and so capitalism moves to conservative ideology and policy. Earlier gains of working peoples' struggles get lost. Socialists call this *fascism*. From a socialist perspective, the so-called second world appears to be simply one part of a global capitalist market system and, because resistant to capitalist patterns, the most vulnerable area of that system. All global sectors ("south," or the so-called third world; "second," or postcapitalist; and "first," or capitalist) have to accommodate, because the refusal of any nation to do so means that nation cannot buy and sell goods and services in "the world market." The "wrath" of the newly created "real" power centers of the changing capitalist world system—the World Bank, the International Monetary Fund, and GATT (Global Agreement on Tariffs and Trade)—will be directed toward any policies except capitalist ones. Currently, there are no political ways to impact on these new power centers that determine everyone's fate.

In this historical scenario, socialism, or policies that move toward economic democracy, is understood to be in its very earliest phase of historical development. The collapsed second-world economies were internal to a global capitalist system and therefore were not well suited to resist and survive so inclusive and catastrophic a "crisis" as global capitalism is now undergoing. However, socialists, especially feminist socialists, also insist that the large, state-centered "command economies" that were generated by communist movements were in critical respects a betrayal of the historical vocation of socialism itself.

Feminists insist that one-party political systems, even if justified in moments of revolutionary historical chaos, quickly betray the socialist goal of extending democracy to include democratic participation in setting economic priorities. This defeats socialism from within. In light of recent experience, most contemporary socialists also believe that this greater political openness must develop simultaneously with new modes of decentralizing economic activity. Centralization and bureaucratic rigidity make ecological destruction, which must be curtailed, harder to stop.

As noted, these controversies strongly affected the first movements of feminism, at least in Europe. Most European feminists were socialists. Most remain so, even though, beginning in the 1970s, the postmodernist controversies and what is known as French feminism disconnected feminist work from socialist or radical theories of political economy. French feminism connected instead to a socially constructed, gendered version of Freudian psychology and a nonsocial conception of embodiment and materialism.

U.S. feminists, particularly white feminists, often suspicious of a radical political economy because of their cultural contexts, have nevertheless carried on extended discussions of how feminism and radical social theory relate. Perhaps the central challenge to feminist liberation theology and ethics in the twenty-first century will be to formulate more holistic theories, ones that neglect neither genuine political-economic change that increases democracy at every level nor the versions of sacredness generated by religio-moral-cultural communities. We must learn not to deny or minimize concrete physical or material need, while celebrating the spirituality of all our longings for connectedness in and through sacred power.

Chapter 19

Social Justice and Economic Orthodoxy: Structural Evils Neglected

This essay first appeared in 1985 in Christianity and Crisis, *part of a special issue devoted to discussing the first draft of the U.S. Conference of Catholic Bishops pastoral letter,* Economic Justice for All: Catholic Social Teaching and the U.S. Economy. *Readers should note that these remarks were aimed at an early draft of the pastoral that was more sympathetic to critical liberationist readings of the U.S. economy than was the final statement the bishops adopted (see the following essay, "Theology, Economics, and the Church"). In this response, Harrison first challenges right-wing accusations that the pastoral is too radical as a political tactic aimed at pushing an already centrist statement further to the right. Then, providing her own critique, she argues that the document is still too beholden to neoclassical economic theory and does not adequately include perspectives of racial minorities and economically marginalized people. From* Christianity and Crisis *44 (January 21, 1985): 513–15.*

Reading the first draft of the bishops' pastoral after scanning the media-hyped, highly orchestrated, prerelease attack on it launched by William Simon, Michael Novak, and other American Enterprise Institute groupies comes as something of a surprise. The well-organized neoconservative barrage led me to expect that the bishops had let the liberation theologians run amok with the text. No such luck!

To be sure, the letter gives normative moral priority to the poor, but, as every informed observer knows, so does the present pope in his instruction aimed at reining in the liberation theologians.

In fact, any honest interpreter of Roman Catholic moral theology would have to concede that at the theological level this first draft builds on the spirit and substance of Vatican II theology, working within a broadly neoorthodox methodology. Its theological presumption is that elucidating the positive themes of Christian Scripture and tradition as they relate to the Christian vision of economic life is the proper starting point of theological analysis, and this presupposition is fully consistent with neoorthodox methodology. Nor has the methodological challenge of liberation theologies made any great inroads on the pastoral. The liberationist exegesis of early Christian tradition has influenced *how* early Christian tradition is understood, but at the level of method, there is no evidence of a liberationist "hermeneutic of suspicion" about the possibility of speaking universally about *the* Christian tradition; nor is there any disposition to acknowledge Christian complicity in economic evil.

What is impressive about the pastoral is how successfully it correlates the reigning Catholic theological method with Thomist social ethical teaching. From a strictly academic perspective, the bishops' first draft deserves its highest marks for its conceptually rich reformulation of the Thomistic theory of justice. The pastoral's representation of commutative justice as social participation should warm the heart of every Christian concerned for social justice, and, because the text will be widely read, it could well lead to a recovery of interest in that tradition among non-Catholics.

In short, the bishops' draft stays well within present papal perimeters. The moral principles invoked have figured centrally in Catholic teaching on modern economic life since its inception over a century ago. Moreover, while some of the economic analysis and policy discussion does *not* present so seamless a garment as do the initial theological sections, the irenic spirit in which the entire text is cast hardly warrants a wrathful response. Since all of this is so demonstrably true, therefore, one is bound to wonder anew how so conceptually and rhetorically measured a work could meet with such hysterical dissent.

So thoroughly prepared were the neoconservatives to batter the first draft of the pastoral, that their strategy seemed rather crass. One could even sympathize with members and staff of the National Conference of Catholic Bishops (NCCB) who reportedly protested that all this criticism was undeserved. After all, the NCCB had tried to avoid the ire of the Reagan Raiders—the pastoral was delayed so as not to influence the presidential election. Furthermore, the cordial alliance between certain Roman Catholic archbishops and some persons in the New Right in the crusade for "traditional values" (which, when all is said and done, translates into blocking women's reproductive control and strongly enforcing compulsory heterosexuality) would seem to augur some consideration from the right. On the issue of economic morality, at least, the bishops were bending over backward to create a climate of public civility for the discussion, and to make it clear that their draft aimed to increase deliberation, not preclude it. (Oh, how we who oppose them on abortion covet this stance of respectful recognition of complexity and disagreement.) Little wonder, then, that the enmity that greeted the release of the document left some of its drafters stunned and unnerved.

It is clear by now what the strategy is: Depict the pastoral as profoundly radical, thereby forcing all subsequent negotiation over it toward the political right. The worrisome thing is that so far this strategy has worked fairly well. A good many (by no means all) spokesmen for the first draft have sounded badly defensive. The media meanwhile have focused largely on smoking out the question of whether the letter intends a criticism of capitalism.

'REALISM' AND 'IDEALISM' AGAIN

The debate over the pastoral is further confused by the neoconservatives' rereading of the old argument, so familiar to readers of this journal, over "realism" and "idealism" in Christian ethics. Not surprisingly, they have trumpeted our "need for Niebuhr" again, but with a twist: Resurrecting the conceptual structure of Niebuhr's social ethics (with, of course, neither the exact substance nor anything of the spirit), they have used it to trash any clear expression of dissent from the reigning political economy. They conveniently overlook the fact that Niebuhr's was a critique launched during a specific historical period and from *within* the Social Gospel wing of the mainstream Protestant churches. The realism-idealism debate was between Christians at the political center and those *on the left*, and both groups were clear in their opposition to the more egregious forms of fascism on the rise at the time. In our very different historical context, the claim by neoconservatives that they, not the political center, represent the "realism" pole—indeed, their claim to be the center—is a ploy to keep those further to the left out of the debate altogether.

Those of us who are to the left of the pastoral—namely, those of us who are persuaded that the core of our "economic problem" is the structure of the global political economy itself—are bound to be a little bored with this retread debate about realism. But we do see that the argument is intended to keep us invisible and silenced. (The "friendly face of fascism" at the industrial center of the global economy—unlike the forms utilized at the periphery—requires only that the left be silenced, not exterminated.) It also leaves us—and, I hope, some of those who worked on the pastoral—asking, "Where will the dissent on the left come from to offset the barrage from the right?"

That, I submit, is a real dilemma. I was reluctant to challenge this draft precisely because it is far better than anything I had hoped for, because pinpointing its analytic inconsistencies and policy problems could weaken the hand of those (myself included) who want its moral challenge to stand uncompromised, because I don't want my discontent to serve as fuel for criticism from the right, and because it is most likely that what is best in the pastoral from my viewpoint will be the most challenged and changed (witness the subsequent drafts of the pastoral on war and peace).

Even so, some criticisms must be made. First, the analytic and programmatic sections of the pastoral read as if its drafters saw no need to come to terms with the current major ideological and methodological debates within the social sciences. Instead of choosing clearly among competing theoretical paradigms, they attempted to extend the artful appeal to Catholic consensus at the level of theological and moral heritage into discussions over the U.S. and global economies. The result is that the various policy sections of the draft reflect unresolved differences among social theories, not only in analytical method and theoretical assumptions but also in diagnoses of why these problems exist and in the evaluation of the seriousness of the moral dilemmas at hand.

To offer but one obvious illustration: On the basis of the moral priority given to labor over capital in Catholic social thought, the draft affirms the goal of full employment as a clear presumption of Catholic moral teaching. However, the important opening policy section on full employment treats this issue without stepping outside the boundaries of the standard welfare-economics analysis of the causes and remedies for unemployment. Nor does the draft put forth any coherent historical or theoretical explanation of unemployment. It embraces unequivocally the right of labor to organize, but it also urges less antagonistic relations between workers and management without making reference to current efforts to crush or domesticate organized labor. Finally, it reaffirms the morally principled character of full employment but ends by conceding the complexity of it all. (Idealism and realism again!) The truth is that in this section (as in far too many others) the bishops have chosen to stay within the policy perimeters of neoclassical economics. And as long as they do, moral imperatives and the limits of economic possibility will conflict. In neoclassical terms, "rational" economic activity is "utility maximizing," and that means that production must be governed by profit considerations. Nothing else is substantively "economic." Nor is there any recognition that unemployment serves the interests of producers by forcing down wages. Structural unemployment due to the adoption of high technology is barely mentioned, and inflation is, for the most part, presumed to be related chiefly to wage rates rather than to profit margins and capital shifts.

The section on poverty is far superior. The analysis is substantively informed by the work of social theoreticians operating from a broadly neo-Marxian paradigm, in which economic suffering is viewed as a consequence of historical-structural dynamics. Here also for the first time, the perspectives of black and feminist social theorists are given some voice. But even that inclusion is problematic. For when the discussion moves from analysis to policy prescriptions, the neoclassical paradigm again prevails. Racial/ethnic women and men, and white women, are seen as *victims* of economic injustice, not as full participants in the process of formulating prescriptions for change.

This section of the draft, were it not for its predominantly neoclassical policy slant, could also have served as the basis for analyzing the effects of our economic system, not just on the poor but on the vast middle strata in this society. The draft (inadvertently) lumps the middle class together with the rich, seeing both groups as beneficiaries of the system. It badly neglects the working poor, wage laborers, and even those fully employed in modest-income white-collar work. This oversight is serious and, I suspect, due in part to the failure to respect the liberationist method I earlier identified. The victims of injustice must enter into the analytic dialogue.

MORAL PRIORITIES, LIBERAL ANALYSIS

The bishops are not alone here, however. It is not yet widely understood, even among progressives, that talking about the moral priority of the well-being of the poor while remaining tied to a liberal analysis that treats "class" as synonymous with "strata" (upper/middle/lower) does not clarify how institutional policy plays the poor off against the middle, and requires both to pay dearly for economic acceleration. This makes it seem that the poor stand over against the rest of us, as though we had few common interests. While everything in the moral discussion stresses our social relationality, there are aspects of the policy discussion that obscure this.

The draft would serve us all better if its analytic perspective were consistently deep enough to illuminate the extent to which the now global economic system interlinks us all, also within the domestic economy. Otherwise, we will be left with a lingering early capitalist prescriptive morality: charity for the middle sectors, radical hope for the poor. To be sure, the draft certainly avoids the most patronizing forms of this ethic. Its counsel to the affluent about their lifestyles is wise, but "voluntary relinquishment" is a better ethic for the really well-off than for those just barely making it. We who want a deeper economic morality had better learn a lot more about the impoverishment of life our economic system has brought to broad reaches of this society. It runs very deep indeed—far, far beyond the core problem of consumerism that gets some specification in this draft of the pastoral. The deterioration of conditions for meaningful work and the growth of low-scale and non-career-track work are examples that deserve more than a mere mention.

The constant shifting of theoretical perspective—with the neoclassical always paramount—is also evident in the various discussions of the international economic order. The pastoral attempts a strikingly detailed discussion of steps required to move toward a more just economic order. Some of this analysis is on target, but several of the policy prescriptions endorsed are simply wrongheaded. A case in point is the bishops' proposal to strengthen existing control mechanisms such as the International Monetary Fund and World Bank. To do so without also shifting the locus of political control toward the poor nations would reduce self-determination in the third world even further.

Much more could be said about the promise and problems of this first draft. One further thing *must* be said. The various social theorists, even critical ones, the dominant theological theorists given voice, most of the consultants, and others whose views were listened to in hearings on the document all share a glaring weakness: They are nearly all white, chiefly Euro-North American (cultural imperialism gets a nod from the Hispanic sector only toward the end), and they are mostly male. Irenic tone is no substitute for the perceptual sensibility that genuine pluralism creates.

Given the situation of women in Roman Catholicism, I was not surprised that serious feminist theory was taken into account only in the section on poverty, but I was shocked at the largely liberal—that is, nonstructuralist—diagnosis (or lack of it) of racism, except again, as noted, in the analysis of poverty. Failure to grasp that racism is an intrinsic aspect of our political economy and a source of its success, not just an "exogenous" issue of interpersonal discrimination, suffuses any analysis with "idealism." It is inexcusable among morally sensitive whites today.

In the best of all possible worlds we might even expect the bishops not to relegate to the margins either sexism or cultural imperialism. At the level of domestic economy, and globally, the wealth of white males is sustained by the unpaid or underpaid labor or enforced leisure of everybody else. That has been true throughout U.S. history. Not only racism but sexism and cultural imperialism are intrinsic systemic dimensions of our political economy. That the wealth (not to be equated with income) of the world is controlled by rich, white, male Europeans and North Americans, and a very limited number of confreres in East Asia and elsewhere, needs to become explicit in our theology, morality, and social theory. It does not shape this document adequately.

So let no one imagine that this promisingly progressive draft is the last word, or a good-enough word. The bishops have done well. They could do a lot better.

Chapter 20

Theology, Economics, and the Church

This piece was originally given on May 5, 1986, at the Episcopal Divinity School in Boston as part of the annual Kellogg Lecture Series. Harrison gave one of three lectures, along with David Hollenbach and Byron Rushing. The theme for their collective discussion was "Theology, Economics, and the Church," and Harrison's lecture was, in part, a response to the final draft of the U.S. bishop's pastoral on economic justice titled "Economic Justice for All" (Hollenbach had been one of the drafters of that document). The essay offers a pointed objection to misreadings of socialism and the allegiance to what she calls late monopoly capitalism and inadequate versions of Christian realism that shaped the final document.

The topic assigned for this year's Kellogg Lectures, "Theology, Economics, and the Church," when properly formulated, interconnects with every aspect of our theological understanding and every dimension of Christian ministry today. Even so, within most Protestant and Catholic theological education, there is little reflection on economic life—so little as to make the issue appear much like premodern alchemy, an esoteric arena of knowledge, a gnosis, a set of secrets comprehended only by the few. My thesis is that in a world where institutional shifts in the economic order are daily transforming the lives of every woman, child, and man on this globe, we U.S. Christians are as poorly equipped as any even to comprehend what is occurring. Even less are we prepared to grasp the *urgency* of the matter before us and to reflect upon its implications for our theological integrity and ongoing ministry. Among us, economics is a mystified dimension of our lives.

Within a feminist liberation theological vision, we stress that this planet, indeed the whole cosmos that we inhabit, is not merely a gracious home. It is an interactive web of life that is as much a part of us as we of it. The wholistic theological vision of total interrelationship we insist upon makes it inconceivable that nature, with its resources for abundant life, can be conceived as something external, as something merely to be manipulated and dominated. With the Catholic bishops, we deny that it can be turned into the possession of a very few. We tolerate no dualism of matter and spirit. From a feminist perspective, we are all sensuous and embodied beings, separated from the cosmic whole and from others of our species-being only by the fragile skin that separates us from each other and the created and creative processes of nature of which we are a part. Feminists rejoice that the first two drafts of the U.S. Conference of Catholic Bishops' pastoral letter, *Economic Justice for All: Catholic Social Teaching and the U.S. Economy*, reflect positive steps in official Catholic teaching to overcome the debilitating dualism of matter and spirit that has so long beset Western patriarchal Christianity. Only when we escape from life-denying forms of spirituality can we have anything genuine and powerful to say, anything that is "good news" to anyone's ears. This will not happen until Christians finally cease to take it for granted that food, shelter, health care, and the genuine liberation of the human spirit that comes from both good, sensuous, physical and intellectual labor are fundamental conditions of the spiritual life. This is an uncompromising assumption of feminist liberation theology. We can affirm human dignity until we are blue in the face, but if we do so from a theological perspective that divides material and spiritual well-being, our moral rhetoric will be vacuous. Fortunately, the bishops do not do so when they address economic life.

The legacy that enabled the bishops to see the importance of economic justice arose from pastoral concern. Modern papal social teaching also arose, under Leo XIII, as a pastoral response to the appalling conditions of urban workers in a much earlier phase of capitalist institutional realignment. In the late nineteenth century, Leo XIII's annunciation of the moral primacy of labor over capital, now so important in Catholic teaching, was not an embrace of modern democratic life.[1] Leo XIII feared the secularizing effect of the rising tide of worker militancy that led eventually in Europe to some mitigation of the worst effects of newly centralized capitalist industrial production (a mitigating effect never registered in the United States). The numbers of socialist political movements that were pressuring for greater economic democracy also frightened him. Leo XIII possessed a static worldview of society as an inherited system of orders. Nevertheless, he cared about the well-being of his people.

Catholic social thought has a clear history of rootedness in genuine pastoral concern. The sort of moral criteria formulated in the pastoral can only emerge from authentic pastoral engagement. That all aspects of economic life are to be evaluated morally by the way that they affect "the dignity of the human person, realized in community" reflects this engagement. The central moral criterion of liberation theology, then, is close to that of the U.S. bishops: How do economic life and economic institutions affect concrete human life, and how do they function to reduce concrete human suffering engendered by structural and institutional forms of domination? If we feminist liberation theologians focus upon the systematic exclusions of whole groups because of racism, sexism, heterosexism, and class dynamics, we do so because we know that no one is truly a "mere individual." We share the bishops' concern for personal dignity, and we also insist with them that human persons come to dignity only when we are deeply and richly related to one another. In spite of great similarity, however, I want now to attempt to locate some differences between a feminist liberation approach and the bishops' approach.

The core disagreement, as I have already indicated, is not a disagreement about moral principles. (Genuine and serious moral conflict rarely is about principles, which is why contemporary moral philosophy is often rather boring!) If there were time enough, I might locate some of the differences at the level of theological imagery—feminists and Catholic bishops rarely envision divine power in the same way! However, I believe it is more urgent here to lay before you some examples, albeit brief ones, of how a feminist liberation theo-social analysis differs from the one the bishops make, because my deepest worry about the pastoral is focused there. Social analysis is a process intrinsic to the theological-hermeneutical circle within a liberation methodology, and the terms of that social analysis must be consistent with one's moral and theological vision.[2] In light of the social analysis present in the pastoral, there is, I submit, reason to suspect that the moral radicalism of the bishops' norms of justice is at some points more rhetorical than actual.

This analytic comparison is not easy precisely because at some points in this draft the bishops have appropriated aspects of the critical analysis of contemporary political and economic dynamics done by third-world[3] Christians, black liberation theologians, and feminist theologians, among others. Large portions of the present draft of the pastoral aptly describe the devastating effects on women, children, persons of color, and people in the so-called third world of our now globally integrated political and economic system. However, in this draft, it is the way in which their social analysis places the political economy of the United States in global history that is suspect. The key point of their analysis with which liberationists must quarrel appears at the beginning of chapter 3, where the bishops turn to selected policy recommendations:

> [127] . . . We situate our discussion within a context of diverse and competing views of how to understand the American economic system. One such analysis assumes that an unfettered free-market economy—where owners, workers and consumers are allowed to pursue their individual self-interest—provides the greatest possible liberty, material welfare and equity. The policy implication of this view is to intervene in the economy as little as possible because it is such a delicate mechanism that any attempts to improve it are likely to

have the opposite effect. *A second view argues that current economic problems are inherent in the very nature of the capitalist system. In this view capitalism cannot be reformed, but must be replaced by a radically different system that abolishes private property and the market system.* [128] *Catholic social teaching has traditionally rejected both of these ideological extremes, for they are likely to produce results contrary to human dignity and economic justice.* Nor is it the role of the church to create or promote a "third way" or a specific new economic system. Starting with the assumption that the economy has been created by human beings and can be changed by them, the church works for reforms in a variety of economic and political contexts.

[129] Therefore, our approach in analyzing the U.S. economy is pragmatic and evolutionary in nature. We live in a "mixed" economic system that is the product of a long history of reform and adjustment. It is in the spirit of this American pragmatic tradition of reform that we seek to continue the search for a more just economy. (Emphasis mine)

CRITIQUING THE MISREPRESENTATION OF THE POLITICAL LEFT

At the risk of turning some people off, I confess that I am one of these extremists referred to. I represent the second extreme: those who believe "that current economic problems are inherent in the very nature of the capitalist system." I believe this, as do most feminist liberation theologians. The further characterization of this "extremist" viewpoint is, however, not one I recognize. I have never known or read a single twentieth-century socialist theorist who believes what the pastoral says we believe, namely, that private property must be abolished along with the total market system. Nor, I would add, do most Communists believe it. This characterization, along with that of the U.S. economy that follows, is based on a caricature of left-wing politics that first developed in the Protestant social ethic known as Christian realism.

Before turning to an analysis of some of the dubious effects of some versions of Christian realism on contemporary Christian economic ethics and on the bishops' assessment of the U.S. economy, I do need to enter a further caveat against this deep misrepresentation of the views of the political left. Socialists (and even most Communists) are not and never have been opponents of personal private property. In the third world, none oppose the limited use of markets. We believe that what must be socialized, or brought under the direction of society and its people, is not private property but the means of production (i.e., the means by which the wealth of a society is produced). Let us also remember that this means that wealth is *not* just a lot of income. It is ownership of the means to create wealth. In the advanced stages of capitalism, one can have more than enough income but little social power, as many really affluent people are only too well aware.

When capitalist Christians characterize and/or confuse modern socialist or communist views with the early religious socialist belief that all private property is "wrong," we need to remember that it was late eighteenth- and early nineteenth-century socialists, including religious socialists, who developed the idea that a propertyless society could be an economic goal. These people, believing that the Bible teaches Christians to hold all things in common, were distressed by the deep social and cultural dislocation and social violence that nineteenth-century capitalism generated. They responded by envisioning a propertyless society. Most so-called "secular" socialists disagreed with this. People forget that much later a nineteenth-century German Jewish philosopher, Karl Marx, became the major critic of religious socialism. Angry about this sort of pacifist, romantic, religious envisagement of socialism, he insisted that the vision of a propertyless society was based on a superficial analysis of capitalism in its historical context.

It is a sad irony that we Christians so frequently blame Marx for what some of our coreligionists have urged. Marx inveighed against this view even though he believed that capitalism had begun to create some of the conditions of human liberation. He also believed that the most exploitative feature of capitalism was not the great disparities in the amount of property people owned, which was only a *symptom* of what was wrong with capitalism. Marx felt that a more systemic problem was not having a say in what we work for and in the capacity to experience meaningful work within antidemocratic working conditions. Marx also believed that capitalism created alienation as people had to work to live rather than to express their human essence. At a later point, his analysis became more specific regarding the basic dynamic that created the intensified social antagonism and alienation. Capitalism, argued Marx, was the sort of economic system that inevitably allowed a few to determine how the *wealth-producing wealth* of a society (i.e., "the mode of production") is to be used to produce more wealth. Therefore, it made real economic democracy impossible. People's use of their own labor as a basic expression of their lives was, he believed, entirely out of their control. His detailed historical analysis of the earlier phases of capitalism showed how, gradually, capitalist economic organization had turned land, natural resources, human labor, and machines into commodities. Soon we ourselves would be commodities, we would have to sell ourselves. As a result, he claimed this mode of economic organization was creating societies in which exploitation was the dominant mode of social interaction between a rather small group of owners and the vast majority, who could only survive by selling their labor.[4]

Let us also remember that no serious student of European urban life in the latter half of the nineteenth century denied the problem that Marx pointed to. *Marx did not invent the idea of class conflict* (i.e., antagonistic relationships created by economic dependency). Every nineteenth-century classical economist, including those heroes of modern capitalist neoclassical economic theory Adam Smith and David Ricardo, concurred with Marx that social antagonism was on the increase because of accelerating industrial capitalism. In fact, what Smith, Ricardo, and Marx agreed upon was that a new "science" of political economy was needed to clarify and address these social antagonisms. Alas, most current neoclassical economists have by now forgotten the reasons their discipline developed in the first place—i.e., to shape less violent societies.

Karl Marx was a great admirer of capitalism's productive capacity. (Some of us today, in light of the ecological crisis and the rape of the environment, would say that he was too admiring.) Many forget that Marx was for a brief time a European correspondent to the *New York Tribune*, and he dared to hope that the transformations of capitalism toward socialism would come in the United States, where productive resources were many and institutions of liberal political democracy had already been established. (It should be noted that he did not adequately understand the history of our slave labor system or the exploitation of native peoples through land expropriation.)

Needless to say, his hope was in vain. Most of the few postcapitalism economic experiments the world has so far seen in the last fifty years have emerged in appallingly poor peasant societies. In every case, these economic transformations have followed upon bloody civil wars aimed to bring down horribly repressive political tyrannies and in cultures with powerfully resistant elites, closely identified with dominant religions. We need to remember these historical realities when we purport to measure the successes and failures of the noncapitalist economic systems, such as Russia, China, Cuba, and so on. You do not understand the appeal of communism in many areas of the world today if you do not understand that, for all of its mistakes, the Chinese Communists moved their quarter of the globe's population from abject poverty to near subsistence in one generation.

There is another statement in this section of the pastoral that is analytically off base. It proclaims, "Ours is a mixed economy." This, I submit, is from any historically adequate reading of U.S. history a *perfectly preposterous assertion*. No U.S. government initiative (except the Tennessee Valley Authority) ever aimed to socialize any dimension of economic production. A few European countries went so far as to bring a few basic productive sectors under public control, and they may, perhaps, be characterized as "mixed economies." The United States did not socialize any basic productive functions. Only one given to fantasy could describe the changes the United States went through during the New Deal as having led to a "mixed economy." The United States moved, very begrudgingly, and through intense political struggle, to become a *regulatory-state system*—that is, a system in which the state attempts to prevent by administrative rule and law some of the worst social effects of business activity. We also gradually adopted a minimalist government-administered set of welfare net functions—social security, limited unemployment insurance—and, at *the state rather than the federal level*, a degrading set of charity policies for children and indigent mothers based on "merit."

I defy anyone to show me one productive function that is genuinely under the control of U.S. citizens as such. *Nothing could be more off target than the claim that ours is a mixed economy.* Make no mistake—our political-economic evolution has been the reverse of a move to a mixed economy. Our solution to capitalist political-economic crisis always has been to use the state to shore up or strengthen existing patterns of the private ownership of the means of production at whatever price to the wider society. We have the most minimalist welfare system in the world today, and its bureaucratic problems are due to the fact that everyone has to prove they deserve help. These are not economic rights; they are begrudging capitalist charity.

More importantly, the state has now become more or less beholden to the modern advanced industrial corporate complex. The state has not taken over corporations; rather, the reverse has occurred. The corporations now largely control the state. The bishops' worries about the dangers of statism are touchingly beside the point. This very week, the *New York Times* reported on its front pages that a federal district court has declared the rights we are guaranteed by the U.S. Constitution apply only to citizens dealing with the government, not to citizens' relations to corporations. In this era of the Reagan Supreme Court, the least observed social revolution in U.S. history has taken place in interpretations of corporate law. Corporations now have *fuller* political rights than even the richest citizen possesses. Let no one miss the point: The state is now far more an instrument of corporate will than it is of the will of the people. This is evident in the congressional rhetoric over the last twenty years in which the historic concern for attending to "the will of the people" has been replaced by an emphasis on "protecting the interests of consumers." I submit that most of us have less and less control over the social policy of the nation, but more and more choice about which is the best brand of toothpaste to purchase!

CRITIQUING CHRISTIAN REALISM

I take no pleasure in the judgment that the sort of thinking reflected in the section of the pastoral I read has some roots in Christian realism, since that is the movement most closely associated with my former teacher Reinhold Niebuhr. In its most creative period, Christian realism was a complex theological response to earlier Protestant Social Gospel Christianity, but it was also the movement that kept much of the justice passion of Social Gospel Christianity alive in mainstream U.S. Protestant churches. The source of the problem rests in the mode of social analysis that Niebuhr developed.[5]

Reinhold Niebuhr became a creative force in Christian social ethics through his early writings, most especially his book *Moral Man and Immoral Society*, precisely because, among other things, he faulted Christian ethicists for their idealist moralizing and for their failure to take into account the rising power of economic forces in society. Later, as his attention turned, first, to the rising threat of fascism in Germany and then to the questions posed by the confrontations between the United States and Russia, the terms of his social analysis also shifted. In his early phase, Niebuhr believed passionately that all social power, including economic power, should be power accountable to people. He also advocated that Christians should support those political movements that forged such accountability. In his later phase, he adopted the ahistorical theory of invariant power dynamics between nation-states as his mode of analysis. In so doing, he ceased to attend to economic-institutional dynamics. In his time, Niebuhr perceived fascism and communism as equally totalitarian. He himself had a tepid preference for a mixed economy and perceived the United States as moving in such a direction. Niebuhr observed our nation's economic recovery from the Great Depression and the economic boom of the post-World War II period. He seemed to believe in his later years that the institutions of liberal democracy, once in place, would withstand any threats of economic concentration to our national life. He offered no justification for this complacent view. I am not now interested in trashing Niebuhr, but in showing how some of his dubious assumptions still shape the current debate.

Today a bizarre range of folks embrace the Christian realist label. Neoconservatives such as Michael Novak and Robert Benne have elided its political ethic to a passionate defense of the morality of capitalism. This would have appalled Niebuhr. However, there is another group that strongly emphasizes that it is a matter of indifference whether Christianity supports capitalism or socialism so long as the formal structure of earlier constitutional democracy exists. I find this position strongly present in the pastoral. This view, it must be said, was probably Reinhold Niebuhr's view late in life. Where he would be today, no one knows. Anyone can claim him. But it should be noticed that his closest collaborators, such as John Bennett and Roger Shinn, have ceased to use the label "Christian realist" at all. As Bennett once said in a personal conversation, the term functions now chiefly as a polemical boast about the moral adequacy of one's own point of view.

By the 1960s, when the now accelerating economic power of the first-world capitalist nations began to reshape the globe in directions different from the nineteenth-century system, those who followed Niebuhr's systemic neutrality failed to understand what was occurring. It is not surprising that they missed it. Like Niebuhr, contemporary neutralists start with the assumption that *we* have arrived at a mixed economy. The problem here is that if we accept the ahistorical assumption that the existence of formal liberal constitutional and electoral political institutions are an invariably adequate definition of democracy, one need not see our modes of economic life as dangerous. To such men, the menacing forces are exclusively political, and societies are to be judged solely by political criteria. Nations are deemed democratic based on the presence of constitutions and elections, not by the extent to which people are fed, clothed, housed, or have a role in shaping social priorities. From this perspective, economic colonialism is a thing of the past, and the worst effects of economic imperialism have ended. In the immediate post-World War II period, most nations gained their formal political independence, did they not? The vast majority even adopted political constitutions modeled on our own, in some cases even expanding the rather limited definitions of political rights that we have! The failure of people who read the world this way to note the shifting dynamics of capitalist economic power is a disastrous mistake, one that creates a deeply misguided ethical analysis.

Realists then tend invariably to frame social policy options only in terms of the eighteenth- and nineteenth-century definitions of "politics"—that is, formal constitutional and elective functions. They also fail to see society as involved in and undergoing dynamic processes of change. For them, the political "extremes" are invariant—left and right. Go too far in either direction and the earth will tip and we will fall off. They do not notice that the laissez-faire ideology is clearly a fabrication vis-à-vis history! A "free market" was never anything but a *theoretical construct of early capitalist economic theory.* Even Adam Smith knew that it was a theoretical construct, and was not and never had been a historical reality. While Milton Friedman and a certain group of social philosophers have refurbished the myth for late twentieth-century academics to admire, no working businessperson or philosophically sophisticated neoclassical economist presumes its empirical existence. Every businessperson knows that you fail in business if you do not move to capture the market! I must add that Milton Friedman does not think free markets should exist in the third world. Witness his advice to General Pinochet of Chile about how to implement his state-centered economic planning: Send out the military to keep the workforce going at low wages, if you must, in order to accept the conditions of the not-so-free global market system.

The other bugaboo that neo-Christian realism describes as extremism is, of course, collectivized state socialism of the Russian variety. I have already explained how far from socialism this is. In my view, the Russian system turned out to be state capitalist.[6] The latter-day realist spirit urges Christians to conclude that anyone who criticizes the spontaneous, internally generated evolution of capitalist institutions is a pinko, Communist sympathizer, a supporter of gulags, an adamant collectivist. Furthermore, it encourages Christians to think, with Reagan's Rambos, that everything the U.S. industrial-military state does to destroy any small nation's efforts to find an alternative to full and total integration into the global capitalist system is a great victory for the democratic way of life. Witness the barrage of propaganda that aims to shape our perceptions of what is going on in South Africa, the Philippines, Nicaragua, Cuba, Haiti—to name a few societies where the rising of people for political and economic justice is giving us trouble.

For some time now, liberationist Christians in many areas of the third world have been trying to get a message through to us that we U.S. Christians have not heard very clearly. It is a twofold message. On the one hand, they insist that the second phase of global, capitalist, political-economic imperialism is worse than the first. In the eighteenth and nineteenth centuries, colonial states only lost their formal political independence. In the late twentieth, even with liberal constitutions, these former colonies have lost the capacity to work for their own personal and national material well-being. The transnational capitalist system now penetrates to control their lives directly at every point. Not only must all their natural resources and the cream of what their domestic labor produces be transferred to the first world, as in the first era of imperialism, but now their own domestic economies are totally skewed to produce not what they need but what the first world requires. The best food that hungry people produce comes to us!

There is also a second aspect of the third-world liberationists' message to us, one we have heard even less than the first: The political and economic dynamics that are now ripping apart their societies and destroying their ancient and valued cultures are beginning to move back from the periphery of the global capitalist system—for that is what the third world is—to the center, that is, to the United States. The same dynamics of the political economy that are reshaping their lives are now reshaping ours. Every liberation theologian from Latin America, Africa, and Asia that I have ever met or read has pressed this plea: *Do not imagine that what is going on in your lives is a separate or unrelated dynamic. Begin your own analysis of the interconnections.* Understand that the acceleration of racism, sexism, and class stratification of your society is not unrelated to our struggle. Recognize that the escalation of the poverty of women and children, the deindustrialization of the seventeen states of the U.S. Northeast, your farm crisis, the growing impotence of your city, regional, and even regulative sectors of your federal government to impact your situation are related to that against which we struggle!

It is this message that neoconservative and moderate Christian realists call Christian naïveté and evidence of the dangerous and uncritical use of Marxism.[7] Few liberation theologians in the world today, certainly none in Latin America, look uncritically at the second-world or Russian model as a desirable alternative to their captivity. Recently I was on a panel with Venezuelan liberation theologian Oscar Maduro as he detailed for a group of U.S. socialist scholars the long history of antagonism between, on the one hand, Latin American liberation movements and Latin American liberation theologians, and, on the other, the old-line Communist parties of Latin America. The suggestion of some realists that liberation theology leads to collectivism is preposterous. Any who seek a full Christian gospel of hope must stop being bullied by such accusations.

Let me stress again that my criticisms of realism here are not aimed at the bishops or the vast body of the draft of the pastoral before us. That document is only flawed by a touch of these assumptions! And they certainly avoid any Red-baiting, save in the characterization of noncapitalist economic views. They have embraced the moral right of political self-determination clearly enough. Still, their policy analysis has a stress on the responsibility of our existing dominant political and economic institutions to shape a new domestic and global economic order. And by placing domestic economic policy questions in a framework that urges development through a cooperative approach that will link existing political and economic institutions—most especially government and the corporations—some of their policy recommendations could well lock us further into the corporate statism that already exists. Believe me, the state and the corporations are already deeply locked in "cooperative" ventures. That is our problem! And the question to be asked is, How do we gain some access to make change in this massive cooperative corporate-statist venture?!

I am, of course, still enough of an authentic Christian realist to agree with the bishops' plea for a pragmatic approach to social change. Authentic practiced pragmatism is a willingness to experiment and learn from the spirit of experimentation. Furthermore, looked at from one point of view, all social change, particularly when it involves authentic change in dominant patterns of social life, is

Need a good analysis

evolutionary. But if we do not get our analysis of where we are in history clear, social policy becomes not authentic incremental change but social palliatives that do not touch our deepest needs and that reinforce existing imbalances of power. The bishops do see that we need to accept the legitimacy of economic rights. However, at this point I doubt that they yet see that political democracy will not survive in Western societies unless we realign economic institutions to make them genuinely accountable to people. Economic participation is now the most important form of political participation.

I have little problem with the classic Catholic principle of subsidiarity—that is, the principle that social organization should evolve at the level closest to the needs such organization is designed to serve—*if* it is invoked to support a spirit of local and regional experimentation. There is much in this principle that should commend itself as we begin to ask what we can do to return social power to communities and groups whose lives are being devastated by corporatist decisions they do not control. Even so, it is dangerous not to recognize that the agenda of an adequate Christian economic ethic must also commit us to a road that carries us beyond the liberal, ideologically loaded misinterpretation that there actually now exists in this nation a separation of economic and political power.

I submit that Christian intellectuals need to be clear that whether we like it or not, the historical direction in which we must move is the line originally staked out historically by European socialism. In Western history, until some realists, both Christians and others, confused the issue, *socialism* always meant democracy inclusive of our economic life. After realism, we socialists always have had to use the label "democratic socialist," but historically that label was redundant. I am not a fool, and I do not mean to suggest that today everyone needs to wrap ourselves in a socialist label. But Christian intellectuals in the United States at least must have enough integrity to challenge the Red-baiting always going on. What we must seek is a political order that provides citizen control over how resources, including human resources, are used. Unaccountable economic power must be seen and made accountable precisely to the norms of human dignity and well-being that the bishops embrace. We must find our way to a situation in which people have some direct say in how social wealth is used.

Liberation theologians understand what realists have missed—that our global political economy has been centuries in the making. To find our way to alternatives is not the work merely of a lifetime, but, if our planet survives, the work of all of our and our children's foreseeable futures. I do not care what political labels anyone uses to move toward this agenda of economic democracy that the bishops have called "economic participation." *But move we must.*

CONCLUSION

To this point, I have done my analysis chiefly at the global macrolevel. As a liberation theologian, however, I am obliged to take my cues not from this level but from the daily struggle and suffering of people, and especially women, to gain human dignity. I want to conclude with a few notes on what all of this means for the Christian people with whom all of us live and for our ministries.

We are living in a profoundly repressive political climate. We cannot imagine, as dominant theologians so often do, that an authentic practice of the Christian gospel of living hope in abundant life will be readily welcomed. Our situation is much like that of the Brazilian peasants among whom Paulo Freire worked. We too live in a social situation where reality is mystified and the power even to name our dilemma has been largely taken from us. Vast, vast numbers of people in this society have come to identify with the Rambo-like myths about our history that our rulers urge upon us. In this dominant myth, hard work and responsible support of the system gains its reward—the absolute assurance of upward mobility. White people in particular perceive that for the most part this great American dream has worked and is working still.

What such identification with the dominant ideology does is encourage people (in this case, most especially, white people) to forget our roots—especially if where we come from is not where we think we are headed. (Blacks and other racial ethnic people do not forget their forebears' struggles for dignity as readily as many white people do.) Ours is a society in which those who suffer from ideological identification with dominant groups forget their own history. Many of us live in a condition of *social amnesia* in which we have disconnected from anything in our past, including our family histories or the cultures from which we came, that does not pass muster in the dream of upward mobility. In vast reaches of "the muddled middle" of this society, a historical amnesia prevails, and because we need a scapegoat for the rising tide of powerlessness that threatens, we project those fears onto those we perceive as unlike us and blame those more victimized by the system than ourselves.

In situations such as these, the work of liberating ministry becomes a combination of grief work on the one hand and empowerment and conscientization on the other. We must help people to begin to recover the hope for dignity that comes from understanding that the social, political, and economic malaise in which we are enmeshed is not due to the personal failure of others and is not blind fate. We must work to enable people who do not even know they are grieving for their broken dreams to do so and then to move on, to *begin to struggle once more for life.* We must learn to encourage any and every stirring of a *praxis of resistance* to what is life thwarting to vast numbers of people. In such a situation, clergy dare not moralize about being charitable to the poor, as if your own people who live somewhat above the poverty line (often on two salaries) are rich. We must help them make the connections between the deeper suffering of those totally marginated and their own malaise. We must help them understand the genuine solidarity of human need that links our lives!

I do not romanticize about what hard work this is. We cannot even begin it unless we are aware of some of the deficiencies of the liberal Christianity to which we are heir. We radicalized Christians (those trying to get to the root of the matter) face an immense pilgrimage even to enter into a ministry of genuine empowerment in our time. Among other things, latter-day liberalism (the centrist, "balanced" position) sees its vocation as peacekeeping—not *peacemaking*, but peacekeeping. Many of us are psychologically inclined to deny the reality of social conflict. Let's face the fact that it is far easier to join the new religious right's strategy of offering personal palliatives and encouraging a preoccupation with interiorized, otherworldly spirituality. In fact, many in the formerly liberal churches are doing just that.

As we learn how to join more effectively in a struggle for abundant life in this society, let us remember that this struggle does not begin with us, and it will not end with us. A Christian spirituality grounded in a global and cosmic vision of abundant life is necessary both to help us maintain our own resolve in the struggle as well as to help us build our vision of the future that we seek. It is to that task that I hope the bishops and the churches will focus our efforts.

Notes

1. See Christine Gudorf, *Catholic Social Teaching on Liberation Themes* (Lanham, Md.: University Press of America, 1980). Also helpful is the work of the Canadian Catholic theologian Gregory Baum regarding the development of modern Catholic social teaching.
2. For a fuller statement of this point, see Beverly Wildung Harrison, *Making the Connections: Essays in Feminist Social Ethics*, ed. Carol Robb (Boston: Beacon Press, 1985), 245–49.
3. Since writing this lecture, I have learned from the voices of many around the world and now refer to the "two-thirds world" or "the South."
4. I am no longer interested in arguments about whether Marx's dialectical materialism is adequate. If, as some scholars still contend, Marx's views were based on a naturalistically reductionist view of nature, then his metatheory was premodern and can be rejected. Einstein taught us that nature can be viewed as matter or as energy, *simultaneously*. The nineteenth-century debate over "materialism" can be set aside.
5. For a more detailed critique of Niebuhr, see Harrison, *Making the Connections*, 58–74.
6. This is a complex claim that I cannot defend here. What is notable has been the degree of centralized economic power in both the U.S. and Soviet economies. Single-party state socialism and so-called private (i.e., corporate) capitalism are both inimical to democracy.
7. I cannot here describe the unbelievable misunderstandings of Marxism and neo-Marxism that have been spawned to justify these caricatures. An excellent interpretation of what Marx actually said is Anglican theologian Nicholas Lash's *A Matter of Hope: A Theologian's Reflections on the Thought of Karl Marx* (London: Darton, Longman & Todd, 1981). To understand the complex relationship between Marx and what later Marxists have done with his perspective, begin by reading non-Marxist David McLellan's book *Marxism after Marx: An Introduction* (London: Macmillan, 1979).

Chapter 21

Toward a Christian Feminist Liberation Hermeneutic for Demystifying Class Reality in Local Congregations

This essay grew out of a presentation Harrison made during a week-long meeting at Emory University, organized by Barbara Wheeler, that focused on local congregations. Here Harrison addresses the impact of social class on the lives of congregations. She offers questions to help inquire into the ways economic realities deform the lives of people in the community and guidance on how to develop strategies of resistance. This edited version of her presentation appeared in Beyond Clericalism: The Congregation as a Focus for Theological Education, *edited by Joseph C. Hough, Jr., and Barbara G. Wheeler (Atlanta: Scholars Press, 1988), 137–51.*

LIBERATION HERMENEUTICS AND THE REIGNING THEOLOGICAL AND SOCIAL-SCIENTIFIC PARADIGMS

I do not believe that Christian ethics is a discipline in either the classic or the modern sense of that term.[1] In my view, it is, rather, a high art form, a praxis[2] that integrates—and must integrate—several streams of intellectual theory, themselves compounds of disciplines or heuristics of inquiry and interpretation.

To insist on this view of Christian ethics already signals that in mode and methodology I fall within the genre of liberation theology. This means that I understand all theory to be related dialectically to human experience and that I am committed to shaping my own theoretical choices in accordance with an active posture of resistance to domination.[3] Such resistance is not possible in isolation; it becomes a life option only in and through the experience of communities of resistance. It also acknowledges that such a vocation is to refuse dehumanization and to resist conditions that thwart life.

The streams of theory required to practice Christian ethics are (1) theological theories of historical Christian communities, (2) moral theories of both Christian communities and the cultural and intellectual traditions integrated into them, and (3) the various streams of social theory—the disciplines of human self-understanding that are, today, perceived as separate from Christian theological-ethical theory, including modes of social science, and also philosophical and scientific perspectives that have not otherwise been woven into existing Christian self-understanding by earlier integration.

Practitioners of Christian ethics today can develop a normative theory about what Christian ethics should be only through either an implicit or an explicit integration of these three strands. An explicit integration is preferable, because it makes clear one's assumptions. But every normative theological-ethical perspective is, simultaneously, a normative evaluation of theological-moral social relations.[4] Though I disagree with some of the theses advanced by David Pacini in an article on congregations, I agree with his dissent from the prevailing notion that theological investigations cannot arise from the analysis of social conditions:

> What is right about [this viewpoint] is the notion that there are distinctions between the analogies of social science and theology. What is wrong is the presumption that sociological analyses do not already contain an implicit theological view point, or that theological analyses are not contingent upon an implicit sociological meeting.[5]

Though I would substitute the term *social* for *sociological* here, I concur that all notions of divine-human and human-human relations imply a conception of social relations and that all conceptions of social relations imply notions of what is benevolent cohumanity and sacred power. They also imply at least minimal moral notions about the obligations, values, and virtues that should characterize human interaction.[6] It is not possible to practice Christian ethics as a reflective action without an integrating of these theoretical streams.

None of us—seminary professors, social scientists, or lay Christians—can ignore the inclusive normative force of what we articulate, whether we speak of how we experience God or what we are to do in the church and world.[7] Furthermore, theology, moral theory, and social theory are embedded in ideological conflict, the fundamental human debate about the nature and direction of social change.[8] Christian ethics and the wider theological enterprise would be made clearer if more attention were paid to these epistemological issues.

My discussion pertains to the relationship of professional theologians to the life of congregations. Christian theologians and ethicists must accept, as they now do not, responsibility for forming their theories at the concrete loci of Christian praxis—local communities of believers. Like theologians, liberation theologians accept the normative character of theological-ethical reflection and do not claim to approach congregations disinterestedly. Unlike those who take other, more idealist positions, however, we assume the existence of resistance to domination in these communities. A liberation theological hermeneutic aims to enable members of the congregation to become more explicitly engaged in such resistance.

From a liberation perspective, what needs to be recognized is that the problem of many theologians' positions is not so much their excessive "accountability to the academy" per se. Rather, many inadvertently mimic reigning academic theories of knowledge by embracing conceptions of theological truth that assume that Christian theology already has established and incontrovertible norms. As a result, the professional theologian's normative role becomes a protection against dissent. Theological theory is often appropriated idealistically, and the social context of praxis that produced it is forgotten. Rarely is the ideological role of past theological-ethical utterances made clear. Consequently, too many theologians join other academic elites in approaching the "object" of their research or the "subjects" of their consultation with much to teach and little to learn.

The difference between a liberation theological epistemology and the predominant ethos of academic theology is dramatic. Here I can identify only a few salient divergences. Although few dispute the appropriateness of normativity in theology, many dispute the locus of theological normativity. In a liberation hermeneutic, it rests not in confidence regarding the past theological truth but in the faith praxis of existing faith communities insofar as that faith praxis concretely transforms human life in the direction of nonalienating experiences of power and relations, of and to God, the world, and neighbor. Theology, like all humanly constructed perspectives, is here understood to function dialectically. It either masks or reveals power and relationships; it is life giving or it is life denying.[9] In its masking function, the theological perspective perpetuates and reproduces existing alienated relationships; in its revealing function, it opens the way to realizing concrete good as shared power and a deeper relationship with God, world, and neighbor. According to this view, the concrete locus and generating center of all theology is in the particularity of people's real lives in their struggles. Appeals to orthodoxy as established truth do not admit the reception of fresh revelation or novel human experience. Theology ceases to be a self-critical discipline—one that can both challenge and unmask and incorporate new value as truth. The refusal itself of Christian theology to use resistance to oppression as the starting point, expecting new theological insight to arise from such a struggle, testifies to a nondialectical perspective on the relation of theory and praxis.

The literature on local congregations shows social science theorists capable of empathetic engagement with congregations and parishes, as even epistemologically inadequate theories of social science make some room for participation and empirical referents in their recommended modes of inquiry. I am not ready to change hats and cast my lot exclusively with the social theorists, however, because a liberation hermeneutic creates as deep epistemological differences with the reigning conceptions of social science theory[10] as with the reigning conceptions of theological-ethical theory.

I agree with many Latin American liberation theologians and embrace the radical conception of the role of social theory and science associated with a broadly Marxian view of human science.[11] That is, the aim of human science should not be to understand the world but to enable us to change it, and to do so with the aim of greater justice for members of our species and the wider environment in which we are set.[12] Marx is persistently misunderstood in the North American context, and so I insist that identifying with the Marxian genre of radical social science means denying that there can be any positive or noncontingent knowledge of the human social world and rejecting the view that there are "iron laws" in human history.[13] Radicals believe that the goal of social-theoretical inquiry is the greatest possible precision in comprehending how past social relations have enmeshed current human relationships in alienation and violence. From this perspective, human alienation is the result of exploitative social relationships. "Scientific" knowledge is a descriptive mode of "critical" knowledge, that is, knowledge that "unmasks" how the interpretations of the past are read to show that the social relations of the present cannot be changed. The test of "scientific" knowledge's adequacy, then, is whether it discerns the mechanisms of exploitation precisely enough to identify the patterns that must be altered in order for justice to occur.

Because theological and social-scientific theory must converge in a critical hermeneutic aimed toward justice (that is, mutual empowerment and right relationship), the theorist must understand his or her relationship to a community of believers not as didactic but as reciprocal. Critical theory, theological-ethical and social, must be tested and transformed in dialectical relation to the ongoing praxis and faith claims of other believers. In other words, my accountability as a theorist is to my own well-being and to those with whom I stand, and to what will happen to us in shared transformation as we struggle together for life-giving change. This does not mean that constructive social change is within our grasp or even possible in a given circumstance. A liberation hermeneutic presumes neither the simple malleability of our common life nor the amenability of existing alignments of power to genuine human fulfillment.[14] But it does posit the necessity of unending struggle for fulfillment and the godly presence that such a struggle promises. The proclamation of the divine promise of deliverance is truthful only when this struggle for shared, abundant life occurs. But such an annunciation is only mystifying double-talk without struggle. And this means that liberation theological rhetoric can mystify as much as any other can.

A LIBERATION HERMENEUTIC FOR CONGREGATIONS

I can only roughly describe here the meaning of a liberation hermeneutic for the role of the Christian ethicist vis-à-vis the local congregation. One assumption of this hermeneutic is that its analytic point of departure must be the concrete life contradictions that operate in the church and the world to prevent human fulfillment. Over the last decade and a half, I have tried to locate and express solidarity with those local congregations whose entry point in this struggle has been resistance to the subjugation created by male supremacy in Christian tradition and praxis, a subjugation that renders women and their faith praxis all but invisible, whether in the literature on local congregations (in which women are hardly a minority),[15] or in the images, metaphors, and narratives of theological confessions and liturgy. A feminist liberation theological hermeneutic, however, relates to more than gender relations: Feminist theory and struggle must answer to the oppression of all women and thus become a critique of all human domination in light of women's experience, a faith praxis that can unmask whatever threatens the well-being of the poorest, nonwhite woman.[16]

From a liberation stance, the guiding questions for congregational life are these: What contradictions deform the lives of those gathered in this community, and what forms does the resistance to these contradictions take? The patterns and structures of domination operate upon and within Christian communities, for a community of believers is never less or more than a community that shares the life of the world. But such a community may also—if it lives its praxis of faith—actively experience the divine presence in resisting disempowerment and alienation. Whether it does depends on the availability of critical resources, including theoretical ones, for demystifying domination. This is when theological, ethical, and social theory may help, not as a substitute for an ongoing praxis of resistance but as an analytic component of this unmasking and annunciatory process. Communities of believers need the intellectual resources of theological-ethical-social traditions, not as imposed theory but as a resource for a process that empowers them as agents of faith.

My experience working with the contradiction of gender among women in local congregations has taught me that the key to liberation hermeneutics rests in a process of self-naming, or conscientization, whereby women learn to trust their own capacities as analysts and agents. Feminism has been a creative spiritual force in much mainstream Protestant congregational church life in the last fifteen years (and although male commentators have mostly missed this fact, it has been nearly the only dynamic spiritual force in predominantly white Protestant mainstream churches) because so many women have actually had this conscientization experience of empowerment. And despite the well-orchestrated effort to discredit feminist sensibility as a cultural and political force and to coopt women to reinforce traditional values, the spiritual health of any congregation can, more often than not, be measured by the changes taking place in women's roles.

My work with congregations has led me increasingly to the conviction that the major drawback to the presence of liberation hermeneutics in local parishes, including the development of an inclusive feminist hermeneutic among the women in these churches, rests with the pervasive mystification of other contradictions in congregational life. One, obviously, is the mystification of white supremacy. I do not know how to correct it in the predominantly white churches in which I work. My own conviction is that nothing works against the emergence of a genuine faith praxis among white Christian communities as much as does our failure to grasp the full meaning of "white privilege" on this planet at this juncture in history. At the same time, I believe that we cannot develop a faith praxis that resists white supremacy in its personal and political guises unless we discover far more about the particularity of the contradictions in our own lives. Using an inclusive feminist hermeneutic has deepened my conviction that insensitivity to others' suffering and to our own cultural destructiveness is conditioned by our failure to appropriate and accept the reality of our own pain and to comprehend how existing historical contradictions affect us. Because white Christians in the dominant culture have lost touch with the courage and struggle that have been part of our own heritage, a struggle that has grounded the most authentic values of that heritage, we neither see nor respect the contradictions and struggles of Afro-Americans, Latinos, Native Americans, Asians, and others who are culturally marginal to the dominant ethos.

Accordingly, I have worked to develop a specific liberation hermeneutic process vis-à-vis white mainstream congregations that focuses on the contradictions most common in the lives of middle-American white people, whether in local communities of believers or in our wider common life. These contradictions and their attendant mystifications are related to the socioeconomic dynamics that shape our lives. Increasingly, I am interested in the possibility of conscientization with respect to the issue of class. What I propose to do in the space remaining in this paper is to clarify how a methodology might be conceived that aims at conscientization in class, a methodology formulated to enable local communities of believers to begin to name the alienations and disempowerments occurring in their lives today.

TOWARD A CRITICAL KNOWLEDGE OF CLASS
DYNAMICS IN LOCAL CONGREGATIONS

I do not accept most of the current characterizations of the socioeconomic situation of most mainstream local congregations and parishes. Nor do I believe that the fairly well-educated rank and file of church members is equipped to revise social relations in this society. The privileged status of Christians is less a factor than most believe; more important is the identification of Christians and non-Christian "middle" Americans with the dominant ideology of the United States as "the promised land" and as a society characterized by "the individual as central sensibility."[17] By contrast, I believe that middle Americans live in a world in which we are growing more powerless to shape even local conditions of well-being. But should we identify with the dominant ideology, an identification that is secured in many ways? One characteristic of our life is a "social amnesia"[18] through which we lose touch with the particular struggles of our families and communities. Such an amnesia alienates us from anything in our present and past that does not correlate with the "American Dream" and upward mobility. There-fore, we require a concept of class that resists reinforcing the dominant ideology.

Current social science blends the notion of class with social status and renders the concept heuristically empty by treating "class" as equivalent to "stratum," as in upper, middle, and lower. A stratified society permits the mobility of some, but stratification, because it is viewed as inexorable, has no historical import. Many factors—income, educational level, employment prestige—coalesce to cre-ate a class position, and a change of position results from a change in these fac-tors. A more useful notion of class, however, does not merely identify stratum location, but rather identifies what the concept of stratum location hides, namely, how socioeconomic dynamics enhance or prevent people's participation in shap-ing their lives and the life of their communities.[19]

In teaching economic justice I have discovered that morally sensitive people, perhaps especially conscientious Christian people, have been encouraged to over-look their families' struggles for material survival by identifying with some sec-tor of the middle class. Having an adequate, even if moderate, family income is assumed to be a guaranty of middle-class status, and an income of $60,000 for a family of six that enables the parents to own a home and two cars and to pay the full costs of private higher education for the children is interpreted as affluence. Not infrequently, students in my seminary classes acknowledge that coming to appreciate the dynamics of the global and the U.S. economy has led to reconcil-iation with their parents, whose anxieties about money they had previously writ-ten off as greed! When I ask my students to locate more relevant indices of class—in either their family's income-producing wealth or their power to deter-mine the goals of their work—few claim an upper status of any kind.

When a stratum-status notion of class prevails, a social theorist can charac-terize a congregation's class status by determining the group's average income and other relevant factors. The literature on congregations abounds in such charac-terizations and also the assumption that a given congregation is homogeneous at the socio-economic level. To be sure, most mainstream, predominantly white congregations or parishes are homogeneous in one sense: Most of the members of a given congregation belong to the same statistical class stratum. But I submit that a critical consciousness, one that is aware of contradiction and mystification, requires us both to be suspicious of the dominant liberal theory of class and to fear the further repression of particularity that follows from any easy diagnosis of homogeneity.[20] If empowerment lies in the simultaneous recovery of both particularity and deepened relationship, do we dare to analyze congregations in this way?

The prevailing theory of class has other problems. A stratum-status analysis by family units, for example, hides women's economic vulnerability. The full-time homemaker is always economically vulnerable, as high poverty rates among recently divorced homemakers attest. (Conclusions about the homogeneity of congregations usually leave women out of the picture altogether. A woman pastor told me that the percentage of older widows in her upper-middle-class congregations who, for financial reasons, lived on cat food is staggering.) Furthermore, family income figures invariably mask the deep differences in male income levels in apparently similar, but actually different, "white collar employment." Most families have "middle incomes" because two salaries, not one, are involved. There are other objections to the stratum-status theory. More to the point, however, is that its emphasis on income masks rather than reveals the basic questions that concern for "class" should foster: Who controls the resources shaping our lives, and who participates, or is excluded from participation, in socially generated power? Both men's and women's lives are mystified and misrepresented by a stratum-status analysis. Increasingly, this mystification is the one that most threatens the spiritual integrity of congregation life.

I cannot outline an alternative theory of class here. But as in so many other analytic matters, I agree with Karl Marx that classes are antagonistic groups created by the patterns of social relations conditioned by the organization of the social means of production.[21] Marx insisted that society's organization of the means of production would affect social relations more directly than would other factors because material well-being is so basic to species survival.[22] Such organization will most directly determine the extent to which a society's social fabric is characterized by alienation. Unless human sensuous labor joins control of the goals of production, exploitation will be intense. To demystify this exploitation, the relationship of work, ownership, and control must be seen in historical perspective.

Marx's insight that economic activity is principally human work—not, as in capitalist economic theory, the buying and selling of goods and the exchange of money—is critical to an adequate theological method.[23] Even though we now live in a capitalist, global political economy, in which most labor (an exception is household work) is turned into a commodity—something we do in order to make money—it is still important to consider the theological-ethical significance of the nature and quality of people's work as basic to their spiritual and moral well-being. It is all the more important at a time when life in the workplace is deteriorating for everyone and the prospects for meaningful work for most people are eroding.

Marx's class analysis of early industrial capitalism clearly has been preempted by the dramatic changes in the now-global capitalist system.[24] The antagonistic and exploitative relations that Marx identified in middle-period capitalist Europe between the owners of the means of production and the wage laborers they employed continue to generate conflict wherever capitalist modes of production are introduced into a society. At the heart of the late global capitalist system, however, structural realignments in the political economy are only one conflict in the owners' (transnational corporations) exploitation of wage laborers.

The newer dynamics of exploitation relevant to the daily life of middle Americans in congregations include capital shifts, via the corporate state, that are making obsolete all decentralized economic life. That is, small independently owned businesses and farms and small, locally based corporations are becoming untenable or are maintained as costly ventures in family loyalty to local communities. Everywhere large industries capitalize only very profitable ventures. Exceedingly profitable high technology shapes life in the workplace. New jobs, when they are created, are either high-income, high-technology positions or insecure, low-wage, service-sector positions.[25] The national budget is slashing expenditures for education, social programs, and human welfare expenditures in order to increase high-technology military production. Moral questions aside, the increased military expenditures provide only a few jobs per number of dollars expended. Government welfare functions are increasingly being returned to the private sector. Our national leadership disguises this counterrevolution against the modest gains achieved by earlier political struggles for justice with a rhetoric about private charity and the erosion of traditional values.[26] Such language manipulates the fears and nostalgia of people who do not comprehend what is happening. Because they are identified with an amorphous middle stratum or status, Christians are as susceptible as is everybody else to this rhetoric, especially when political leaders ritually embrace those Christian leaders and groups who most often turn theology and ministry to the service of celebrating "tradition."

All this is affecting the daily life of every person in every Christian parish and is placing incredible pressures for conformity on the congregations themselves. At best, we have only a few components of an analytic approach that can help Christian people comprehend this situation.

My work with local church people has taught me that their resistance to examining these issues has less to do with political ideology and identification than with their mistrust of the church as the sort of community in which such revelation may occur. The laity and clergy both feel this mistrust, for very different reasons. Furthermore, my feminist commitment has led me to deal simultaneously with gender and sexuality and with economic justice and class in my work with clergy and laity. As a result, my work with congregations has revealed that sex and money are taboo subjects in the parish because nearly everyone feels vulnerable to them. Very few believe that, as experienced in their congregation, Christian love includes attention to people's suffering in these areas. In order to overcome this mistrust, the development of a critical consciousness of class issues requires participation and mutuality at all levels of congregational life.

The ability to develop a critical class consciousness is not much affected by a congregation's theological perspective. Self-identified liberal congregations and clergy usually have a strong, historically conditioned resistance to accepting struggle and conflict in the community, and far more powerful mechanisms operate within such congregations to identify with the dominant cultural ethos. The social amnesia characteristic of "middle-stratum-identified" groups is especially prominent in liberal churches because job mobility and education obscure connections with family roots. Conservative churches are not much different.

I am still hopeful that approaches to developing a critical class consciousness will emerge from the personal narrative on which a liberation hermeneutic depends. In my work, I use both social and personal cross-generational narratives of individuals and their families and historical narratives about socioeconomic changes in the United States. I then ask the participants to trace the theological-ethical-social biography of their own families across at least three, and if possible, five generations. I ask them to record the socioeconomic factors, cultural sensibilities, and religious convictions, praxis, and observance of past generations of their families. I have them describe the geographic location and type of homes the family occupied, their personal possessions, the work they did, and their access to and attitudes toward money, education, and social status. I ask them to look at patterns of gender relations in their families and how their situations related to the profiles of neighbors in the communities where they lived. I urge them to explore the effect of all these factors on their families' piety and religious practice. In reconstructing their stories, I have my students note experiences of poverty, deprivation, and natural disaster, struggles against illness, personal and social tragedies, and the positive values that helped them in these struggles.

Not surprisingly, this assignment, even when carried out over a period of time that allows for digging and research, confronts participants with a dramatic map of their own and their families' collective social amnesia. Frequently, the result is the discovery that families seem to remember only their "successes" and to forget the "failures." Often relatives' personal problems, such as educational failures, family violence, divorce, and alcoholism, are related to indices of downward socioeconomic mobility, a relationship that no one in most families ever considered when dealing with those who were "problems."

When the narratives have been reconstructed and shared with the other participants, I ask the group to relate their familial-personal narratives to a broader critical analytic, drawn from the work of historians and political economists who share neither the "promised land" reading of U.S. history nor the myth of perpetual upward mobility. The narrative I use shifts somewhat from group to group. Among rural congregations, I highlight the history of U.S. agriculture and the impact of business cycles and government policy on farmers, as well as the cultural impact of urbanization on rural cultural and social life. With urban congregations in the Northeast, I highlight the effect of central capitalist institutions such as banks and corporations on urban centers as well as their role in deindustrialization. In every historical narrative, I describe the effect of war and government policy on veterans, education, land and resource use, and labor.

From these sessions, I have learned that many clergy and laypersons are familiar with the history of their communities and regions but that they understand only little about the impact of national governmental policy. (This is an index, I suspect, of how little they fear the long-term consequences of the Reagan administration's actions.) Few appreciate how much presumed social mobility, in nearly all families, is tied to shifting government policies and to government activism in social welfare. A few examples will suffice. Most autobiographical narratives highlight two points in a family's pilgrimage: the beginning of educational achievement and the first ownership of land or a home. Both are perceived as the crossing of a class threshold. What most people do not realize is that home or land ownership for most American families is made possible by either government land grants or low-interest housing loans for veterans. Except for those who enjoy corporate or more affluent professional income levels, home ownership is chiefly enabled by inheritance, a pattern likely to become more common in the future. Higher educational levels are also related closely to state and federal policies, but by examining the differences between their parents' educational experience and their own and their children's, participants learn that education by itself is no longer a guaranty of upward mobility. Thus, the so-called conservatism of the young and their demand that education respond to the job market is interpreted by some as the result of greed, but these demands are in fact responses to objective and destructive social conditions. A further insight has emerged. What most families experience as periods of upward mobility correlate closely with periods of expansion in the United States economy, especially those following World Wars I and II. That our economic system has become slightly more equitable only when other industrial economics have been decimated by war comes as a shock to most people.

I cannot say much about the broader significance of this sort of conscientization for the ongoing life of congregations. In most instances, this process precipitates a deeper interpersonal respect and a greater ability to identify the roots of powerlessness. Whether such an approach can lead some in the congregation to concern for the well-being of the wider community remains to be seen.[27] What is clear is that for the clergy and laity, the resulting self-respect is not simply personal. It embraces their family forebears, whose life and struggles take on new meaning and power. Their growing capacity to perceive and analyze social dynamics transforms once private pains into public issues with intersubjective grounding in the dynamics of the current political economy. I do believe that those clergy, seminarians, and lay people equipped to engage in this sort of hermeneutical process become more able to relate to what is going on in their congregations. As a result, some have reoriented their pastoral work.

I am not hopeful about the prospects for widespread adoption of this sort of liberation hermeneutic in the life of middle-stratum churches in the United States. Yet I see no alternative except to press on with this process. Such engagement has priority for me as a practitioner of feminist Christian liberation ethics, not because of any particular theological-social theory, as much as I value the theory and practice I have developed. Nor is this priority based on the expectation of success. Rather, it is grounded in my acceptance that these white, Christian middle-stratum folk in the mainstream churches are my people. Like me, my people are capable of empowerment in God as they develop a praxis of justice. Making the connections between my own and others' struggles has also taught me a harder truth, namely, that lacking such empowerment, we pious, white, middle-stratum people in this nation are dangerous to those who share the planet with us. Professing ourselves particularly blessed and truly free, when we are neither, robs us of the capacity to fight for our own lives and also to see and respect the courage, creativity, and transformative power of those many others who struggle for theirs. A liberation hermeneutic in the mainstream churches is a nonnegotiable requirement, not to return these churches to the position of cultural hegemony they once enjoyed but to ensure that the rising tide of "friendly fascism"[28] in our midst will not be able to claim a sanctified Christian face.

Notes

1. I do not understand Christian ethics to be a conceptually discrete body or system of knowledge, or a univocal theoretically informed heuristic of inquiry. Because Christian ethics is practical and moral, it is inherently evaluative and interdisciplinary. The point may seem banal, but in my opinion, much self-flagellation among professional Christian ethicists results from their inability to embrace enthusiastically the interdisciplinary character of their work.

2. The normative force in insisting on a praxis conception of Christian ethics will, I hope, be clarified in what follows. I do not mean to suggest that Christian ethics should be praxis based. My intent is to insist that all Christian ethics reflect at least a latent historical project, hence "a praxis."

3. One of the most helpful expositions of what is involved in a hermeneutic of resistance to domination is found in the work of Elisabeth Schüssler Fiorenza. See especially *In Memory of Her: A Feminist Reconstruction of Christian Origins* (New York: Crossroad, 1983), xiii–65; and *Bread Not Stone: The Challenge of Feminist Biblical Interpretation* (Boston: Beacon Press, 1985), 93–149.

4. Theories that conceptualize the human relationship to sacred power as running directly between God and believer or between God and church, without reference to nature, culture, or history/society often presume to live free of social-theoretical considerations. My perspective classifies such theologies as a species of capitalist social relations theory, even though this theological genre preceded the rise of a fully developed capitalist-political economic theory.

5. David S. Pacini, "Professionalism, Breakdown, and Revelation," in *Building Effective Ministry: Theory and Practice in the Local Church*, ed. Carl S. Dudley (San Francisco: Harper & Row, 1983), 134. I concur with Pacini's call for more concern for metaphorical sensibility and with his unease with mechanistic notions of social process. I take such notions to result from "positivist" conceptions of science. However, I strongly disagree with the assumptions implicit in his "breakdown" thesis. I read him as informed by Alasdair MacIntyre's idealist analysis of our malaise. What we are living through, in my view, are fundamental and humanly destructive institutional social-power realignments, largely invisible to us because of ideological manipulation. People do not just abandon or forget their cultural traditions or values. Rather, the communal forms of life that generate these traditions and values are crushed by a practice based on modes of power and rationality that decimate communities and their cultures. Of course, as a feminist I also cannot be a nostalgic cultural romantic like MacIntyre. Traditional culture also carries contradictions or socially embedded forms of domination. The resistance to struggle against racism and sexism rests precisely in this deep cultural embeddedness, and so a liberation hermeneutic also must be critical at the cultural level.

6. I not only presume the desirability of attending to each of these traditional base points for a Christian ethic but also believe that no genuinely normative ethic is possible without addressing all three.

7. I use the formulation *church and world* to make clear my own assumption, at the epistemological level, that our relationship to God is through nature-culture-society-history and that no one ever actually prescinds from this nexus. There is no "Christ above the culture" option.

8. My point here is simply that there is no way for our theory to float free of "ideological entanglements." Self-awareness of an accountability for the ideological impacts of our work is the only road to the important if modest claims to objectivity we can ever justifiably make.

9. In using the more typical radical conception of ideology here, I do not presume that there is a theoretical standing ground that ensures an ability to demystify. I believe that Marx is misread on this point, not only because of the misinterpretations of his view of science by conservative theorists such as Karl Popper, but also because Marxist academic philosophers, especially of the genre of Paul Althusser, are attempting to return the Marxist tradition to the path of scientific positivism. Marxist academics, every bit as much as Christian theologians, seem incapable of bearing the angst that is required to live with the inherent contestability of human truth claims.

10. Though I shall hereafter use the term *social science* to denote perspectives from academic fields other than theology, I prefer the more complex formulation I use here, in order to avoid identifying my understanding of social science with empiricist notions of it.

11. I do not mean to suggest that there is homogeneity in the interpretation and use of Marxism in Latin American liberation theologies, only that they presume that social analysis must be made explicit in theological work and that the most genuinely historical-critical scientific perspectives should be used.

12. I do not mean to suggest that Marx's own corpus is helpful in conceptualizing a notion of justice. It is not, in part, because Marx denied the possibility of an adequate moral theory under historical conditions of exploitation. Even if he had not, however, he was too preoccupied with analyzing the existing exploitation to reflect on the future. When concern for the future is neglected or suppressed, the dimension of ethical reflection is lost. The best treatment of Marx by a theologian, one that recognizes the point about Marx's failure to consider the future, is by Christopher Lasch, *A Matter of Hope: A Theologian's Reflections on the Thought of Karl Marx* (Notre Dame, Ind.: University of Notre Dame Press, 1982); see esp. 210–30.

13. Marx's satirical uses of this phrase in discussing the "iron laws" of capitalism have been misunderstood by many theologians as defending positivist science, because they do not understand the political-economic view of Marx's contemporaries that he was challenging.

14. I could emphasize this point by insisting on an uncompromising focus on domination and by challenging any "scientific" reading of our situation that renders it resistant to a more adequate human praxis. A liberation hermeneutic breaks completely with the "progressivism" of any social theory that posits evolutionist enlightenment at the scientific, theological, or moral level.

15. Barbara Wheeler observed the absence of women from the company of congregational researchers, in Dudley, ed., *Building Effective Ministry*, 239. I am pointing to the even more notable absence of women from characterizations of the life of congregations and their surrounding communities and also in the conceptualizations of the social world used in these descriptions. What we have here is not merely a failure in human sensitivity but also a theoretically conditioned ineptitude.

16. On this point, see the Mud Flower Collective, *God's Fierce Whimsy: Christian Feminism and Theological Education* (New York: Pilgrim Press, 1985).

17. The term is from Michael Lewis, *The Culture of Inequality* (Amherst, Mass.: University of Massachusetts Press, 1978).

18. The term is from Russell Jacoby, *Social Amnesia* (Boston: Beacon Press, 1975). My own analysis of the sources of social amnesia does not follow Jacoby's, however. Invaluable resources for appreciating how a subjective appropriation of class injuries conditions this process are by Jonathan Cobb and Richard Sennett, *The Hidden Injuries of Class* (New York: Random House, 1972); and Lillian Breslow Rubin, *Worlds of Pain: Life in the Working Class Family* (New York: Basic Books, 1976).

19. See James Stolzman and Herbert Gamberg, "Marxist Class Analysis versus Stratification Analysis as General Approaches to Social Inequality," *Berkeley Journal of Sociology* 18 (1973–1974): 105–25.

20. I do not mean to say that objectivistic-scientific description does not provide valid information. What it does not do is clarify pastoral strategies for helping people avoid "class injury" by not internalizing the dominant ideology.

21. For other reasons to prefer a broadly Marxian approach to social theory, see Beverly Wildung Harrison, "The Use of Social Theory in Christian Ethics," in *Making the Connections: Essays in Feminist Social Ethics*, ed. Carol S. Robb (Boston: Beacon Press, 1985).

22. "Means of production" here means the total complex of land, resources, human labor, and machines needed for any society to produce "surplus value," that is, more value than those resources had before they were used in a productive process. At the risk of either tediousness or tendentiousness in the interpretation of Marx, I want to remind my readers that he neither objects to private ownership of personal property nor implies that markets have no place in a democratized economy. We have no more business holding Marx responsible for the idiocies of some of his followers than we do holding Jesus responsible for the crimes of some of his.

23. It cannot be overstressed how thoroughly we are imbued with the capitalist understanding of the role of economic reality in human life. Even thoughtful efforts to make churches and Christians concerned about economic morality can reinforce this neoclassical paradigm. I have commented on how the pastoral on economic life of the National Conference of Catholic Bishops does this, in "Social Justice and Economic Orthodoxy," *Christianity and Crisis* 44 (January 21, 1985): 513–15. (This article has been reprinted as chapter 19 in this volume.) It should also be noticed that the bad habits of many Christian ethicists in spending most of their energies on questions of distributive justice rather than on communicative justice also reinforces the fallacies of the neoclassical economic paradigm.

24. Unless we connect the analysis of our national economy's dynamics with global structural dynamics, we may also reinforce the wave of nationalistic fervor now orchestrated to discourage dissent. In 1975, a young Latin American economist said to me, "You in North America face a much more difficult task than we do; you must get people to see the direct connections between the sufferings of your people and those of Peruvian peasants." I mark that conversation as the origin of my own participation in economic ethics.

25. An excellent reflection on this matter is by Alan Geyer, "Politics and Ethics of History," *Annual of the Society of Christian Ethics* (1985): 3–17.

26. See William K. Tabb, "The Social, Political, and Ethical Meaning of the 'Reagan Revolution,'" *Annual of the Society of Christian Ethics* (1983): 185–216.

27. Obviously, a movement beyond conscientization and initial analysis to reorienting our broader praxis depends not merely on deepening the life of the congre-

gation but also on making connections with those in the broader community whose praxis is convergent. Because this society is in a situation of severe political repression, such linkages are difficult to make. We must learn to respect the long-term scope of our struggle. Although the prospects for progressive regional and national strategies are dim at present, I believe the new possibilities are emerging locally, if we could only see them.

28. The phrase is from Bertram Gross, *Friendly Fascism: The New Face of Power in America* (New York: M. Evans, 1980).

Chapter 22

The Fate of the Middle
"Class" in Late Capitalism

This essay was originally given as part of a 1987 lecture series on the topic "Rich and Poor: Judeo-Christian Ethics and Market Ethics," sponsored by Agenda for a Prophetic Faith, an interfaith group of Roman Catholic, Protestant, Jewish, and Unitarian clergy and laity in and around Madison, Wisconsin. Harrison presents "an alternative radical reading" of ways the political economy impacts the lives of the vast majority of people in the United States. The essay was originally published in God and Capitalism: A Prophetic Critique of Market Economy, *edited by J. Mark Thomas and Vernon Visick (Madison, Wis.: A-R Editions, 1991), 53–71.*

It is gratifying to participate in a public discussion that aims at careful theological and ethical scrutiny of contemporary economic theory and ideology. While some may mourn the loss of a consensual "public philosophy"[1] in this society, the truth is that there is hardly any public dissent—even in the academy—regarding the theoretical and practical paradigms that underlie policy prescriptions and diagnoses of American political and economic woes.[2] The ostensible disarray at the level of social values is *not* accompanied by a commensurate scepticism about the reigning paradigms of neoclassical economics and of welfare liberal, neoliberal, or neoconservative political theory. Those who are unapologetically radical in their approach to social change have an awesome task before them, especially in view of the ostensibly "social scientific" viewpoints enunciated by the most powerful whom the press and media revere.

To scrutinize the claims and counterclaims of all the ardent defenders of the political economy of the United States is not a task for a single essay. There is too much to be considered concerning both the "neoconservatives" who want less political interference in market exchange and increased government expenditures only for defense, and liberals or "neoliberals" who seek a more "realistic" social interdependence in which the interests of the United States are coordinated with other capitalist, "democratic" nations. What all these mainstream (and "malestream"[3]) analysts share, and what few who take a "radical" stance acknowledge, is that neoclassical economics deserves trust.

To a radical theorist, the neoclassical economic perspective is *the* ideology par excellence of capitalist political economy. It is a theory that explains nothing more than how to assure that capitalism remains capitalism. That is, neoclassical economics demonstrates how wealth and resources may continue to function to the advantage of the minority that controls wealth and the immediate access to political power. It is an ideology because it depicts as "rational" only economic behavior that seeks the "utility maximization" characteristic of market exchange. That other motives and values might deserve priority in our action as economic agents is either unthinkable (ruled out by definition) or, worse, held to be economically "irrational." Neoclassical economic theory is itself a system of morality—and theology and ethics—masquerading as "science." Yet those who dissent from this hidden morality have a difficult task before them, for this debate concerning the ethics of economics is consistently suppressed in public discourse. Reigning economic theory makes calls for the substantive realignment of existing economic power appear as madness. Dissenters are by *definition* "unrealistic," "utopian," or "irresponsible."

The moral and religious implications of neoclassical economic theory have already been explored. The relevant point for this discussion, however, is that this "hidden consensus" on the moral and religious benevolence of our social, political, and economic system leads people to cynicism about public life, and to the sense that it makes little difference who gets elected or what political rhetoric is used. The widespread despair about the impotence of politics, and the escape into privatized values, will continue so long as basic questions about the structural relationships between economic control and political power are ruled out of public debate. Liberals and neoconservatives conspire—by uncritical acceptance of neoclassical economic theory—to keep that issue from serious discussion.

This essay offers an alternative radical reading of how the political economy is affecting the lives of the vast majority in American society—those in the "middle." Such an interpretation of what is happening to the middle "class"[4] in this society is only the beginning of the broader theological and ethical analysis required. But such an analysis can illustrate how public discourse would be improved if those who control the ideological climate permitted serious radical perspectives to be widely heard.

The principle of theological and ethical interpretation employed here is one broadly invoked by Christian and other religious feminists: a "socialist-feminist liberation hermeneutic" that seeks to take seriously the concrete experience of people's lives. Particularly, it adopts a "hermeneutic of suspicion"[5] about the existing order of things. The aim is to illumine the concrete suffering of those victimized by the social orders we human beings have constructed. A "socialist-feminist hermeneutic of suspicion" accepts accountability for the "poorest of the poor"[6]—women and men of marginalized racial, ethnic, and religious cultures excluded from full social empowerment and participation by barriers of class, gender, or sexual orientation and preference. Racism, class and gender privilege, and compulsory heterosexuality constitute powerful structural constraints making people powerless, without access to the minimal conditions for human dignity. Feminist-socialist theological and ethical perspectives seek a complex, interstructural account of human suffering and a praxis[7] that understands human-divine, human to human, and human-cosmic relationships holistically and critically. Such a theological ethic assumes that human life is embedded in cultural, social, political-economic, and cosmic relationships. All basic theological and moral questions are about power-in-relationship. They question what the existing power-in-relationship is, how existing power distorts and alienates relationship and community, and how persons can act together to transform social life into genuine (nonalienated) community.

This theological vision is of a world where there are no excluded ones, but such a world is hardly the present one. The current polemic against liberation theologies vacillates between the claims that it espouses violence, that it neglects the theological task of "reconciliation," and that it is too "utopian" and "unrealistic" in insisting upon policies that transform all forms of social privilege. But social violence is always pervasive (even if invisible to the powerful) wherever social injustice exists. To kill the dream of a just and inclusive society is to entrap humanity in the status quo, to render the power of religious imagination moot, and to rob persons of hope and power to act for change.

This analysis emerges from only one critical category of a feminist liberation hermeneutic: class privilege. It needs to be stressed, therefore, that the sketch of life in the middle of this society requires amplification in other directions not offered here. White racism and ethnocentricity, Christian religious imperialism, Anglocentric European cultural hegemony, and enforced conformity to compulsory heterosexuality all contribute powerfully to the dynamics of exclusion from middle-class life. Women, especially racial ethnic women, and their dependent children are (and increasingly will be) "the poorest of the poor" in this nation and globally. To reinterpret critically the suffering of the middle is no substitute for addressing these broader dynamics. No politics is progressive and no theology or morality genuinely liberationist if it begins and ends with class analysis. Socialist-feminists, black and Hispanic liberationists, and others have rightfully charged that the traditional "radical" social theories generated by the Euro-centered Marxian academic traditions have produced neither theory nor strategies adequate to genuine social transformation. This failure stems precisely from a refusal to take race, gender, and the control of sexuality or cultural hegemony seriously. Nor have the traditional antagonisms of the progressive secular left enabled serious attention to the distinction between alienated and transformative religion in the struggle for liberation.

Even so, it may well be that mystification of class reality is *the* trump card of those who control ideological discourse in this society. Morally speaking, the notion of "fate" used here is suspect in any ethical analysis, if only because fate cannot be resisted in action. But in the absence of a critical theory of class, the ongoing incapacitation of middle-strata people does appear almost as fate. Without a broad understanding of what is happening, it is difficult to resist policies that purport to serve the interests which—we are daily assured—all decent and hard-working people should share.

Neoclassical economics provides no theory of class relations. Unlike *all* classical political economists—including Adam Smith, David Ricardo, and Karl Marx—modern mainstream economists leave such concerns to political scientists, sociologists, and other "soft" (i.e., less "scientific") social perspectives. When liberal or neoconservative theorists of the political economy speak of class at all, they tend to use the term as a synonym for *social stratum*.[8] Since, presumably, every society is "stratified," every society is a "class-stratified" society. By definition, then, this theory of class invites us to think of class relations as a perennial, fixed, and inevitable mode of social differentiation. The chief problem with this conception of class is that it reveals nothing about the relation of human beings to political, economic, or social power.

Recently, one empirically minded sociologist discovered that 80 percent of the people in his statistically viable sample identified themselves as "middle class." Another recent survey reported that 92 percent of people told pollsters that they were members of the "middle class."[9] Yet today, no one willing to discuss poverty in the United States denies that the poor constitute a massive group. Most responsible estimates concede that not less than 20 to 23 percent of our population lives in poverty. Some of these are "working poor," but most live outside of any regular sustained wage-relation to the economy. They are often maintained by welfare or other "safety net" provisions or by alternative improvised arrangements such as petty crime. Still, even the millions of retired persons living on social security and modest fixed retirement incomes opt for "middle class" status when asked to identify their own affiliation.

The alternative radical approach to class hardly constitutes a simple paradigmatic alternative. Radicals—including all who look to insights from Karl Marx for understanding class dynamics in society—are far from a unified mind about what constitutes the class dynamics of late monopoly capitalism. Still, what is shared is a general critical heuristic insight that was central to Marx's polemic against his contemporaries.

Christian theologians and teachers often have profoundly misrepresented Marx's views, and Christians (in the name of respect for truth) must work to avoid perpetuating these dishonest interpretations. Marx is often portrayed as a political radical whose primary aim was to overthrow capitalism and bring in a utopian "classless" society. Based on the one small political tract Marx coauthored, *The Communist Manifesto,* Christians often accuse him of wanting to foment class conflict and "create" social discontent. This is to misunderstand not only Marx but the entire intellectual context of which he was a part.

Karl Marx's basic work as an intellectual was to trace historically how societies organized basic natural resources and human labor to produce wealth. In point of fact, Marx seemed to argue that capitalism was a world-historical phase in the organization of natural, human society and that it had created some of the conditions for genuine social democracy. One may indeed criticize Marx for underestimating capitalism's problems rather than for overestimating them. Among other things, for him capitalism had spurred and accelerated the social creation of wealth and as such was a "necessary" condition for the eradication of poverty.[10] Marx did not fully anticipate the profligate power of industrial capitalism to exhaust natural resources or pollute the earth and biosphere—a point not lost on some of his latter-day followers.

Be that as it may, what Marx aimed to accomplish was a careful analysis of how capitalism worked as a total system of political economy. He was insistent that political economists should aim for a critical (demystifying) interpretation of the past and present in order to enable humanity to avoid reproducing the alienated social relations of the present. "Social theory" (to use the term Marx employed for what most of us call "social science") must be a critical science. Positivistic knowledge of human society—that is, ways of construing present social organization as "inevitable"—presently reigns. Only a critical science enables persons to act effectually to improve social relations.[11]

Marx's view of economic relations is very different from Adam Smith's, whose perspective was adopted by the mainstream defenders of capitalist political economy. To Smith, buying and selling—market relations—are the quintessential economic activities. Marx parodied this view. In a capitalist economy, market relations—buying and selling, or "business"—*appear* to be the basic economic activities. But to define economic activity this way is to misinterpret both human nature and the genuinely distinctive features of capitalism. What makes capitalism capitalism is *the ownership of the means of production by a few,* an "owning class."[12] In contrast to Adam Smith, Marx insisted that the basic distinctive human economic activity was sensuous labor, and that a humanly emancipatory approach to political economy would have to change human political economy so that humans did not literally have to sell themselves in order to live. For Marx the "commodification" of labor power—a process through which persons become self-alienated because they do not control their own labor power—was the defining social relation of capitalism.[13] He predicted rightly that this commodification would penetrate all areas of social life under capitalism. And what was happening in the economic structure was mirrored socially in cultural life.

While one may disapprove of what some followers of Marx have done with his basic insights about capitalism, he was very much on target about class. He argued that antagonistic and conflictual social relations—"class conflict"—would be pervasive where the political economy of capitalism is not altered politically. He insisted that class conflict would continue to be the characterizing feature of such a political economy because some few own the means of production and the vast majority must sell their labor to survive. Marx sought to make those disadvantaged by existing class relations more precisely aware of the social arrangements that oppressed them. This was not an effort to increase class conflict but to give existing victims consciousness of the dynamics of oppression that already shaped their lives.

Of course, modern radical social theorists still debate how Marx's insights concerning class and the social reproduction of alienation should be elaborated, given the dynamic and global changes that have taken place in capitalist political economy. Antagonistic relations between nineteenth- and early twentieth-century owners and the new industrial proletariat in the central capitalist economies have undergone dramatic change. Today, advanced monopoly capitalism is in the process of realigning itself in such a way that antagonistic class relations are reproducing themselves dramatically in every society penetrated by capitalism. This only exacerbates premodern class alignments. Most importantly, antagonistic class lines now run not only *within* nations but *between* them.

Still, how is life in the middle of this society shaped, conditioned, and mystified by the failure to take seriously these antagonistic social relations? From a radical perspective, the "class line" runs between the few who control wealth-creating capacity and the wage-laborers who do not have the conceptual categories to name their growing powerlessness.

Nearly fifteen years ago, a young Latin American economist noted that the task of liberation theology was far more difficult in the United States than in Latin America because here it is much more difficult to see how the political and economic forces that are reshaping the lives of all Latin American peasants are also transforming the lives of every woman, man, and child in this country. From a liberation theology perspective, "critical consciousness," or awareness of subjugation and oppression, must begin with our own experience.[14] The failure to see and name pervasive class dynamics in this society is robbing middle-strata people—especially men—of the critical insight needed to become aware of their subjugation or to act creatively and effectually against human oppression. White feminist women and racial and ethnically marginalized women and men have entree into the sort of critical consciousness required for active resistance to oppression. But white mainstream men, and the women who still shape their way of seeing the world primarily through white male identification, do not have such an entry point. In the absence of the sort of critical theory of class alluded to here, those growing more powerless are particularly susceptible to manipulation and to projection of their fears onto those more powerless still. That "blaming the victim"[15] is a conspicuous social dynamic in our common life, and "meanness mania"[16] a widespread social reality, is not surprising given the ideology that teaches that America is a truly "classless" society where the social antagonisms of political and economic privilege have been largely overcome. Insofar as people believe this, they are enervated. Yet, for the most part, white people in the middle do tend to believe precisely this.

To further discern the current fate of the middle class, brief attention must be given to two matters: some features of advanced monopoly capitalism that are reshaping our domestic economy in a direction that enervates people, and the ideological convictions that maintain the "invisibility" of class relations.

No one denies that capitalist political economy has been "dynamic." But the neoclassical theory of market-state transactions does not attend to the specific history of the restructuring of capital, nor to the political, social, and cultural consequences of such processes. Once again, it must be acknowledged that radical scholars are divided about how the story of capitalist political economy unfolds historically and about how to interpret the current global restructuring of this political and economic system.

There is some consensus about how the United States economy fits into the wider picture, however. Early capitalist economy in the United States developed with "advantages," first of a slave labor system—systems of indentured labor—and later massive immigration of peoples from other nations, many fleeing the effects of the rapid dislocations of Britain's and central Europe's own industrializing process. Land and resources were abundant, and America's decentralized liberal political system favored not only "free enterprise" but the vast private acquisition of land and resources. Until the twentieth century, the United States's geopolitical remoteness from European national political conflict also favored the development of a strong and relatively independent national economy. Technological innovation fueled the dynamic shift from the family firm (upon which Adam Smith's implicit model of microeconomics was predicated) to the regional and national corporation.

Neoclassical economics is predicated on an abstract model of market exchange presupposing competition as the distinctive dynamic of capitalist economy. Radical economic historians contend, to the contrary, that the dynamic of the capitalist business unit is toward monopoly or the effort to enhance profitability through the control of markets.[17] U.S. economic history must be read not only as a story of the acceleration of concentrations of wealth and power but as a story of the increasing mobilization of the state in the service of existing economic power. This latter has been accomplished in spite of massive resistance from those disadvantaged by growing concentrations of wealth. A radical reading of American history recognizes that its economic history is full of crisis.[18] With each crisis, the system itself undergoes structural change and centralization to enhance profitability, no matter the cost to people in terms of joblessness, bankruptcy, and loss of economic security.

There is always political resistance to this accelerated trend toward concentration of wealth and power. Progressive political struggle now and in the past has wrested concessions that mitigate the worst effects of these changes, but not without brutal struggle, as labor, racial ethnic, and agricultural history demonstrates.[19]

In the later nineteenth and twentieth centuries, the political economy of the United States became ever more integrated into the European system of colonialism and political competition. American participation in the "world wars" of the twentieth century—which required "total mobilization"[20] of our political economy—accelerated the liaison between the national state and those sectors of capitalism that were nationally integrated. After the Second World War, the United States had the only remaining fully functional industrialized economy in the world. For over a decade, American society reaped the fruits of this historical anomaly. The high regard most Americans have for capitalism derives in large part from memories of that time of national economic prosperity. During that period, when the productive power of the United States was unrivaled, the total wealth of the society accelerated dramatically. The so-called rising standard of living created a trickle-down effect which increased the economic well-being of millions.

It is undeniable that during that period the expansion of national wealth accelerated and the margin of economic security for many people in the society was increased dramatically. What is frequently forgotten is that, prior to that period, the economic position of the vast majority was profoundly precarious, and few escaped daily anxiety about money and the economic stability of the American system. The "Great Depression" of the 1930s was atypically traumatic in the United States only because it was the first nationally integrated crisis. Regional and local depressions of comparable scale have been frequent.

Significantly, this gain in national wealth became a primary source for the "myth of classlessness." Since the election of President Nixon, neoconservatives have managed an ideological triumph by creating an alternative official history about this economic prosperity. Drawing upon fear and reaction to pressure for change in the 1960s—the Civil Rights and Black Liberation movements, the anti-Vietnam War movement, the early stirrings of women's organized efforts for justice—propagandists of the right portray American affluence as the perennial fruit of unbridled "free enterprise." In point of fact, every objective change in the living standards of citizens of the United States has come from accelerating national wealth, not from the redistribution of that wealth. Periodic national prosperity has enabled political leaders to enact legislation resisted by conservative forces. Without political pressure, growing prosperity would not have been shared to the extent that it has been.

In asking students and others to trace their family histories socially, culturally, and politically, paying close attention to those points in that history when enhanced economic security was noted, their answers frequently turn on occasions when land or home ownership or access to higher education became a reality. Just as frequently, economic shifts were recognized when new government initiatives were enacted. Policies such as G.I. loans, veterans mortgage benefits, or enhanced spending for public education were the source of these positive shifts. Yet today, the self-designated middle class largely credits private enterprise for the generalizing of prosperity. People also increasingly accept the correlative judgment that political organization and effort *cannot* affect the deep injustices of our common life. The ideology of capitalist economic interest has penetrated so deeply into public discourse that even when most "liberal" presidential candidates conceive of strategies for securing economic justice, these strategies involve deepening the liaison between massive corporate wealth and the state.[21]

Meanwhile, the transnational integration of corporate power proceeds apace, fundamentally restructuring our domestic economy. The absorption of the state into this larger global capitalist system has led to a foreign policy that commits the United States to supporting reactionary political forces in other nations that submerge their national economies in the global capitalist system. This places the United States in the position of supporting ruthless military regimes that enforce austerity on their impoverished people and that mis-develop local and national economies to serve the needs of the global system.

Our domestic economy is also undergoing profound mis-development. The much discussed problem of deindustrialization—the loss of basic industries and industrial jobs—is but the tip of the iceberg. Increasingly, this economy has become militarized—shaped and sustained by massive federal expenditures on military technology and hardware. These expenditures create far fewer jobs and no wealth-producing goods or socially beneficial services. And they also negatively affect small enterprises and family farms. The centralized, capital-intensive economy is transforming the lives and economic prospects of millions of people for the worse. Many are losing farms and businesses once thought to be the secure reward of hard work and devoted effort.

Life in the workplace is changing for nearly everyone, as bureaucratization accelerates and demands for so-called productivity increase. The labor market is being transformed in ways that hold little promise for the young who go deeply into debt to gain educations that once promised "upward mobility." The labor market is "segmenting"—producing a few high-income jobs for technical elites and large numbers of low-income jobs in the service and distribution sectors, for instance, in the fast food industry, in retailing, and in the repetitive "low-tech" segment of the "high-tech" economy. Many of these new jobs carry few if any of the traditional benefits and protections won by working people in earlier labor struggles. Is it any wonder that the young are often portrayed as confused, unmotivated, or lacking in traditional values? They often know intuitively that their futures will not fit the American dream, and that the traditional values of hard work and responsibility make little difference in the world in which they live. Fewer and fewer of them can look forward to home ownership, debt-free middle age, or secure retirement.

Underfunding of public-service sectors also results in job cutbacks, downward income trajectories for those who have jobs, and escalating work loads. With fewer jobs available in the industrial sector, and with regional shifts to where industrial jobs are available, organized labor has diminished power to constrain the downward trend in wages in relation to the cost of living. Corporate profit margins are at record highs. U.S. workers, who have long had the lowest rate of unionization of any capitalist, industrialized nation, have virtually no way to resist workplace tyranny because their access to political power is so indirect. Through the two-party system, Democrats vie with Republicans to find solutions to public problems that enhance corporate power.

All of the foregoing is taking place with little public discussion concerning how public policy decisions and the state-corporate relationship are affecting the lives of the people of this country. The culture of capitalism—making consumable things of all relationships and activities—has penetrated American life so totally that politicians speak more of the rights of consumers than of the well-being of citizens. Without a critical conception of class, individuals feel that they are largely on their own economically, and that compassion for others or concern for the common good is naive or foolish. This isolation of human beings represents a spiritual malaise that enervates people and discourages efforts to seek ways of common action. The cultural ideology of an earlier social welfare liberalism now combines with a widespread "social amnesia" regarding past political struggles to keep the myth of being a political economy in place. This cultural ideology that hides class reality must be addressed.

Class may be defined by antagonistic social relations between those who control wealth and have ample political power and those whose economic life is determined by episodic wages and voter participation. Class conflict of this sort can be seen pervasively in this society. Yet that conflict remains largely covert, appearing as alienation or social "anomie,"[22] resentment, addiction, and self-directed or other-directed anger and violence. Class mobility, so often portrayed as a distinctive feature of our political economy, is all but nonexistent. Most radical historians deny that there has been any genuine dynamic of class mobility in our history. To the contrary, the percentage of the total wealth of this society owned and controlled by the richest 2 percent of our population has risen continuously throughout our history, and in the Reagan-Bush era it has reached unparalleled proportions. Simultaneously, the percentage of total wealth owned and controlled by the poorest 20 percent of the population has dropped. Most people in the United States who have enjoyed a greater measure of prosperity have done so because women have gone to work. The wages of working men have been tied to inflation only by labor militancy—and then only in periods of relatively high employment. And the United States has always found high rates of unemployment to be socially tolerable by comparison to other industrialized nations.[23] Upward mobility in America is a chimera, an impression created by rising educational levels and by favorable economic conditions maintained by global political hegemony. The actual course of class mobility is as frequently downward due to loss of job stability, declining income, lower job status, and for most working people, pauperized retirement. Social welfare provisions such as social security have done far more to assure citizens' economic survival than any of the dynamics of free enterprise.

Still, a powerful cultural ideology keeps concealed the alienations of social powerlessness. Thus, political resistance often appears as spasmodic and ineffectual. Among the many progressive social theories providing a formulation for analyzing ideology, Michael Lewis suggests that central to "the culture of inequality" is the pervasive "individual as central sensibility."[24] This conviction is totally inadequate as a description of the situation in this political economy. Yet this liberal sensibility saturates cultural discourse—in church and synagogue, home and school. It is the stuff of our political rhetoric as well. Both Presidents Reagan and Bush have depicted this nation as made up of solitary individuals.

Appeals to the cultural values of home and family—so resonant in neoconservative and neoliberal discourse—aim to convince the public that any change at the cultural level will threaten domestic tranquility. It is late monopoly capitalism that today erodes the nuclear family, just as it was the acceleration of earlier industrial capitalism that outmoded the rural extended family. Yet individualistic rhetoric offers comfort in the face of deep-seated anxiety created by growing powerlessness. This cultural manipulation feeds a nostalgia for a simpler, less-threatening time, but mounting evidence suggests that American homes are as likely to be battle zones as havens, and that intimate relationships are more often the victims of socioeconomic stress than sustainers of happy and upwardly mobile workers.

Because poverty, low wages, and vulnerability to rising unemployment are borne disproportionately by racial ethnic people and divorced white women—especially those who are single parents—it is white male workers who remain somewhat isolated from the most devastating economic impacts. Most white males remain fiercely loyal to the neoconservative cultural scenario, while a healthy hermeneutic of suspicion about the benevolence of our political economy inoculates most victims of racism, cultural imperialism, gender subjugation, and homophobia against it. Even "liberal" feminist consciousness among women, unless it has been forged by theoretical and personal critical reflection, can readily dissipate in the face of this cultural nostalgia. This neoconservative cultural script has as great power for women as it has for unaware white males, especially when "the individual as central sensibility" correlates with sensibilities encouraged by sex-role socialization—as it does with those women who have, until now, lived largely "privatized" or "domiciled" lives.

It is the consciousness of large numbers of such men that most powerfully feeds upon the ideology of individuality and hides the truth about the antipersonal bias of society. In their deservedly acclaimed study of working men's lives, *The Hidden Injuries of Class,* Jonathan Cobb and Richard Sennett isolate this dynamic powerfully.[25] The subjects they interviewed were hardworking men who were nevertheless trapped in jobs at the lower end of the scale. Persuaded that the system is fair and that failure is the fault of the individual, they lived lives of a double consciousness. Harboring deep self-doubt, they used powerful identification with the American Dream to displace such feelings. Rigid and perfectionist in their dealings with wives and children, they sent covert messages to them that read, "Do as I say, but do not be as I am." Self-loathing was manifest in rare moments of candor, the result of measuring their lives by others purportedly more successful than themselves. But a more positive identification required a constant effort to find others below them—those even less deserving of success than they. The vicious circle of blame of others, perfectionist criticism directed at their wives and children, and uncritical identification with those who had "made it" trapped the daily lives of men in the demand for invulnerability, self-reliance, and achievement.

For powerless people, particularly males, deliverance from illusion or "conscientization" requires a hard and painful look at the actual way in which the system functions. It is difficult to face the truth regarding a system that has been romantically admired, particularly in the absence of deeply grounded self-respect. Yet the basis for self-respect is denied people in the workplace at every turn. At least one Christian social ethicist who has looked closely at the lives of working men has described the needed pastoral strategy for liberating such men as "grief work." But such grief work must also be part of a larger strategy of communal resistance to the centralization of political and economic power and to the growing powerlessness of local communities. Without a progressive politics of renewal, without genuine options for struggle against dehumanization, people cannot learn to value their own lives or respect themselves for their efforts at survival.

The cultural mystifications of this society include historical and social "amnesia" concerning how much hard work and genuine struggle there has been to gain the rudiments of economic participation and security. Liberal rhetoric envisions a society in which those who work hard are rewarded and thus are spared the threats of poverty or downward mobility. Those who do not fit this vision are forgotten, the value of their lives denied. And so, as Michael Lewis argues, the surrogate reward of consumer goods supplants genuine equality by providing tangible evidence of "upward mobility." Interestingly, Lewis argues that the pursuit of consumer goods, Americans' purported "materialism," has little to do with gaining these goods for their own sake, but everything to do with feeding the emptiness bred by inequality.

This spiritual situation is a dangerous one. It is exacerbated by the fact that many people in the middle and at the bottom are pitted against each other by government policy requiring individual middle-income wage earners to pay the bulk of the cost for the "social safety net." The result is a moral ethos in which social contempt is rampant.

None of this will change until larger and larger numbers of people are willing to break with the prevailing cultural ideology and to run the risks of reinterpreting the realities of our political economy. Ours is a time of "friendly fascism"[26] in which any who ask genuinely critical questions will be called "Communists." Still, theologically and morally concerned people must not let themselves be silenced, no matter how many waver and rush to join the neoconservative or neoliberal ideological line.

Most needed just now is the reopening of serious public debate on extending democracy to economic life. Historically, the term *socialist* meant one who believed that political rights must be expanded to incorporate genuine participation in decisions regarding national wealth. Today, the political right has succeeded in making *socialism* a dirty word. But whether or not this word is used, the acquiescence to the current state of affairs represents a hopelessness concerning citizen and worker control of economic productive power. When this happens, people assent to captivity in a global system that benefits only the wealthy while it undermines the habitability of this planet for the overwhelming majority of the world's people.

The United States of America is distinct for virtually silencing the debate about democratizing economic life. Here human rights mean only those few rights already granted in our liberal constitution. They are important to those who already have assured income, but insufficient to sustain the conditions of our common humanity. Until and unless political rights come to include economic rights, the minimum physical conditions for human dignity—food, shelter, health, education, and work—the liberal political rights Americans have will be less and less secure. As it is, the freedoms of thought and speech that we celebrate in a self-congratulatory way exist largely for the powerful, while the voices of dissent are confined to the margins. To ignore or obscure this state of affairs is only to chant incantations to the gods of capitalist political economy.

Notes

1. Editor's note: Harrison is referring primarily to the seminar series led by the editors of *God and Capitalism* for the Madison Institute on the question of a "public philosophy." The central problem addressed by that seminar is that a coherent public philosophy of the American (religious) left which avoids both sectarianism and the loose coalition of the left is publicly perceived as a collection of disgruntled "interest groups."
2. It might be more exact to think of the United States as the United States of *North* America. Latin Americans have rightly pointed out that they are "American" too in that they also live on the continent. Nevertheless, for the sake of literary convention and simplicity, the traditional forms of "American" and "America" will be used here to denote the United States of America.
3. This term reflects the feminist criticism that social analysis also has been historically dominated by men and the particular interests they bring to it.
4. Editor's note: The ironic use of "class" here is to indicate the author's belief that American middle strata does not form a "class" in the proper sense of the word. Further use of this ironic sense may be assumed without repetition of the quotation marks.
5. This term, coined by philosopher Paul Ricouer, refers to styles of interpretation that seek the meaning of phenomena in structures that are not in the ostensible text but in some more "basic" structure giving rise to it. As examples of such "hermeneutics of suspicion," Ricouer cites especially Marx and Freud.
6. "The poorest of the poor will find pasture, and the needy will lie down in safety. But your root I will destroy by famine; it will slay your survivors" (Isa. 14:30, NIV).
7. *Praxis* here means a reflective theory and a strategy of action.
8. In his classic text on economics, for instance, Paul A. Samuelson cites "class barriers to opportunity" as one of the explanations for inequality, but his discussion is confined to such status matters as education and religious affiliation (Paul Samuelson, *Economics* [New York: McGraw-Hill, 1973], 807–8).
9. Robert W. Hodge and Steven Lagerfeld, "The Politics of Opportunity," *Wilson Quarterly* 11, no. 5 (Winter 1987): 122.

10. By transcending the material fetters of feudal society, capitalism freed human beings from mere natural necessity, argues Marx. But the very process that unleashed tremendous technological energy now suppresses the further progress of humankind toward the "abolition of labor." "Modern bourgeois society with its relations of production, of exchange and of property, a society that has conjured up such gigantic means of production and of exchange, is like the sorcerer who is no longer able to control the powers of the nether world whom he has called up by his spells" (Karl Marx, *Selected Writings in Sociology and Social Philosophy*, ed. T. B. Bottomore and Maximilien Rubel [New York: McGraw-Hill, 1964], 138).

11. The notion of "critical science" developed here is at least structurally similar to the systematic concept of "critical theory" developed by the Frankfurt school. Both argue for forms of social criticism based upon fundamental analyses of society.

12. It is important to remember that Marx did not inveigh against *privately owned property* but against the private ownership of the "means of production"—of land and resources, machines, and wage-labor control, or human labor power.

13. "Labor-power can appear upon the market as a commodity only if, and so far as, its possessor, the individual whose labor-power it is, offers it for sale, or sees it, as a commodity" (Karl Marx, *Capital*, ed. Frederick Engels [New York: Modern Library, 1906], 186).

14. One may note here not only the "pedagogy of the oppressed" of Paulo Freire, which seeks a "critical awareness" by looking for the real causes for things and which Freire calls "conscientization," but the inculcation of such a critical consciousness into the theology of such liberationists as Gustavo Gutierrez in his work *A Theology of Liberation*, ed. and trans. Sister Caridad Inda and John Eagleson (New York: Orbis Books, 1973), 91–92.

15. See William Ryan, *Blaming the Victim* (New York: Pantheon Books, 1971).

16. See Gerald R. Gill, *The Meanness Mania: The Changed Mood* (Washington, D.C.: Published for ISEP by Howard University Press, 1980).

17. Michael Harrington's analysis of "corporate capitalism" provides only one example. Harry Braverman, *Labor and Monopoly Capital* (New York: Monthly Review Press, 1974); and Earnest Mandel, *Marxist Economic Theory*, 2 vols., trans. Brian Pearce (New York: Monthly Review Press, 1968), offer related formulations.

18. "Crisis" refers here to those periods when the so-called business cycles of neoclassical economics become "depressions" and threaten the profits of existing economic units and cause profound disruptions in people's lives.

19. For an incisive labor history from a radical perspective, see Stanley Aronowitz, *False Promises: The Shaping of American Working Class Consciousness* (New York: McGraw-Hill, 1973).

20. This language, reflecting the complete dedication of the resources of the society to fighting a war, was used not only in Germany but in the United States. See, John Jay Corson, *Manpower for Victory: Total Mobilization for Total War* (New York: Farrar & Rinehart, 1943).

21. Even the Roman Catholic bishops, who are on record morally as giving priority to economic justice as basic to the common welfare, adopt such a position.

22. This term was used by sociologist Emile Durkheim to describe the pathology of advanced organic societies when diverse social functions remain isolated from one another, such as when the division of labor creates conflicts between labor and capital, and when the specialization of knowledge fragments intellectual life.

23. While this remark was accurate in the late 1980s when I originally gave this lecture, it should be noted that increased immigration into Western Europe after the fall of the Berlin Wall has dramatically increased unemployment rates in Europe.

24. See Michael Lewis, *The Culture of Inequality* (Amherst, Mass.: University of Massachusetts Press, 1978).
25. See Jonathan Cobb and Richard Sennett, *The Hidden Injuries of Class* (New York: Alfred A. Knopf, 1972).
26. See Bertram Gross, *Friendly Fascism: The New Face of Power in America* (New York: M. Evans, 1980).

Chapter 23

Living in Resistance

Interview by Pamela K. Brubaker

Brubaker: *You've already mentioned that those in the middle strata of "the first world" have constructed our lives in ways that obfuscate the problems of inequality. What do you see are the possibilities for trying to break through that, or do you see resistance and change coming from the rest of the world despite the so-called first world?*

Harrison: There is no doubt that we in the United States live in the "belly of the whale." I learned that from the young radicals in the sixties, and I've always believed that.[1] I don't think this nation in its present state is going to lead the world in any positive directions; my hope is that the world will be able to lead us away from our obsession with the use of violence as a political strategy. I believe that pressure and resistance from the rest of the world is going to reshape our responses immeasurably. I take great hope from that because people change chiefly when they have to, not merely because they "ought" to.

   In the United States the media and the talking heads in Washington and in the institutions of power have created the public's perception of what the world is like. I think a lot of people in the United States are recognizing that the depiction of the world they were sold is partial and limited. I sense a deep mood of restiveness and doubt. People are really becoming very skeptical about what they are being told. There is a new opening for truth telling and education. All we can do is live toward that. I think that living in resistance to lies and half-truths is more fun and more interesting than pretending that everything is just hunky dory. Our suspicions prompt us to ask questions, and our questioning puts us in touch with different perspectives and images of what is happening around the world.

Brubaker: *How would you theorize economic ethics and the road toward global justice in today's world?*

Harrison: The ethics that we're talking about have to come from some kind of global conversation in which we basically hammer out a new shared interest and mechanisms for accountability. It is clear that we need an international bill of rights that reflects the needs of basic material existence for all. If we are to survive as a human community, we must work toward a model of deeply shared, simplified subsistence existence in which we organize economic and political life from the bottom up, from the grass roots. The United Nations has begun this process by developing its Universal Declaration of Human Rights, which is essentially a political-economic bill of rights. It takes into consideration that what we really need to flourish as a planetary community is recognition that political rights in and of themselves are insufficient. The importance of securing women's rights as human rights is taken up even more forcefully in the United Nation's Convention on the Elimination of All Forms of Discrimination against Women (CEDAW). Political rights must be situated concretely in what I would call a respectful subsistence existence.

In moving toward a model of subsistence existence, everyone will have to learn to resist all that goes on in and between communities that threatens not only our personal flourishing but also our shared life. People must demand conditions of life that allow them and their loved ones to have access to all the education that they want or need, that allow everyone to have secure and safe shelter and at least minimum standards of nutrition and health. I think we have to say that nation states have a primary obligation to the well-being of their own people in terms of political and economic policies. While this is already the case in first world countries, the poorer nations of the world are often forced to compromise the well-being of their citizens (i.e., cuts in education, health care) at the behest of the global financial powers that currently play far too great a political role in the governing of the two-thirds world. This means that situations in which the poor nations of the world produce everything for export to the United States—so that *we* have our pick of all of the fruits and vegetables grown around the world while their own children don't have them—has got to stop. The International Monetary Fund and the World Bank have to adopt policies that allow nations to produce sufficient food for their own people, and they must eliminate policies that force nations to sell commodities badly needed for their own population. Even more difficult to imagine, we must find ways to retheorize and restructure economic life so that powerful corporations understand themselves as participating in the struggle for a shared life.

How we actually get that kind of political policy is, I believe, the struggle of this new century, and I don't think those changes will come easily—but they must be fought for by a high escalation of resistance to what I call political/moral mindlessness. We must develop a clearer understanding that the exploitation of poor nations that benefits wealthy nations or the global class of obscenely wealthy folk is an *economic crime*. We also need an international system of justice to hold people accountable for these crimes, just as we now have international courts addressing war crimes. Of course, at present the idea of recognizing economic crime is almost unthinkable, because capitalist political economy has trained us to be blind to the moral impacts of our economic decisions and ways of acquiring wealth.

Brubaker: *Can you offer specific strategies for making unaccountable economic and financial power accountable in the contemporary global economy?*

Harrison: It might help to have publicly elected corporate boards, for given the wealth and power of the corporate culture, it can be corrupting just to be elected to a board. We need to consider putting public watchdogs on corporate boards, particularly in light of, for example, the Enron scandal. But, it isn't just a few bad corporations like Enron; many of the corporations in this country are creating so-called wealth with smoke and mirrors. It is virtual wealth, though, not actual wealth. Given the classical discussions of nineteenth-century economists of what a good economy should do, what we have is not even sane economic activity. It is not production of any *real* goods and services to meet human need. Instead, what we have in the current economy is wealth being created for the sake of more wealth. If we don't want this hideous reality to increase, we must create structures of accountability that are internal to the corporations. There is also little corporate accountability to general stockholders, those who have an interest in the performance of the company but no real power. However, even these general stockholders still tend to think of the well-being of the corporation without paying attention to the well-being of the wider community in which the corporation exists.

In order to get any social control of these massive corporations we'll have to use completely different strategies than have been tried thus far. I believe strongly that we should make all productive units in our economy pay for the actual social costs of their production. In other words, if a corporation uses nonreplaceable, nonrenewable resources—if, for example, it cuts down four-hundred-year-old forests—then the costs of production should be high and should include direct payments to the community that is being robbed of nonrenewable resources. We should also reward production strategies that are consistent with economic subsistence. Unfortunately, change will not come without specific new mechanisms of social control, and we don't even *think* about accountability for social costs anymore. If we initiated this sort of strategy, immediately there would be some things that would not be produced because the cost of production would be too high. We've got to go in the direction of stopping the obvious ravaging of natural resources to produce things that have very little essential value to sustaining life and meeting human need.

But why should *I* be the one to make these concrete suggestions? *We* can figure this out; we're very smart people. If we want to solve a particular problem regarding corporate culture and power, for instance, maybe we could advertise: "Wanted: the best heads available to figure out how to hold corporations accountable for cutting down ancient tracks of trees." There is no simple plan that we can follow to redress the problems of economic exploitation and injustice in our world; there is no panacea. What we need is simultaneous resistance to the many questionable things that every political unit (i.e., local or state government) does, and we need transparent decision making that allows for open debate and scrutiny. This will not be easy, and the contradictory interests of different peoples and communities around the world will generate a certain amount of gridlock for a long time. We have to move forward, however, and the best way to go is just encourage everybody to say, "Not with our town," "Not with our lives," and see from there if we reach the point where the costs of waste, inefficiency, and insensitivity to other people's well-being just become overwhelming or too high. If we resist, slowly but surely, the paths of justice will open a bit.

Brubaker: *In reflecting on your Kellogg lecture, what aspects of your argument would you modify or change if you were addressing the subject of political economy and accountability today?*

Harrison: In rereading it, I didn't find myself feeling much differently about the problems of political economy. Of course, they are worse today, and those of us who live in the first world have obscene wealth while hundreds of thousands of people are dying. I am pretty much of a mind about the critical things I said in the essay, but there are things missing—most especially the awareness of the *tremendous* and unfettered power of the global economic system—the multinational, transnational, corporate system, and the fiscal and financial institutions that were generated by it in the immediate post World War II period. The power of those institutions to realign the world politically as well as economically is something that I would stress now even more greatly than I did. Certainly one of the problems with the bishop's pastoral and with our current work in Christian ethics in this country is that until recently we have mostly thought about economic justice issues only in the context of our national economy. There is no longer such a thing as an isolated national economy, although, of course there are aspects of national economic life.

Another thing that is seriously missing is a sufficiently widespread understanding that the major constraint now on this global system of production is the environment itself, which we are destroying. The fact that we are eating ourselves up from within is, in an ironic sort of way, a possible sign of hope. It means that the assumption of capitalist political economic theory—that subsistence is poverty—has to give way to the fact that subsistence is the friend and the only friend we have in terms of styles of production. This means that those who may never have given a thought to any alternative besides capitalism are going to have to face the fact that without some constraints on the way we organize our lives politically and economically, we're all dead. That is a wake-up call that gives a lie in some ways to capitalism's revered theory of economic determinism, i.e., its abstract theoretical model of optimum production that most people have never been willing to question.

We are beginning to see a new openness in all quarters to talking about economic alternatives. But now we've got to talk about them in ways that take seriously the need for constraints. Global warming will take us all down; the habitability of the planet is something that we can't ignore. I think that the future is somewhat more promising, that people are beginning to see that if we *don't* have a fair economic system, we will have an ever more violent world. It is imperative that humanity moves in the direction of greater fairness, and by this I don't mean any great abstract notion of justice but just a sense that people can have the conditions for survival of life on the planet and enjoy the bounty of Mother Earth without having their lives destroyed by others' greed. Slowly but surely people have to wake up and rise up.

Note

1. The image of the "belly of the whale" comes from Revelation and was used by first-century Christians to refer to their experience of living in the Roman Empire. This phrase was adopted by counterculture radicals in the 1960s to refer to the United States.

Editors' Afterword

We agreed to end this volume of Beverly Harrison's work by continuing to extend the invitation she has always extended, to join her and so many others in the ethical work of building a more just world. To write a collective statement did not, we believed, express fully the distinctive ways each of us sees this task; there is no one way to realize justice, but a myriad of strategies, suited to particular times and places. Yet neither is justice making an individual task, because only by solidarity, by hard work with one another through our differences, can we begin to make the changes we dream of. So this afterword is a production much like the wonderful quilt made for Beverly when she retired—a collage of colors and visions from so many of her friends that *together* make a statement of love and hope.

Marilyn J. Legge begins with a concise articulation of a current method and agenda for contextualization of feminist commitments to justice making. Pamela K. Brubaker emphasizes a sense of global connectedness, of being informed by and in solidarity with those already engaged in this struggle. Rebecca Todd Peters stresses the pedagogical aspect of liberative ethics that is foundational for creating change and relates it to economic injustice, especially the privileges of material affluence. Jane E. Hicks points out the careful interpretation and interrogation of cultural assumptions necessary when naming our work as specifically *Christian* ethics. Elizabeth M. Bounds identifies core elements in liberative feminist ethics, especially the challenges of integrating theory and practice, framed in a concrete example of working with women prisoners. Traci C. West directly appeals to the reader to take up some form of the justice-making work described here, but acknowledges the drain of injustices such as white domination that discourage activist resistance as well as other factors that might deter participation.

Ongoing Vision for Justice in the Making

Marilyn J. Legge

You may have already discovered why Beverly Harrison has been accused of being a utopian feminist. She focuses on "justice imaginable," not as a blueprint but as the energy to work collaboratively for a day when justice will "roll down like waters, and righteousness like an everflowing stream" (Amos 5:24). You may also be moved, as I am, by her commitment to deep and constructive reimagining of divine-human-cosmic relation. I affirm Beverly's moral claims that we are embodied and relational persons. Therefore, we need to embrace eros and shared power as the proper cues for justice, that is, right relation. The energy to sustain this task of "justice in the making" includes shaping utopian visions and finding moral courage in diversity, with friends and strangers building habitable spaces of human and cosmic well-being.

Feminist ethics undertaken as if persons and communities of global justice and earthly sustainability mattered is part of movements of hope. Utopian visions of alternative futures to current conditions are necessary for feminist and other liberatory ethics. Feminist ethics coalesces around critical consciousness of what in the world is going on and works out shared goals, values, and accountabilities. We know that some have too much and others have not enough. We express discontent and anger as desire for subversion of reigning norms and dynamics. We realize that unjust material realities impact our daily lives, the earth, and generations to come. Feminist religious ethics takes seriously that sin and evil exist in hearts and minds, structures and policies, systems and cultures, but finds them neither immutable nor necessary. Therefore, we are involved in dramatic struggles for visions and practices of abundant life that are rooted in right relation and are flexible, equitable, and effectively inclusive.

Feminist liberatory ethics explores how women's moral agency is variously shaped and active in historical contexts. We problematize notions of home and family, race and ethnicity, nation and religion, class exploitation, gender and sexuality—and aim to make profound connections for the sake of self-critical, empowered, and transformative lives-in-relation. The task of imaging justice is especially difficult under the sway of globalization, that particular expression of postmodern corporate capitalism in the shadow of the American empire. This broad context depletes energies for connection and change and weakens capacities for radical solutions, those that get to the heart of the matter. How to participate in constructing subjectivities, communities, and movements that serve the complex and public good remains a key moral challenge.

Women seeking justice understand their lives as interdependent and mutually accountable, especially to those who suffer most. One's perspective is always partial, one among many that is differently connected to circuits of power and significance for a kaleidoscopic vision of healing and compassion. Resistance to what thwarts well-being is not just an end in itself but a root of renewed energy for the sake of communities' moral life. I live and work in Toronto now, doing social ethics as a feminist theological educator in the midst of many religious, academic, and political agendas, among different groups who define their maps of meaning and their oppressions and obligations in different ways. I do not assume the possibility of an all-inclusive project, but I yearn to participate in and stay connected to movements and communities that are naming and resisting experienced subordination and domination in their own and others' lives. Even as utopian visions are contestable and diverse, they enliven those seeking to create ways of life and social processes that will resist erosions of sustainable, healing, and compassionate communities. Hope is grown in the soils of struggle for non-violent relations. I find hope startling and often an utter surprise.

For example, I find it startling to hear narratives of those battered for being poor, female, racial-ethnic, or lesbian, gay, or bisexual who are resisting the exclusions that harm them and also asking me—a straight, white, first-world, Christian professor—to accompany them and in the process be transformed. I find it startling to witness women's interreligious peace-building initiatives in Sri Lanka, to follow HIV/AIDS activism through both local Canadian and southern African congregations in an ecumenical program called "Beads of Hope," to hear about the Organizacion Femenina Popular in Colombia, a community-based women's organization for reproductive health, peace action, and human rights training. And it is startling to find mainstream religious groups mobilizing to reshape narratives of colonization that do not pretend to innocence in aboriginal residential schools or ongoing white racism and so recognize that feeling sorry is no substitute for repentance or charity for justice, and that friendship alone will not build networks.

Bev Harrison has consistently reminded us that "we act our way into being" and that Holy Power is the power of relation among us. Movements of hope persist because they tend the roots of healing and justice. They reimagine creative ways of empowerment, of dealing with conflict, and are guided by visions of interdependent communities where everyone participates and benefits. As Bev would have it, let us take courage together that all may be well!

Justice Making in the Web of Life

Pamela K. Brubaker

Within a feminist liberation theological vision, we stress that this planet, indeed the whole cosmos that we inhabit, is not merely a gracious home. It is an interactive web of life which is as much a part of us as we of it.
—Beverly Wildung Harrison,
"Theology, Economics, and the Church"

The image of the web of life as the reality in which we are immersed is foundational to the work of feminist ethics. This image often evokes for me a lush earth teeming with a multitude of life-forms harmoniously related to each other and all that is. Yet I know that this is the web for which I and others yearn, *not* the one we inhabit. Rather, we inhabit "a web of oppression and injustice" as described by the Vancouver Assembly of the World Council of Churches (1983), such that racism, sexism, class domination, denial of people's rights, and caste oppression are woven together. Common threads bind women. In reviewing the workshop reports from the Forum at the United Nations Decade for Women Conference in Nairobi (1985), the Society for International Development reported, "[I]t is evident that despite the vast diversity in women's cultural and socio-economic conditions around the world there are common threads of powerlessness, of marginality and dispossession that bind them to their subordinate position in society."[1] I have learned, with Harrison and other feminist ethicists, that although common threads may bind women to a subordinate position, *there is no universal woman*. Women's experience is shaped by complex interstructurings of gender, race, ethnicity, class, sexual orientation, and nationality, as well as other factors. Some of us are in positions of relative power and privilege, while others are disadvantaged and relatively powerless.

My own work in feminist ethics has attempted to respond to the challenge women from the global South made to us women from the global North in Nairobi. They asked us, particularly those of us from the United States, to take on the work of analyzing global political economic dynamics, over which our country has so much control but that impoverishes their countries, particularly women and children. By virtue of my social location as a white, Anglo, middle-strata U.S. woman, I am part of dominant privileged communities. Nevertheless, a vision of imagined communities with those who suffer oppression and exploitation is critical to my justice-making work. These are the communities to whom I am accountable, while working for change in the dominant communities of which I am a part. I also try to hold these dominant communities accountable to their best values—liberty and justice for all, love of neighbor as self. I envision threads connecting me to women and men from around the world with whom I have participated in the Forum and other international gatherings, such as the World Council of Churches Celebration of the Ecumenical Decade of Churches in Solidarity with Women (Harare, 1998). These threads not only connect us as individuals but also link our communities, social and ecological. I am—*we all are*—part of webs of connection, whose nodes may represent those with whom we have had face-to-face dialogue, more personal encounters. The threads that connect us are threads of exploitation and domination but also of compassion and solidarity, like the multiple strands of fiber optic networks. Those of us who join in the work of justice in the making need to *deconstruct* our own position in the web as well as *construct* ways we are connected to others. We must deepen our analysis, strengthen our solidarity, and together continue the work of transforming the web of life into one where all may flourish.

Preparing Ourselves for Making Justice

Rebecca Todd Peters

In a feminist moral theology, good questions are answered by something we must do.

—Beverly Wildung Harrison,
"The Power of Anger in the Work of Love"

The task of Christian social ethics is intimately connected to our ability to ask good questions. I often tell my students that I am more interested that they learn how to ask good questions than that they memorize history, information, and other people's ideas. While these things are important, the critical thinking skills that help one to formulate good questions are less easily forgotten at the end of the semester. One of the downsides of the information age is that we expect to be able to find answers to our questions quickly and easily. When one is searching for *information* this is often a reasonable expectation. But I fear that many people are losing the ability (or not being taught how) to ask the kind of good questions that Harrison refers to—questions that can only be answered *by something we must do*. This task is often very difficult for those who want to believe that there are right and wrong answers to life's hard questions, particularly when there are many religious leaders in the world willing to tell people quite plainly what their vision of "right" and "wrong" is.

My own life and work have been formatively shaped by learning how to ask precisely the kind of questions that Harrison raises—of myself, my community, and my world. I believe that this is the art of Christian social ethics, for the questions that we ask can so often play a critical role in helping to define the terms of a debate and thus often the range of possibilities for resolution as well. It is not enough to ask, "How can we help those who are poor?" (or hungry or hurting). The social ethicist must ask questions like "Why is the poverty of the two-thirds world so debilitating? Why is AIDS decimating Africa when it is treatable? Why is it that I (and my 'people') live so well and comfortably while so many of the world's people live in abject poverty?"

The questions of the Christian social ethicist ought to be crafted so that they open people's eyes to injustice and spur our constituencies to action, to the task of making justice. Unfortunately, justice is often a hard sell in the communities in which I live, work, and teach. Questions like the ones articulated above often make comfortable people uncomfortable. They are, in fact, often designed to do just that. People have to open their eyes to injustice before they can begin to imagine making justice. It's not that comfortable people don't believe in justice; it's rather that, well, they—we—like being comfortable. It's nice, it's easy. The relative affluence of many white Americans is a narcotic. The comforts of our lives—food, clothes, entertainment of various sorts—dull our senses. We don't really *want* to know about poverty, injustice, racism, disease (at least in other places) precisely because they threaten our coziness, our contentment with our own situation. This capacity for escapism is one of the most dangerous evils of privilege that come with economic stability, whiteness, education, and other dominant social positions. One of the challenges of our current age is to break through the narcotic of material comfort in order to help the majority of first-world people recognize the ways in which our comfort is being bought at the price of the planet and the people of the two-thirds world (as well as many people in our midst).

In reality, the call to justice in the making does not have to be the call of Jesus to the rich young man. Asking the affluent, the well-off, and the simply comfortable to give up all that they have and to take a vow of poverty in solidarity with the poor, while perhaps ideal, is simply not realistic. Nor is it necessary. In the world of plenty in which we live, there is enough to go around. This does not, however, mean that our lives do not need to change. There is a distinct difference between modesty and poverty. Of course, the obvious issue is one of definition, and this is always where my students balk. Who gets to decide how much is enough? How many cars/houses/TVs/children/clothes are enough? And this is precisely the kind of "good" question that ought to spur us to action, to justice. Yet the fiercely individual essence of American identity often rears its ugly head when such questions are raised. If we are able to see that our first-world lifestyles are killing our planet (directly) and killing other people (indirectly), then the task of deliberating together as the people of God, as a human community, to determine *how much is enough* really ought to be on the agenda of all communities of faith in the first world, for these are communal questions that all the world's people ought to have a voice in discussing.

A question such as "How are we to live our lives in ways that are sustainable for the earth and all its creatures?" is precisely the kind of question that requires us to *do* something, that requires us to participate in justice in the making. While this kind of question does not necessarily have a "right" answer, there are definitely better and worse answers. These answers can only be crafted within the context of faithful and caring communities who are willing to hold themselves accountable for their actions and who are committed to justice in the making. If you are not currently part of such a community, I urge you to join one, to make one, or turn one of your own communities into one and together learn how to generate your own "good" questions that spur you to action.

Faithful Justice Making

Jane E. Hicks

By virtue of our engaging in the struggle for justice . . . we gain intimations
of what rightly ordered community and God's transcendence may mean.
—Beverly Wildung Harrison,
"Dream of a Common Language"

Appeals to distinctively Christian language and commitments run throughout
this volume. As a Christian, I celebrate Harrison's theological reading of Jesus'
radical regard for the neighbor. Our neighbors are those most "outsider" to us.
Christian faith is thus not mere intellectual assent to a series of static proposi-
tions. Rather, faith entails active solidarity with oppressed peoples and openness
to new horizons made possible in the struggle for justice.

My hope is that the theological and moral vision presented in this collection
will resonate with readers across a variety of traditions while remaining clear in
its particularity. For readers who do not embrace Christianity, some expressions
will, no doubt, require interpretation, imaginative leaps, and refusals in relation
to other religious and philosophical frameworks.

To be sure, feminist liberative ethics need not be Christian. The longing for
justice so essential to feminist spirituality takes many forms, and Christian feminism itself has been influenced by a range of religious and social viewpoints. As
Harrison puts it, "Morality is the work of our *common* life, and the particularities
of my convictions and my participation as a Christian, grounded in the way I have
experienced revelation in my community, must answer not only to my community's sense of narrative and vocation but also to the sensibilities, principles, and
values which inform the conscientious efforts of other morally serious beings."[2]

The ecumenical, interfaith promise of feminist ethics has been instructive for my own thinking about religion in American public life. Today the merits of faith-based initiatives are often framed as simple value questions: Do we hold religion dear? How might we promote greater civility in our daily interactions? Institutional arrangements between religion and government, however, must also be considered in relation to larger economic and cultural patterns, where concern for gender inequality, racism, poverty, and Christian cultural hegemony come together in a very different set of questions: What protections for religious, sexual, and ethnic minorities will be lost, especially for women and girls, when public responsibilities are given over to private religious groups? What of our common life, if education and social welfare are no longer our collective responsibility? Whose faith is *actually* funded through faith-based initiatives? As Judith Plaskow argues, the very rhetoric of faith may obscure a Christian bias, as most Jews, among others, would not express their religious commitment in terms of "practicing a faith."[3] For Christians who hold cultural and political dominance in the United States, respect for neighbor traditions may require careful restraint in matters of religion and government. Such steps toward justice in the making provide a necessary context for knowing God and one another more fully.

Realist Dreams

Elizabeth M. Bounds

It is important to remember that feminist moral theology is utopian, as all good theology is, in that it envisages *a society, a world, a cosmos, in which . . . there are "no excluded ones." But feminist theology is also mightily realistic, in that it takes with complete seriousness the radical freedom we human beings have for doing good* or evil.

—Beverly Wildung Harrison,
"The Power of Anger in the Work of Love"

"I just can't take it any more." I watch D's face squeeze together, as she tries to explain what is going on. "I am tired, I just am tired." We are a circle of women, sitting in a fluorescent-lit, cinderblock square room, with windows on either side revealing rooms that are just the same as this one. All but two of us are prisoners, with names and numbers printed on rough beige cotton shirts. About half of us are black, half are white. All of the women in the circle nod at D's remark. As far as I can tell, most of them have been tired all of their lives, since the people around them, their parents or teachers or lovers, have told them they weren't worth very much. Sometimes these women were told this by being made invisible, and sometimes they were told this directly through harsh words or physical blows. They have come here every Tuesday night, to this little weekly class about spiritual journeys to hear something else, to hear some good news.

As my teaching partner and I sit there each week, I wonder, How are we doing feminist moral theology or feminist ethics? How do we live these words on the ground? Engaging in the words Beverly Harrison has given us, here and elsewhere, I can begin to figure some of this out. As I have pondered, I have come up with some possible base points, markers that can help me sort out the complexity in which we all live.

Doing feminist liberative ethics requires

—interrogating my own location, understanding the ways I am oppressed, the ways I am privileged, the ways I oppress

In this prison classroom, I can identify so many ways that my privilege allows me to live in a different world: I am white, well-educated, earning a good income, partnered with someone who supports me. These factors have made it very unlikely that I will be incarcerated. But for most of these women, a life without these supports has led them here. Yet there are also places where I stand with many of these women: I do know what it means to be called worthless; I do know what it means to stand in the midst of constraints simply because I am female.

—using knowledge of my location as an entry point that helps me analyze the world and sort out my solidarities

I recognize that I have to step outside of my usual responses—perhaps disgust or pity at some aspects of these women's lives, or relief at the privilege of my own. I need to see the complex forces at work that have profoundly shaped our individual choices and that both bring us together and drive us apart.

—seeking complex theoretical frameworks that do justice to the multifaceted nature of social reality

If I simply stay with this knowledge of myself, I run the risk of staying within a crippling narcissism. The only way I can step outside is through analysis, through working with social theories that help me explain better what I am experiencing in that room. Analyses of class and race oppression help me understand the composition of the room—the disproportionate number of women from poorer families, the disproportionate number of women who are black. Analysis of gender can explain why many of these women are imprisoned for crimes related to their male partners (some ran drugs for their lovers while others killed them in the midst of abuse). This is the realism Beverly speaks of in the quote above, a realism about the structures human beings have created, and also a realism about the capacity we all have as individuals to choose evil or good within these structures.

— recognizing the inseparability or mutual interplay of theory and action and choosing to engage issues arising from the places of suffering and oppression (especially the places where women suffer and are oppressed)

Feminist liberative ethics requires not only reflection but also action. What do I *do*? How do I avoid what happens to so many well-intentioned, privileged white people like myself, becoming either paralyzed by guilt or overwhelmed by the enormity of the structures I face? First, *I choose to do something rather than nothing*—even a little step is empowering. Second, *I use my analysis to make better choices*. For example, I and my teaching partner in the prison, who is black, joined forces because both of us know that this is one way to counter the racism that surrounds us—that is, to insist to these women and to ourselves that black and white women are leaders and leaders who can work together. Third, *I recognize my limitations*. I cannot change the world alone and am not required to. But I *am* required to do what I can. Recognition of my limitations leads to the fourth point, that *I try to find others*. One class at one prison does something, but joining an organization that tries to change prison conditions does even more.

—appropriating resources from Christian traditions, acknowledging both the exclusion through which these traditions have been formed and the powerful vision they embody

This is one more base point that arises from my own particular convictions, the vision that animates my world and helps me—and the women with me in this room—to keep on keeping on. If we were Jewish or Muslim or agnostic this step would look different, but it would, I am convinced, lead in the same direction: Many of the women in this prison have been *abused* by Christianity—by ministers and churches that have continued the message that they are no good. Yet they hold on to a vision of a God and a Jesus who is with them in their struggles, who loves them madly and who wants them to be whole. I can do no better than to stand with them in this dream of a world where there are no excluded ones.

Justice Making Even When You Don't Feel Like It

Traci C. West

I'd like to talk directly to you.

Listen, I know that there are many concerns that demand our attention each day. As adults, young or old, we are busy trying to create a meaningful life for ourselves, trying to make sure that we have material necessities to survive, some caring relationships, and some activities that give us a sense of purpose—at least a few of which bring pleasure into our lives. Many of us carry a heavy burden of responsibility for our families, our religious groups, and our jobs. If you are invited to take up the task of justice making, it may seem like either just another burden that you have no time for, or like something that you already do all of the time without needing to think about it (if only in your own small, individual way).

But justice-making work, especially insofar as it challenges evils such as white domination, is directly related to your existing, daily efforts to maintain a decent life and respond to the personal responsibilities that you have. Moreover, it is never something that can be assumed on an individual basis, nor unconsciously done in the course of one's routine, courteous exchanges with others.

I also want you to know that I do appreciate how tiring the burden of injustice itself can be. For instance, when you are a person of color in U.S. society, it takes tremendous perseverance to cope with the myriad of indignities that the unjust realities of white domination foist upon you. These realities range from small daily slights such as cab drivers refusing to stop for you or store clerks "not seeing you" as you wait for assistance, to insidious mainstream lies about which there seems to be general consensus in our society, such as claims about the ubiquity of freedom and democracy in the history and fabric of our nation. You may feel that there is sufficient challenge in just surviving ongoing forms of injustice with your physical and mental health reasonably intact—so much so, that finding the energy to *transform* the injustice seems too hard.

Moreover, some of you feel worn out by the nature of justice-making work itself. Perhaps what is most debilitating about this work is the consistent occurrence of betrayal by one's allies who also work for social change. Some of us already feel too exhausted by the black church civil rights leaders who want to deny the civil rights of black gay men, lesbians, bisexuals, and transgendered persons; the white feminists and white gay activists whose racist arrogance seems impermeable even after their "diversity" and antiracism training; the ecological activists who have finished their work when public or private lands are "saved," while toxic poisoning of Native American children on reservations or industry's poisoning of Latino/a immigrant farm workers are not even considered for their agenda; peace activists who decry the insane violence and emotional torment inflicted by both international terrorist groups and state-sponsored wars on terrorism but ignore the everyday battering and rape of women and girls that occurs within families; Christians who are insistent about religious freedoms except for certain discriminatory, restrictive policies for Muslims that "are necessary right now."

When I think about how to respond to the weariness of just trying to survive, of injustice itself, of betrayal by allies, I think of Fannie Lou Hamer. She was a courageous civil rights leader who organized beleaguered grassroots people in Mississippi and declared, "I'm sick and tired of being sick and tired." I think about Hamer at that 1964 Democratic National Convention. After all of her hard work and leadership in the Mississippi Freedom Democratic Party that had helped to create the confrontation over white racist disenfranchisement of blacks at that convention, she was excluded in an agreement reached at a closed, crucial decision-making meeting, betrayed supposedly because she was not formally educated and because her style was "too emotional."[4] I am inspired by Hamer's example in so many ways, but especially by how she tried to teach people to turn the times when you are most "sick and tired" of unjust conditions into a resource for refusing to continue to be made "sick and tired" anymore.

For myself, as I respond to the need for justice making based upon my Christian faith, I find the bonds of oppression as well as restorative resources of faith and community reproduced in church life. Communally developed Christian biblical interpretation and theological notions of evil, sin, Jesus' incarnation, and God's grace help me to sort out those realities in church and society. Even disappointment and weariness can be empowering resources when they bring recognition of dehumanizing practices and self-destructive means often used to cope.

The only way that we can be assured that injustice will prevail with ever more costs to ourselves and our children is if you and I refuse to take up the tasks of justice making. I need you in order to even imagine the range of liberative tools necessary for social transformation. There are so many creative possibilities for resistance that we can learn from each other. I can't accomplish this work without you.

Notes

1. Society for International Development, "World Crisis and Women: Risk of Dis-possession or an Opportunity for Empowerment?" *Compass* 27 (April 1986): 1.
2. Beverly Wildung Harrison, "The Dream of a Common Language: Toward a Nor-mative Theory of Justice in Christian Ethics," p. 16 in this volume.
3. Judith Plaskow, " Whose Initiative? Whose Faith?" *Journal of the American Acad-emy of Religion* 70, no. 4 (December 2002): 863–67.
4. Taylor Branch, *Pillar of Fire: America in the King Years, 1963–65* (New York: Simon & Schuster, 1998), 470; see also Chana Kai Lee, *For Freedom's Sake: The Life of Fannie Lou Hamer* (Champaign, Ill. University of Illinois Press, 1999), 95.

Editors' Biographies

Elizabeth M. Bounds is Coordinator of the Initiative in Religious Practices and Practical Theology at Emory University, where she is also Associate Director of the Graduate Division of Religion and Associate Professor of Christian Ethics. Along with the volume *Coming Together/Coming Apart: Religion, Community, and Modernity* (Routledge, 1997), she has published various articles on welfare reform, pedagogy, and racism. She is a graduate of Harvard University (B.A., classics and history), Cambridge University (M.A., English), and Union Theological Seminary in New York (M.Div.; Ph.D., Christian social ethics).

Pamela K. Brubaker is Professor of Religion at California Lutheran University, where she teaches courses in ethics and gender studies. Before coming to Cal Lutheran in the fall of 1994, she was at Cleveland State University in Ohio. She has published several articles and three books on various topics in Christian ethics and women's religious history, including *Women Don't Count: The Challenge of Women's Poverty to Christian Ethics* (Scholars Press, 1994), and *Globalization at What Price? Economic Change and Daily Life* (Pilgrim Press, 2001). She is coeditor of *Welfare Policy: Feminist Critiques* (Pilgrim Press, 1999). She is a graduate of Roosevelt University in Chicago (B.A., sociology) and Union Theological Seminary in New York (Ph.D., Christian social ethics).

Jane E. Hicks is Assistant Professor of Ethics in the Department of Religious Studies at St. John Fisher College in Rochester, New York. Her teaching and research interests include religion in American public life, Christian social ethics, women's studies in religion, and biomedical ethics. She is the author of recent articles in *Word and World* and *Teaching Theology and Religion* and currently serves on the steering committee for the Ethics Section of the American Academy of

Religion. She is a graduate of Trinity University (B.A.), University of Florida College of Law (J.D.), Harvard Divinity School (M.T.S.), and Union Theological Seminary in New York (Ph.D.).

Marilyn J. Legge is Associate Professor of Christian Ethics at Emmanuel College of Victoria University in the University of Toronto. She teaches and has published on various topics in social ethics with reference to religion, political economy, and global and Canadian contexts. She is the author of *The Grace of Difference: A Canadian Feminist Theological Ethic* (Scholars Press, 1992) and has coedited *Liberation Theology: An Introductory Reader* (Orbis Press, 1992) and *Doing Ethics in a Pluralist World: Essays in Honour of Roger Hutchinson* (Wilfrid Laurier University Press, 2002). She has been President of the Canadian Theological Society, a member of the World Council of Churches' Women's Advisory Group, and coordinating editor of *Studies in Women and Religion*. She is a graduate of Victoria University (Hons. B.A., history and religious studies; M.Div.) and Union Theological Seminary in New York (S.T.M.; Ph.D., Christian social ethics).

Rebecca Todd Peters is Distinguished Emerging Scholar and Assistant Professor of Religious Studies at Elon University in Elon, North Carolina. She is also a member of the environmental studies faculty and offers courses in the honors program and the women and gender studies programs. Research and teaching areas include economic and environmental ethics, sexuality issues, and reproductive concerns. She is the author of *In Search of the Good Life: The Ethics of Globalization* (Continuum, 2004), which won the 2003 Trinity Prize. She is a graduate of Rhodes College (B.A. with honors, Art; B.A., English) and Union Theological Seminary in New York (M.Div.; Ph.D., Christian social ethics). She is an ordained minister in the Presbyterian Church (U.S.A.), and worked in their national office of Women's Ministries for six years.

Traci C. West is Associate Professor of Ethics and African American Studies at Drew University in Madison, New Jersey. She teaches ethics courses in the areas of religion and society, church and society, and women's studies. She is the author of *Wounds of the Spirit: Black Women, Violence, and Resistance Ethics* (New York University Press, 1999), as well as many published articles on issues related to race, gender, and justice in church and society. One of her more recent articles is "Constructing Ethics: Reinhold Niebuhr and Harlem Women Activists" (*Journal of the Society of Christian Ethics*, 2004). She is a graduate of Yale University (B.A., religious studies), Pacific School of Religion (M.Div.), and Union Theological Seminary in New York (Ph.D., Christian social ethics). She is an ordained minister in the United Methodist Church and previously served as a parish pastor and campus minister.

Beverly Wildung Harrison: Bibliography of Writings

Compiled by Jennifer L. Janzen-Ball

BOOKS

Our Right to Choose: Toward a New Ethic of Abortion. Boston: Beacon Press, 1983.

Making the Connections: Essays in Feminist Social Ethics. Edited by Carol S. Robb. Boston: Beacon Press, 1985.

God's Fierce Whimsy: Christian Feminism and Theological Education. Katie G. Cannon, Beverly W. Harrison, Carter Heyward, Ada Maria Isasi-Diaz, Bess B. Johnson, Mary D. Pellauer, Nancy D. Richardson (The Mud Flower Collective). Cleveland: Pilgrim Press, 1985.

The Public Vocation of Christian Ethics. Edited with Robert L. Stivers and Ronald H. Stone. New York: Pilgrim Press, 1986.

Die neue Ethik der Frauen: Kraftvolle Beziehungen statt blossen Gehorsams. Stuttgart: Kreuz, 1991 (translation of portions of *Our Right to Choose* and *Making the Connections*).

CHAPTERS IN BOOKS

1974

"Sexism and the Contemporary Church: When Evasion Becomes Complicity." In *Sexist Religion and Women in the Church, No More Silence!* edited by Alice L. Hageman in collaboration with the Women's Caucus of Harvard Divinity School, 195–216. New York: Association Press.

1978

"Feminist Theology: Class and Labor Perspectives." In *Is Liberation Theology for North America? The Response of First World Churches to Third World Theologies,* edited by Sergio Torres, 21–27. New York: Theology in the Americas.

1979

"The Politics of Energy Policy." In *Energy Ethics: A Christian Response,* edited by Dieter T. Hessel, 56–71. New York: Friendship Press. An adapted version appears in *Making the Connections.*

1982

"The Reality of the Churches in the US." In *Theology in the Americas: Detroit II Conference Papers,* edited by Cornel West, Caridad Guidote, and Margaret Coakley, 72–79. Maryknoll, N.Y.: Orbis Books.

1986

"Agendas for a New Theological Ethic." In *Churches in Struggle: Liberation Theologies and Social Changes in North America,* edited by William K. Tabb, 89–98. New York: Monthly Review Press.

"The Quest for Justice." In *The Public Vocation of Christian Ethics,* edited by Beverly W. Harrison, Robert L. Stivers, and Ronald H. Stone, 289–310. New York: Pilgrim Press.

"Sex Discrimination." In *Westminster Dictionary of Christian Ethics,* edited by James F. Childress and John MacQuarrie, 578–79. Philadelphia: Westminster Press.

"Women, Status of." In *Westminster Dictionary of Christian Ethics,* edited by James F. Childress and John MacQuarrie, 663–66. Philadelphia: Westminster Press.

1988

"Toward a Christian Feminist Liberation Hermeneutic for Demystifying Class Reality in Local Congregations." In *Beyond Clericalism: The Congregation as a Focus for Theological Education,* edited by Joseph C. Hough, Jr., and Barbara G. Wheeler, 137–51. Atlanta: Scholars Press. Reprinted in this volume as chapter 21.

1989

"Pain and Pleasure: Avoiding the Confusions of Christian Tradition in Feminist Theory" (with Carter Heyward). In *Christianity, Patriarchy, and Abuse,* edited by Joanne Carlson Brown and Carole R. Bohn, 148–73. New York: Pilgrim Press. Reprinted in *Sexuality and the Sacred: Sources for Theological Reflection,* edited by James B. Nelson and Sandra P. Longfellow, 131–48. Louisville, Ky.: Westminster John Knox Press.

1991

"The 'Fate' of the Middle Class in Late Capitalism." In *God and Capitalism: A Prophetic Critique of Market Economy,* edited by Norman K. Gottwald, J. Mark Thomas, and Vernon Visick, 53–71. Madison, Wis.: A-R Editions. Reprinted in this volume as chapter 22.

1994

"Sexuality and Social Policy." In *Sexuality and the Sacred: Sources for Theological Reflection,* edited by James B. Nelson and Sandra P. Longfellow, 242–55. Louisville, Ky.: Westminster John Knox Press. Reprinted from *Making the Connections.*

"Women-church and Similar Support Groups in Mainline Protestant and Catholic Churches: Comments on the Hartford Study." In *Defecting in Place: Women Claiming Responsibility for Their Own Spiritual Lives,* edited by Miriam Therese Winter, Adair Lummis, and Allison Stokes, 227–30. New York: Crossroad.

1996

"Anger/Wrath." In *Dictionary of Feminist Theologies*, edited by Letty Russell and J. Shannon Clarkson, 6–8. Louisville, Ky.: Westminster John Knox Press.

"Socialism-Capitalism." In *Dictionary of Feminist Theologies*, edited by Letty Russell and J. Shannon Clarkson, 264–66. Louisville, Ky.: Westminster John Knox Press. Reprinted in this volume as chapter 18.

"Theology and Morality of Procreative Choice" (with Shirley Cloyes). In *Abortion: A Reader*, edited by Lloyd Steffen. Cleveland: Pilgrim Press. Reprinted from *Making the Connections*. Reprinted in *Moral Issues and Christian Responses*, 7th ed., edited by Patricia Beattie Jung and Shannon Jung. Florence, Ky.: Wadsworth Publishing, 2003.

1999

"Feminist Thea(o)logies at the Millenium: 'Messy' Continued Resistance or Surrender to Post-Modern Academic Culture." In *Liberating Eschatology: Essays in Honor of Letty M. Russell*, edited by Margaret A. Farley and Serene Jones, 156–71. Louisville, Ky.: Westminster John Knox Press. Reprinted in this volume as chapter 14.

Foreword to *Welfare Policy [feminist critiques]*, edited by Elizabeth M. Bounds, Pamela K. Brubaker, and Mary E. Hobgood, vii–xi. Cleveland: Pilgrim Press. Reprinted in this volume as chapter 6.

2003

"Christianity's Indecent Decency: Why a Holistic Vision of Justice Eludes Us." In *Body and Soul: Rethinking Sexuality as Justice-Love*, edited by Marvin M. Ellison and Sylvia Thorson-Smith, 25–44. Cleveland: Pilgrim Press.

"Dorothee Soelle as Pioneering Postmodernist." In *The Theology of Dorothee Soelle*, edited by Sarah K. Pinnock, 239–55. Harrisburg, Pa.: Trinity Press International. Reprinted in this volume as chapter 15.

ESSAYS AND ARTICLES

1972

"Response [to G. Williamson, Jr., pp. 99–104]." *Christianity and Crisis* 32 (May 1, 1972): 104–6.

"Advocate's Guide to Seminary Discussions of the Woman Question." *Theological Education* 8 (Summer 1972): 225–32.

"That Earth Might Be Fair: When Fruitfulness and Blessedness Diverge." *Religion in Life* 41, no. 4 (Winter 1972): 480–96.

1975

"Challenging the Western Paradigm: Theology in the Americas Conference [Sacred Heart Seminary, Detroit, August 17–23, 1975]." *Christianity and Crisis* 35 (October 27, 1975): 251–54.

"The Early Feminists and the Clergy: A Case Study in the Dynamics of Secularization." *Review and Expositor* 72 (Winter 1975): 41–52. Reprinted in *Making the Connections: Essays in Feminist Social Ethics.*

1976

"The Effect of Industrialization on the Role of Women in Society." *Concilium, Sociologie de la Religion* 3 (1976): 91–103. Reprinted in *Making the Connections: Essays in Feminist Social Ethics.*

1977

"Continuing the Discussion: How to Argue about Abortion: II [reply to J. Burtchaell, with rejoinder]." *Christianity and Crisis* 37 (December 26, 1977): 311–13.

1979

"Does the First Amendment Bar the Hyde Amendment?" *Christianity and Crisis* 39 (March 5, 1979): 38–40.

1981

"Free Choice: A Feminist Perspective." *Church and Society* 71 (March-April 1981): 6–21.

"A Theology of Pro-Choice: A Feminist Perspective on Abortion." This is a two-part article that appears in *Witness* 64 (July 1981): 14–18 and *Witness* 64 (September 1981): 18–21. A later version of this essay, written with Shirley Cloyes, appears in *Abortion: The Moral Issues*, edited by Edward Batchelor, 210–26. New York: Pilgrim Press, 1982. This same version also appears in *Speaking of Faith: Global Perspectives on Women, Religion, and Social Change,* edited by Diana L. Eck and Devaki Jain, 215–24. Philadelphia: New Society Publishers, 1987.

"The Power of Anger in the Work of Love: Christian Ethics for Women and Other Strangers." In *Union Seminary Quarterly Review* 36 (Supplement 1981): 41–57. Reprinted in *Making the Connections* and in *Weaving the Visions: New Patterns in Feminist Spirituality,* edited by Judith Plaskow and Carol P. Christ, 214–25. San Francisco: Harper & Row, 1989.

1982

"Misogyny and Homophobia: The Unexplored Connections [excerpt from *Integrity Forum* 7, no. 2 (1981)]." In *Church and Society* 73, no. 2 (November-December 1982): 20–33. Reprinted in *Making the Connections.*

1983

"Abortion Has Made a Difference in the Lives of Women." In *Engage/Social Action* 11, no. 3 (March 1983): 37–40.

"Human Sexuality and Mutuality." In *Journal of Presbyterian History* 61 (Spring 1983): 142–61. Reprinted in *Christian Feminism: Visions of a New Humanity,* edited by Judith L. Weidman, 141–57. San Francisco: Harper & Row, 1984. Reprinted in this volume as chapter 7.

"The Dream of a Common Language: Towards a Normative Theory of Justice in Christian Ethics [Presidential Address, Society of Christian Ethics, 1983]." In the *Annual of the Society of Christian Ethics* (1983): 1–25. Reprinted in this volume as chapter 2.

"Restoring the Tapestry of Life: The Vocation of Feminist Theology." In *Drew Gateway* 54, no. 1 (1983): 39–48. Reprinted in this volume as chapter 13.

1984

"A Feminist Perspective on Moral Responsibility." *Conscience* (1984/1985): no pages given.

1985

"Social Justice and Economic Orthodoxy: Structural Evils Neglected [Bishop's Pastoral Letter]." In *Christianity and Crisis* 44 (January 21, 1985): 513–15. Reprinted in this volume as chapter 19.

1986

"Feminist Realism." In *Christianity and Crisis* 46, no. 10 (July 14, 1986): 233–36. Reprinted in this volume as chapter 4.

1987

"Respondent." In *Journal of Feminist Studies in Religion* 3, no. 1 (Spring 1987): 95–98.

"An Overview of Basic Issues in Theological Education in the United States of North America Today." In *Journal of the Interdenominational Theological Center* 15, nos. 1–2 (1987–1988): 13–22.

1989

"Agents with Integrity." In *WATERwheel* 2, no. 2 (Spring-Summer 1989): 1–2.

"The Politics of Reproduction" (interview by Mary Lou Suhor). *Witness* 72 (June 1989): 12–15.

1990

"Abortion Perspective: Third Presentation." *Church and Society* 80 (January-February 1990): 60–71.

1991

"Trust Women." In *WATERwheel* 4, no. 4 (Winter 1991–1992): 1–3.

1994

"Roundtable Discussion: Backlash" (with Carter Heyward). *Journal of Feminist Studies in Religion* 10, no. 1 (Spring 1994): 91.

1995

"Rhetorics, Rituals, and Conflicts over Women's Reproductive Power." Edited by Beverly Harrison. *Journal of Feminist Studies in Religion* 11 (Fall 1995): 1–135.

2000

"Interview by Carter Heyward with Beverly W. Harrison." *Feminist Theology* 25 (Summer 2000): 103–4.

REVIEWS

"Feminism and Process Thought" (review of *Feminism and Process Thought,* edited by Sheila Greeve Davaney). *Signs: Journal of Women in Culture and Society* 7, no. 3 (1982): 704.

"Labour-Religion Prophet: The Times and Life of Harry F. Ward" (review of *Labor-Religion Prophet: The Times and Life of Harry F. Ward,* by Eugene P. Link). *Union Seminary Quarterly Review* 39, no. 4 (1984): 316–22. Reprinted in this volume as chapter 11.

"Niebuhr: Locating the Limits" (review of *Reinhold Niebuhr: A Biography,* by R. W. Fox). *Christianity and Crisis* 46, no. 2 (February 17, 1986): 35–39. Reprinted in this volume as chapter 10.

"Vintage Adams" (review of *The Prophethood of All Believers,* by J. L. Adams, edited and with an introduction by George K. Beach and *Voluntary Associations,* by J. L. Adams, edited by J. Ron Engel). *The World* (January/February 1988): 44–45. Reprinted in this volume as chapter 12.

REVIEWS OF HARRISON'S WORKS

Our Right to Choose

Segers, M. C. *Christianity and Crisis* 43 (October 31, 1983): 410–13.
Weidman, J. *Christian Century* 100 (November 16, 1983): 1057.
Cahill, Lisa Sowle. *Horizons* 11 (Spring 1984): 202.
Robb, Carol S. *Union Seminary Quarterly Review* 40, no. 3 (1985): 69–72.
O'Connor, June. *Religious Studies Review* 11 (January 1985): 105–14.
Brauning, Joan. *Reformed Journal* 35, no. 11 (November 1985): 26–30.
Bolton, Martha. *Ethics* 96, no. 2 (January 1986): 467.
Lambert, Jean. *Journal of Religion* 66, no. 1 (January 1986): 90–91.
Kollar, Nathan R. *Journal of the American Academy of Religion* 54, no. 1 (Spring 1986): 175–76.
Tillman, William M., Jr. *Southwestern Journal of Theology,* n.s. 28, no. 3 (Summer 1986): 69.
West, Mary. *Sojourners* 15, no. 2 (Fall 1986): 44–45.
Bruland, Esther Byle. *Theological Students Fellowship Bulletin* 10, no. 2 (November-December 1986): 33–34.
Paris, Peter J. *Theological Education* 24 (Autumn 1987): 135–36.

Making the Connections

Bettenhausen, Elizabeth. *Christianity and Crisis* 45 (September 30, 1985): 379–81.
Bellis, Alice Ogden. *Christian Century* 102 (October 9, 1985): 898.
Sands, Kathleen. *Signs: Journal of Women in Culture and Society* 12, no. 1 (Autumn 1986): 178–81.
Cahill, Lisa Sowle. *Journal of the American Academy of Religion* 54, no. 3 (Fall 1986): 584–86.
Hinze, Christine Firer. *Journal of Religion* 66, no. 4 (October 1986): 465–66.
Peck, Jane C. *Theology Today* 43, no. 3 (October 1986): 454–58.
Saunders, Martha J. *Studies in Religion/Sciences religieuses* 16, no. 1 (1987): 124–25.
Gudorf, Christine E. *Religious Studies Review* 14 (April 1988): 125–27.
Carr, Anne E. *Critical Review of Books in Religion* 1 (1988): 280–82.

Die neue Ethik der Frauen: Kraftvolle Beziehungen statt blossen Gehorsams

Hofmann, Bernhard F. *Journal of Empirical Theology* 5, no. 2 (1992): 105–6.

RESPONSES TO BEVERLY W. HARRISON

Kelly, James J. "Tracking the Intractable: A Survey on the Abortion Controversy." *Cross-Currents* 35, nos. 2–3 (Summer-Fall 1985): 212–18.
Gallagher, Janet. "Response to Beverly Harrison, 60–71." *Church and Society* 80 (January-February 1990): 72–75.
Schlossberg, Jerry. "Response to Beverly Harrison, 60–71." *Church and Society* 80 (January-February 1990): 76–79.

"Feminists, Religion, and Ethics in New York City: The Roman Catholic Example." In *New York Glory*, edited by Susan A. Farrell, 322–32. New York: New York University Press, 2001.

FESTSCHRIFTS

"Special Issue in Honor of Beverly Wildung Harrison." Edited by Elizabeth M. Bounds. *Journal of Feminist Studies in Religion* 9 (Spring-Fall 1993): 7–245.
"Festschrift for Beverly Harrison." Edited by Marvin M. Ellison and Marilyn J. Legge. *Union Seminary Quarterly Review* 53, nos. 3–4 (1999): 1–218.

Index